Marvellous
Mince &
Sensational
Sausages

100 Easy & Delicious Recipes by **Simon & Alison Holst**

Published by Hyndman Publishing
325 Purchas Road
RD 2 Amberley 7482

ISBN: 1-877382-56-6

TEXT: © Simon & Alison Holst

DESIGN: Dileva Design Ltd.

PHOTOGRAPHY MINCE & SAUSAGES:
Lindsay Keats except page 68, 71 and 83.
©Hyndman Publishing except 16 and 52
©New Holland Publishers (NZ) Ltd and page
25 ©Chanel & Stylus Publishing.

PHOTOGRAPHY POTATOES: Lindsay Keats
(except page 123, 170, 174 and 175
Sal Criscillo) Additional potato images
from vegetables.co.nz

FOOD STYLING: Simon & Alison Holst

The recipes in this book have been carefully tested
by the authors. The publisher and the authors have
made every effort to ensure that the instructions
are accurate and safe, but they cannot accept
liability for any resulting injury or loss or damage to
property, whether direct or consequential.

Because ovens and slow cookers vary, you should
take the cooking times suggested in our recipes as
guides only. The first time you make a recipe, check
it towards the end of the suggested time to see if it
is cooking faster, or more slowly than expected.

Always follow the detailed instructions given by
manufacturers of your appliances and equipment,
rather than the more general instructions given in
these recipes.

Before You Start Cooking!

For best results use standard metric measuring cups and spoons when you
use these recipes. 1 metric cup holds 250ml. 1 tablespoon holds 15ml. 1
teaspoon holds 5ml. All of our cup and spoon measures are level unless
otherwise stated.

Large amounts of butter are given by weight. Butter packs usually have 50g
or 100g markings on the pack. 1 Tbsp butter weighs 15g.

Abbreviations used:

cm	centimeter	g	grams
°C	Celsius	tsp	teaspoon
ml	millilitre	Tbsp	tablespoon

If you use a loaf tin or baking dish which is bigger than the one specified the
contents will probably cook in less time. If you use a smaller dish the cooking
time may be a little longer.

When parsley is specified use fresh parsley. If you use dried herbs instead
of the fresh herbs specified use about half as much. It is not the end of the
world if you make the recipe without the herbs specifically listed or replace
them with similar amounts of other herbs that you have and like.

We use microwave ovens of 700-750 watts. If your microwave is of a higher
wattage the food will require a shorter cooking time. Use our cooking times
as a guide only. When tomatoes are specified in a recipe they are fresh
tomatoes. Canned tomatoes are always specified when they are required.
Tomato paste is available in cans and tubes, suit yourself.

When chicken or other stock is specified make your own, use stock from
your freezer, or use packets, jars or cans of stock, or use instant stock and
water, one level tsp to 1 cup. If you stir too much instant stock or too many
stock cubes into hot water the mixture will be too salty.

For more information about other Holst titles, visit
www.holst.co.nz or **www.hyndman.co.nz**

Which type of mince shall I use?

There is now quite a range of minced meat on sale. Although most of the
recipes in this book list one or two possibilities, you may like to experiment
with other types too. Look for minced lamb, chicken and pork, as well as
minced beef.

About this Book

No wonder mince and sausages are so popular!

They are both great value for money, can be quickly cooked in a wide variety of ways, and best of all, they are popular with all age groups!

MINCE is especially versatile! You can cook it quickly as a burger on a grill, pan or barbecue, just as you would cook expensive steak. You can form it into a loaf and cook it in the oven in the same way you would cook a roast, you can encase it in pastry and make

ever-popular pies, or you can pop it into a pan with vegetables and rice, potatoes or pasta and make an easy one pan family dinner. You can also cook it with interesting spices and herbs to make exciting dishes from many different parts of the world.

Whatever you do with mince, you know that your meal will have plenty of flavour and wide appeal for you and for children. If you follow our instructions, you can expect good results, even if you are not a very experienced cook!

When you are shopping for mince, make sure that you look around and see all the varieties that are available. You may find minced chicken, pork, and lamb as well as different packs of minced beef, and decide to experiment with something a little different. If you are not sure what is best for you, choose a quiet time and ask to speak to an experienced butcher. Butchers in supermarkets as well as those in butchers' shops can be very helpful and friendly – we have learned a great deal from them, over the years.

Remember that some fat is needed in all minced meat if you want a succulent meat dish with good flavour. While you don't want minced meat so lean it will have a "dry as sawdust" texture when cooked, you also don't want beef mince which has a pale colour, because it is flecked with too much fat.

SAUSAGES have always been popular with our families, too! Why? They are quick and easy to cook, cheaper than most other meats, and again, are very versatile. We have found them very good when cooked in slow cookers, and hope you will try them this way, too! We don't make our own sausages often, but when we do we are always delighted, so we have included some recipes in case you would like to try them sometime, too!

Whether you are planning to cook mince or sausages (or other meat), we hope that you will remember, and teach your family that the main meal of your day should be well balanced, with some meat, something starchy like potatoes, rice or pasta, and a variety of colourful vegetables. These can be in various piles on your plate, or all mixed up together in a one pan dinner.

We hope that you and your families will enjoy our mince and sausage recipes.

Good cooking!

Simon and Alison Holst

Mince & Sausage contents

Satisfying Soups

Mexican Beef, Lime & Tortilla Soup

This spicy soup makes an interesting and warming meal. Corn tortillas may sound like an unusual addition to a soup, but after simmering in liquid for a while they soften and swell, becoming almost like pasta. If you have a choice, use lime rather than lemon juice – it'll give a particularly good flavour.

FOR 4 SERVINGS:

2 Tbsp olive or canola oil
1 large onion, peeled and diced
2 cloves garlic, crushed, peeled and chopped
1 medium green pepper, cored and diced
500g lean minced beef (see page 2)
2 tsp ground cumin
1 tsp ground coriander
½–1 tsp chilli powder to taste
½ tsp oregano
2–3 medium tomatoes, diced
4 cups chicken stock
6 soft corn tortillas
juice of 2 limes or lemons
½–1 tsp salt
¼ cup chopped coriander
1–2 Tbsp olive or canola oil

Heat the oil in a large pot. Stir in the onion and garlic and cook, stirring frequently, for 3–5 minutes until the onion is soft and just beginning to brown. Add the green pepper and the minced beef to the pot and cook, stirring occasionally, for about 5 minutes until the beef is lightly browned. Sprinkle in the spices and cook, stirring frequently, for about 1 minute longer. Add the oregano, tomatoes and stock. Bring the soup to the boil, then reduce the heat to a simmer and cook for about 10 minutes.

While the soup simmers, chop five of the tortillas into pieces about 2.5cm square, then stir into the soup along with the lime or lemon juice and salt to taste. Simmer for about 5 minutes longer, then stir in most of the chopped coriander.

To make an attractive garnish while the soup simmers, cut the remaining tortilla into strips about 5mm wide. Heat the second measure of oil in a medium non-stick frypan, add the tortilla strips and cook until golden brown. Remove from the pan and drain on paper towels; they will crisp up as they cool.

Serve the soup, garnished with the crisp tortilla strips and the reserved chopped coriander. An avocado and tomato salad and perhaps some additional warmed tortillas make excellent accompaniments.

NOTE: Soft (i.e. not fried or baked until crisp) corn tortillas used to be relatively hard to come by, but now they can be found vacuum-packed in the Mexican foods section of most supermarkets.

Quick Mince & Vegetable Chowder

You can make this wonderfully warming, nutritious and filling chowder (a cross between a soup and a stew) in less than half an hour. Serve it plain for an easy meal, or turn it into something really special by adding exciting toppings.

FOR 4 LARGE SERVINGS (8 CUPS):

1 Tbsp oil
1 large onion
500g minced beef (see page 2)
1 clove garlic, finely chopped
1 medium carrot, finely chopped
2 stalks celery, finely chopped
½ red or yellow pepper, finely chopped (optional)
1 x 400g can whole tomatoes in juice
2 cups chicken stock + 2 cups water or 4 cups water
    + 2 tsp instant chicken stock powder
½ tsp oregano
1 tsp each salt and sugar
½ cup orzo (rice-shaped pasta) or other small pasta
2 Tbsp tomato paste
about ¼ cup chopped parsley or other fresh herbs

Heat the oil in a large pot. Finely chop the onion, then add it to the pot and cook for 1–2 minutes until lightly browned, then add the minced beef and cook over fairly high heat until no longer pink. Add the vegetables as you prepare them. Stir in the tomatoes in juice, the stock and water and remaining seasonings. Bring to the boil, then add the pasta. Bring back to the boil, then reduce heat and simmer, covered, for 15 minutes or until the pasta is tender. Stir in the tomato paste and the fresh herbs.

This chowder is best if left to stand for 10 minutes until it cools a little. During this time, taste and add extra salt, pepper if required, and a little lemon juice if it seems bland.

Serve in large bowls, accompanied by crusty bread, bread rolls or toast.

If the chowder is the main part of the meal, serve a variety of toppings, added in generous spoonfuls to individual servings, such as:

- unsweetened yoghurt or sour cream
- chopped coriander leaves or more parsley
- chopped raw tomato
- chopped avocado in lemon juice
- tiny croutons or tiny crackers
- basil (or other) pesto
- grated parmesan cheese
- hot sauce

Asian-style Meatball & Noodle Soup

Simon recalls that his love of Asian-style soups stretches back to his childhood, when for a special treat the family would go out to dinner at a local Chinese restaurant. Enjoying a bowl of Long and Short Soup, a clear broth full of long noodles and deliciously slippery wontons, remains one of his clearest memories. This soup captures many of the same flavours and textures, without having to go to the trouble of making wontons first. Served in large bowls, this soup can easily serve as the main part of a meal.

FOR 2–3 SERVINGS:

BROTH:
2 cups chicken stock
2 cups water
2 dried shiitake mushrooms, chopped or sliced
2.5cm piece fresh root ginger, quartered
1 Tbsp light soy sauce

MEATBALLS:
1 clove garlic, peeled
2.5cm fresh root ginger, peeled and roughly chopped
2 Tbsp roughly chopped coriander
400g pork mince (see page 2)
2 tsp cornflour
1 large egg
1 Tbsp light soy sauce
2 tsp sesame oil

100–150g rice noodles
1 large carrot, peeled and finely julienned
about 20 spinach leaves or 1 cup thinly sliced cabbage
1–2 Tbsp chopped coriander

Combine the ingredients for the broth in a large pot, then place on the stove over low – medium heat to simmer.

To make the meatballs, put the garlic, ginger and coriander in a food processor fitted with the metal chopping blade. Process until finely chopped, then add the mince, broken into four or six smaller lumps, cornflour, egg, soy sauce and sesame oil. Process in short bursts until evenly mixed. Working with wet hands to prevent the mixture sticking, form the meat mixture into 10–12 golf ball-sized balls. Carefully drop the balls into the boiling broth mixture, and boil gently for about 10 minutes, turning the meatballs two or three times as they cook.

While the meatballs cook, place the rice noodles in a large bowl or pot and cover with boiling water. Leave to stand for 5 minutes or until tender, then drain and set aside.

When the meatballs are cooked (cut one in half after 10 minutes to check), add the prepared vegetables to the pot and cook for 1–2 minutes until they have softened, then stir in the chopped coriander.

Add the noodles to the pot (a good option if they have cooled), then ladle the soup into bowls or you can divide the noodles between the serving bowls and top with the steaming broth and other goodies. Serve immediately.

Frankfurter & Vegetable Soup

All sorts of vegetables may be used in this soup, but it's especially good in autumn when there are so many to choose from.

FOR 6 SERVINGS:

2–3 Tbsp butter or oil
1 onion, finely chopped
1 stalk celery, finely chopped
1 carrot, finely chopped
1–2 cups coarsely grated pumpkin or marrow
1 cup chopped green beans
1 cup finely chopped cabbage
6 cups cold water
½ tsp salt
pepper to taste
1 packet cream of chicken or onion soup
3–4 frankfurters, sliced 5mm thick
¼ cup chopped parsley

Heat the butter or oil in a large pot and cook the prepared vegetables, stirring frequently, for 5 minutes without letting them brown. Add 1 cup of the water, and salt and pepper to taste. Cover and simmer for 15 minutes or until the vegetables are tender. Mix the packet soup with the remaining water, add to the pot and return to the boil. Simmer for a further 15 minutes, then taste and adjust seasonings.

Five minutes before serving add the sliced frankfurters to heat through, then just before serving stir in the chopped parsley. Serve immediately in bowls or mugs with crusty bread rolls or toast.

NOTE: Do not grate potato into the soup since it spoils the texture. Add finely diced potato with other vegetables, if desired.

Spanish Sausage Soup

This tasty "meal-in-a-bowl" soup is flavoured with the herbs and spices found in chorizos, which are Spanish-style spicy sausages. Mix the flavourings through the sausage-meat or, more simply, just add the flavourings to the soup itself.

FOR 6–8 GENEROUS SERVINGS:

chorizo flavourings (see page 87)
450–500g sausage-meat
1 large onion
1 large carrot
2 stalks celery
2 large potatoes
8 cups chicken or other stock
2 Tbsp tomato paste
2 cups prepared green vegetables, e.g. chopped
    zucchini, chopped cabbage or chopped broccoli
    and frozen peas
2 Tbsp each chopped parsley and coriander leaves

Measure into a small container the chorizo flavourings as listed on page 87. Either mix these thoroughly through the sausage-meat at this stage or set them aside.

Form the sausage-meat into walnut-sized balls with wet hands. Brown the balls evenly, in several batches, over moderate heat in a large pot with a non-stick surface. Remove from the pot and set aside until required.

Chop the onion, carrot and celery into small cubes and cook in the fat left in the pot from the sausage meat until the onion is transparent. If you haven't already added the chorizo flavourings, stir them into the pot now along with the unpeeled potato cut into cubes. Return the sausage balls to the pot and gently shake over moderate heat for 2–3 minutes. Add the stock. (If home-made stock is not available, mix 5–6 level teaspoons of instant stock with hot water – it tastes best if you mix two or three different instant stocks.) Add the tomato paste, then simmer for 30 minutes.

Skim off all visible fat from the top of the soup and add the prepared green vegetables. Simmer for a further 10 minutes, then adjust the seasonings if necessary, add the chopped herbs and serve in large bowls with crusty bread rolls.

Pea Soup with Sausages ▶

This substantial cold weather soup is ready to serve in less than an hour. By thickening the cooked purée you'll get a smooth creamy soup.

FOR 4 SERVINGS:

½ cup split peas
1 large onion, chopped
2 slices bacon, chopped
3 cups water
1 Tbsp butter
1 Tbsp flour
½ cup milk
salt and pepper
2–4 precooked sausages, sliced

Combine the first four ingredients in a fairly large pot. Cover and simmer until the peas are tender, about 45 minutes.

Purée the contents of the pot along with the cooking water, preferably in a food processor, or sieve or mash with a potato masher.

In another pot melt the butter, stir in the flour and heat until bubbling. Stir in the milk, then cook until thick and boiling vigorously, stirring constantly. Mix in the puréed pea mixture, then stir until the mixture boils again. Add salt and pepper to taste.

While the soup cooks, brown the cooked sausages in a non-stick frypan, adding a little oil if necessary. Drop the sliced sausages into the cooked soup and serve immediately.

Lentil Soup with Sausages

This soup recipe goes back many years – it's a hard one to beat on a cold blustery day. For really smooth soup process it in batches, before you make the little sausage balls.

FOR 6–8 SERVINGS:

2 large onions, chopped
2–4 cloves garlic, chopped
1 Tbsp butter or oil
2 cups red lentils
9 cups water
1 Tbsp butter
2 Tbsp flour
1–1½ tsp salt

SAUSAGE BALLS:

2 thick slices stale bread
¼ cup milk
500g sausage meat
1 tsp instant vegetable stock
½ tsp curry powder

Cook the onion and garlic in the butter or oil in a large, heavy-bottomed pot with a tight-fitting lid until golden, but not brown. Add the lentils and water, cover and cook gently for 30–45 minutes until the lentils are really tender.

Work the second measure of butter into the flour with your fingertips, then drop it into the soup in little bits, stirring with a whisk or a wooden spoon, until the soup boils and thickens. Add salt to taste.

While the soup cooks, make the little sausage balls which give extra flavour.

To make the sausage balls, crumble the bread into a bowl. Add the milk and mash with a fork. Mix in the sausage meat and the remaining ingredients. Using a teaspoon and wet hands, make marble-sized balls. Heat an oiled frypan and shake the sausage balls over moderate heat until they have browned on all sides.

Although it looks nicer to add sausage balls to the soup at the table, it tastes better if you drop them into the soup as they are cooked, then reheat both soup and meatballs – suit yourself! Serve with toast or crusty bread rolls.

Mighty
Meat Loaves

Slow-cooked Nacho-flavoured Meat Loaf

Using crushed corn chips to bind the mixture – plus the other seasonings – gives this an interesting, slightly Mexican flavour. It doesn't matter if the corn chips you use are a little stale – in fact it's a great way to use up opened bags or party leftovers.

FOR 4–6 SERVINGS:

75g corn chips
1kg minced beef (see page 2)
½ cup prepared tomato salsa (see page 91)
1 large egg
1 tsp ground cumin
½ tsp dried oregano
½ tsp salt
2 finely chopped spring onions

GLAZE:

2 Tbsp tomato sauce
1 Tbsp dark soy sauce

Roughly crush the corn chips. Place the crushed chips in a food processor fitted with the chopping blade and process until they resemble coarse breadcrumbs.

Transfer the crumbed corn chips to a large bowl and add the next seven ingredients. Mix until evenly combined. Alternatively, if you have a large food processor, you can do this in small batches in the machine, processing each batch in short bursts until evenly combined. Avoid over-mixing as this will toughen the loaf.

Place a 50–60cm length of baking paper on a board. Tip the meat mixture onto the middle of the baking paper, then pat it into a loaf shape that will fit into your slow cooker.

To make the glaze, combine the tomato and soy sauces in a small bowl, then brush the loaf with the mixture.

Holding the ends of the baking paper, lift the loaf into the slow cooker. Cover and set to LOW and cook for 6 hours (or HIGH for 3 hours). Repositioning the lid so it sits slightly ajar for the last 15–20 minutes will help the loaf brown a little.

Lift the loaf from the cooker, once again using the baking paper as a sling. Cut into thick slices and serve with either lightly cooked vegetables or a salad, and rice or mashed potatoes.

VARIATION TO COOK THIS LOAF CONVENTIONALLY:
Bake in the oven as for American Meat Loaf, page 12.

Tomato-topped Meat Loaf

This family-pleasing meat loaf is especially easy to mix in a food processor but it can also be done by hand provided you grate the onion very finely. The loaf has a very good flavour, even though it has few added seasonings, and it always looks inviting, due to its colourful topping.

FOR 4 SERVINGS:

1 medium onion, roughly chopped
1 egg
½ cup skim milk powder
½ cup water
½ cup quick-cooking rolled oats
1 Tbsp light soy sauce
1 tsp salt
500g minced beef or lamb (see page 2)

TOPPING:

¼ cup tomato or barbecue sauce
¼–½ cup grated tasty cheese

Preheat the oven to 180°C.

Put the onion in a food processor and process in bursts until it is chopped into small pieces. Add the next six ingredients to the processor and mix until the onion is finely chopped and everything is mixed together thoroughly. Break the minced beef into golf ball–sized pieces and drop into the food processor. Process in brief bursts until evenly mixed.

Spread the mixture into a non-stick sprayed or baking paper-lined 20cm-square cake tin or a medium-sized loaf tin.

Bake uncovered for 30 minutes for the square tin or 40–50 minutes if using a loaf tin, or until the centre springs back when pressed and the top is evenly browned. Spread the top of the loaf with the sauce, followed by the grated cheese and return to the oven for 5 minutes.

Cut into four squares or into thick slices and serve with mashed potatoes and green peas, beans or broccoli. Use leftovers for sandwich fillings.

VARIATIONS: Brush with chipotle sauce instead of tomato sauce and cheese.

American Meat Loaf

We often take our high quality lamb and beef for granted. In many other countries the prospect of eating a roast of lamb or beef are impossible dreams for most families. Back when she was living in North America on a tight budget, Alison learned how to make this traditional "comfort food" loaf instead of cooking roast meat.

FOR 4 SERVINGS:

¾ cup fine dry breadcrumbs
1 packet onion soup mix
¼ cup hot water
¼ cup tomato or barbecue sauce
1 egg
450–550g minced beef or lamb

OPTIONAL TOPPING:

1–2 rashers bacon
1 Tbsp tomato paste
2 Tbsp water

Preheat the oven to 180°C.

Stir together the crumbs and soup mix in a medium to large bowl. Add the hot water and stir with a fork to mix. Add the tomato sauce and egg and mix again with the fork, then add the minced meat. Using a damp hand, mix the minced meat as evenly as possible through the other ingredients, then form the mixture into an oval shape about 20cm long and place it on a sponge roll or any other flattish baking tray lined with baking paper or a non-stick liner.

To make the optional topping, cut any rinds off the bacon and snip the flesh around the edges so that it lies flat. Lay the bacon over the shaped roll, smoothing it down evenly. Mix the tomato paste with the water and brush or rub over the bacon and exposed meat.

Bake, uncovered, for 1 hour if using fan-bake or for 1¼ hours without a fan. (Check if it is cooked by cutting into it – there should be no pinkness in the centre.)

To serve, cut into eight thick slices and serve with gravy (see below), mashed potatoes, your favourite green vegetable, and carrots.

Gravy

Although gravy is not essential, it is very nice with meat loaf. You may have enough pan drippings, but if not, add a tablespoon of butter to the baking pan, brown 2–3 tablespoons flour in it over moderate heat, then add about 1 cup of the lightly salted liquid in which you cooked the accompanying vegetables. Stir until the gravy thickens and comes to the boil. Leave to simmer for a couple of minutes. Pour through a sieve to get rid of any lumps, or thin if necessary, adjust seasonings, and serve with the loaf.

If time is short, serve with instant gravy or tomato sauce.

FOR A SLOW-COOKED MEAT LOAF: Place the uncooked loaf crosswise on a doubled strip of baking paper and lower the paper and loaf into the slow cooker. Cook at HIGH for 3–4 hours or LOW for 6–8 hours.

Confetti Meat Loaf

The flecks of colourful vegetables through this delicious family loaf give it an attractive appearance as well as a good flavour. It cooks in the microwave in 30 minutes and may be served hot or cold.

FOR 8–10 SERVINGS:

1 egg
2 thick slices stale bread
1 tsp curry powder
1 tsp instant vegetable stock
1 tsp instant beef stock
1 onion, finely chopped
1 red pepper, chopped
1 yellow or orange pepper, chopped
500g minced beef
450–500g sausage-meat
fine dry breadcrumbs for coating

Break the egg into a mixing bowl and crumble in the bread, crusts and all. When the bread softens, mix it to a smooth consistency with a fork. Add the remaining ingredients except the dry breadcrumbs. Mix thoroughly, then using wet hands form the mixture into a sausage shape and coat with the dry breadcrumbs.

Put the loaf into a microwaveable loaf dish or on a long flat plate. Cover with cling film, leaving a small gap for the air to escape. Stand the dish on an inverted plate so the meatloaf is raised from the bottom of the oven. Microwave on Medium (50%) power for 30 minutes, then leave to stand for 5 minutes if serving hot, or uncover and leave to cool.

VARIATION: Replace the peppers with 1½ cups thawed mixed vegetables and up to 1 cup raw chopped celery if desired.

Slow-cooked Cracker Meat Loaf

This is a loaf that requires only store-cupboard ingredients mixed with the mince. An easy way to crush crackers is to put them into a plastic bag and beat or flatten them with a rolling pin. You can use whatever crackers you have for this recipe – it doesn't matter at all if they are a bit stale or if you mix several different varieties.

FOR 3–4 SERVINGS:

500g minced beef (see page 2)
¼ cup crushed crackers
1 onion, finely chopped
¼ cup tomato or barbecue sauce
1 Tbsp Dijon mustard
1 large egg

Turn your slow cooker (2.5 litres or larger) on to HIGH and coat the bowl with non-stick spray.

Put all the ingredients into a large mixing bowl, then using wet hands mix everything together (or if you prefer to keep your hands clean, put all the ingredients together in a large, unpunctured plastic bag and knead or squish the bag until well mixed).

Shape the mixture into a loaf that will fit in your cooker. Brush the top and sides of the loaf with a little extra tomato or barbecue sauce. Tear off a strip of baking paper, about 10cm longer than twice the height of the bowl, and fold it in half lengthwise (or use a Teflon liner, see page 96). Place the loaf crosswise onto the folded piece of baking paper or Teflon liner, and lower it into the prepared slow cooker.

Cover and cook on HIGH for about 3–4 hours or turn down to LOW and cook for about 6–8 hours. Sprinkle a little grated cheese on the loaf in the last 15–30 minutes if desired. Test with a food thermometer if you have one; the loaf will be cooked when the internal temperature reaches 80°C.

Serve hot with extra tomato sauce, cold in sandwiches or with salad, or reheat sliced, leftover meat loaf (covered with cling film) in the microwave.

NOTE: Double this quantity for a large loaf. A thicker or round loaf will need a longer cooking time.

POTATOES: If you have space in the cooker bowl, scrub, halve and oil some medium-sized potatoes and place in the bowl around the meat loaf. Potatoes do not have to be surrounded by liquid to cook well in a slow cooker.

Apricot & Sausage Loaf

This flavourful loaf is baked in an oven bag, surrounded by an easy but interesting sauce which coats, flavours and glazes it.

FOR 6–8 SERVINGS:

LOAF:

8 dried apricots, chopped
½ cup boiling water
4 thick slices stale bread, roughly crumbled including crusts
1 egg
¼ cup orange juice
½ tsp grated orange rind (optional)
450–500g sausage-meat
1 packet cream of chicken soup
1 onion, finely chopped

SAUCE:

1 Tbsp tomato sauce
1 Tbsp sweet Thai chilli sauce
1 Tbsp Worcestershire sauce

Chop the dried apricots into thin strips and place in a bowl. Pour the boiling water over them and leave to stand a couple of minutes. Drain, reserving the soaking water.

Preheat the oven to 150°C.

Measure and mix the sauce ingredients in an unpunctured medium-sized oven bag. Stand the bag upright in a loaf tin or other suitable baking dish. Add the reserved apricot soaking water.

Combine the rehydrated apricots with the crumbled bread, the egg and the orange juice and rind, if using. Mash the bread with a fork to soften it. Add the sausage-meat, soup mix, and onion. Mix together thoroughly using your hand, then form the mixture into a large egg-shaped loaf.

Place the uncooked loaf in the bottom of the oven bag. Move it around within the bag so all the surfaces are coated with the sauce (you may have to reshape it a little), then stand the bag upright in the baking tin, with the top of the bag loosely folded over several times.

Bake for 45 minutes, then open the bag to allow the top of the loaf to dry. Bake for a further 15 minutes. Leave to stand in the bag for 5–10 minutes before removing and slicing.

Serve hot or cold with rice or a rice salad, and broccoli or a green salad.

Savoury Sausage Roll

This roll looks and tastes good. Serve it with vegetables for an economical family dinner and serve leftovers cold with a salad for an easy weekend lunch.

FOR 4–6 SERVINGS:

2 Tbsp butter
1 cup chopped onion
1 cup sliced celery
1 cup grated apple
2 thick slices stale bread, crumbled
1 Tbsp chopped parsley
½ tsp salt
450–500g sausage-meat
½ cup fine dry breadcrumbs

Heat the butter in a large pot and cook the onion, celery and apple over high heat, stirring occasionally, until the ingredients start to turn golden. Remove from the heat. Mix in the crumbled bread, parsley and salt.

Sprinkle the dry breadcrumbs over a sheet of cling film. Pat out the sausage-meat on top of the breadcrumbs to form a 25cm square. Spread the cooked vegetable mixture over the sausage-meat, leaving an uncovered 3cm border along one side. Brush this border with water, then using the plastic to help you, roll up the whole lot so that you finish with the damp border at the end. Press the damp border firmly to seal.

Cook, seam-side down, over a low heat in a covered non-stick frypan with ½ cup water for 20–30 minutes or place in a shallow dish, cover with a tent of foil, and bake at 150°C for 30–45 minutes.

Serve with your favourite chutney, tomato or barbecue sauce or brown gravy, colourful vegetables and mashed potatoes.

NOTE: If higher cooking temperatures are used the sausage meat will shrink and the roll will split during cooking.

Curried Meat Loaf

This prize-winning, economical meat loaf is as good microwaved as it is cooked conventionally. It may be served hot or cold, and travels well, whether to your favourite picnic spot or to a potluck dinner.

FOR 4–6 SERVINGS:

1 onion
1 small carrot
1 Sturmer or Granny Smith apple
2 cloves garlic (optional)
1 egg
½ cup milk
1 Tbsp soy sauce
1–2 tsp curry powder
1 tsp sugar
½ tsp salt
2 sprigs parsley
500g minced beef or lamb (see page 2)
1 cup rolled oats
¼ cup sultanas

Preheat the oven to 190°C.

Quarter the onion, carrot and apple and roughly chop the garlic if using. Place in a food processor fitted with the metal chopping blade and process until finely and evenly chopped. Add the next seven ingredients and process again until well mixed.

Break the mince into golf ball-sized pieces and add to the food processor, then sprinkle in the rolled oats. Process in short bursts, just enough to blend, then stir in the sultanas.

OR if mixing by hand, grate the onion, carrot and unpeeled apple into a large bowl. Add the finely chopped garlic, then the next six ingredients. Chop the parsley, and add with the minced beef, oats, and sultanas. Use your hands to mix everything together thoroughly.

Press the mixture into a loaf tin that has had the base and sides lined with greaseproof paper.

Bake for 1 hour or cover a microwaveable loaf pan with cling film and microwave on Medium-High (70% power) for 20 minutes or until the loaf feels firm in the middle. Leave the baked or microwaved loaf to stand for 10 minutes before slicing.

Serve hot with your favourite sauce, ketchup, chutney, etc, and hot vegetables, or cold with salads or sliced in sandwiches.

Good Old Meat Loaf Slow-cooked

You may be surprised to find how well your slow cooker will cook meat loaves. The carrot and zucchini hidden in this meat loaf add extra nutrients and give it a light texture that often appeals to young children. Adults find it particularly delicious when served with a spicy plum sauce.

FOR 6–8 SERVINGS:

500g minced beef
500g sausage-meat
1 large carrot, grated
2 medium zucchini, grated
1 x packet (about 45g) tomato or onion soup mix
    (or 1 x 45g packet Tomato & onion soup mix)

Turn the slow cooker on to HIGH and coat the bowl with non-stick spray.

Put all the ingredients into a large mixing bowl, then using wet hands, mix everything together (or if you prefer to keep your hands clean, put all the ingredients together in a large, unpunctured plastic bag and knead or squish the bag until well mixed).

Shape the mixture into a loaf or ball that will fit in your slow cooker. For a browner loaf, brush the top and sides with dark soy sauce. Tear off a strip of baking paper, about 10cm longer than twice the height of the bowl, and fold it in half lengthwise (or use a Teflon liner, see page 96). Put the loaf crosswise on the centre of the baking paper strip or liner and, holding the ends, lower it into the prepared cooker.

Cover and cook on HIGH for 4–6 hours. Serve with mashed potatoes and lightly cooked vegetables or coleslaw. Serve leftovers reheated or cold.

TO COOK THIS LOAF IN THE OVEN: Bake it uncovered at 180° for 40 to 50 minutes in a shallow baking dish.

NOTE: To check whether the centre of a loaf is cooked, lift it onto a board and cut it in half crosswise. If the centre looks as if it needs more cooking, replace the loaf in the slow cooker, turning each half 180° so the cut surfaces touch the sides of the cooker. Cook for 30 minutes longer.

Home-style Hamburgers
with Mince or Sausage Meat

Home-made Hamburgers

A good hamburger is delicious. It is worth experimenting with seasonings, cooking times and cooking methods until you arrive at a personal formula that really suits you.

Unless you like your hamburger patty rare, don't leave out the breadcrumbs, because they keep a hamburger cooked beyond the rare stage moist and juicy.

Vary hamburger seasonings as you do the flavours you add to roasts, steaks, stews and casseroles. Use combinations to characterise the cooking of different countries. Choose glazes and garnishes appropriate to these.

Serve interesting and unusual combinations of raw or cooked vegetables and fruits with hamburger patties, whether you are slipping them into buns etc. or serving them without bread on a plate with vegetables. Many steak accompaniments and sauces are delicious with hamburgers. You may not consider hamburgers as "poor man's steak", but this is not a bad way of looking at them!

If your children like hamburgers, it pays to streamline your production line. If you shape more hamburgers than you need and freeze them individually, you can have a "fast food" bar in your own kitchen. Hamburger patties thaw quickly in a warm kitchen.

If you feel that you are competing with fast-food outlets for your children's custom, make sure you add the trimmings they like. Find and freeze the type of rolls which they consider acceptable, and don't hide any unwanted "surprises" between the burger and the bun, even though you might think it will improve the end product. Point out that it is often quicker to make your own hamburgers rather than stand in a queue waiting for someone else to make them for you!

Basic Burgers

Home-made burgers make a great quick and easy meal. It sounds clichéd but hot off your own stove or barbecue they really are quite different to anything you can buy from a fast food counter. What makes home-made burgers are the extras, but it's better not to go too far.

FOR 4 "QUARTER-POUND" BURGERS:

500g minced beef
1 cup soft breadcrumbs
1 large egg
1 tsp garlic salt
black pepper to taste

TOPPINGS:

sliced tomato
lettuce leaves or coleslaw
sliced cheese
fried egg
red, yellow and green peppers, raw or roasted
sautéed mushrooms
sliced gherkins or dill pickles
thinly sliced red onion
sliced avocado
sliced beetroot
watercress or other fresh herbs
chilli beans and sour cream

Place the ingredients for the burgers in a large bowl, then mix thoroughly (clean wet hands work best for this). Divide the mixture into four balls, then flatten each into a roundish patty – it doesn't matter if they're not perfectly round.

Grill or barbecue the patties about 8–12cm from the heat, turning when browned (or brown the patties on both sides in a hot, lightly oiled frypan). Lower the heat and cook until the centre of each patty is firm when pressed.

Serve in lightly toasted plain or sesame buns with three or four of the toppings given opposite (of course, no burger is complete without tomato sauce and/or mustard).

Home-made potato wedges make an ideal accompaniment. Preheat the oven to 220°C. Quarter scrubbed, unpeeled potatoes lengthwise (allow 1 to 1½ medium potatoes per person), then cut each quarter (again lengthwise) into three wedges. Place the wedges in an unpunctured plastic bag and toss with 1–2 teaspoons of vegetable oil per potato. Arrange the wedges in a single layer on a non-stick sprayed (or Teflon or baking-paper lined) tray. Sprinkle lightly with garlic salt, paprika and pepper, then bake for 12–15 minutes or until golden brown.

Family Favourite Burgers

FOR 4–8 PATTIES:

1 slice stale bread
¼ cup milk
2 spring onions or 1–2 tsp onion juice
2 tsp instant beef stock powder or ¾ tsp salt
1 tsp Worcestershire sauce
1 tsp chopped fresh herbs (optional)
½ tsp garlic salt
500g minced beef or lamb

Crumble the bread into a bowl. Add half the milk, stir with a fork, then add the next five ingredients. Mix well with a fork, then add the minced meat in walnut-sized pieces. Mix well, using wet hands, adding enough of the remaining milk until the mixture is moist enough to shape into patties without cracked edges (this can be done in a food processor but take care not to over-mix).

Shape into four large patties (be sure to tell the kids they will be getting patties that are considerably bigger than a "quarter pounder"!) or up to eight smaller patties if serving two per person alongside vegetables or salad, or if serving smaller burgers for children or not-so-hungry adults.

VARIATIONS:

- Add to the basic mixture ¼–1 cup grated cheddar cheese, or 2 Tbsp parmesan, or 2–4 Tbsp crumbled blue vein cheese.
- Replace the garlic salt and milk with finely chopped relish, tomato sauce, etc. Start with 2 Tbsp, then add more if necessary, or add extra water.
- Replace the Worcestershire sauce with grated horseradish, your favourite mixed mustard, or with soy sauce.
- Leave out the herbs and replace with ½ tsp sesame oil or 1 Tbsp toasted sesame seeds.
- Press some cracked peppercorns onto the surface of large hamburgers before cooking.

TO GRILL OR BARBECUE: Cook the patties about 8–12cm from the heat, turning when browned. Adjust the distance from the heat if necessary – the aim is to produce a nicely browned burger cooked to the stage you like in the centre.

TO COOK IN A FRYPAN OR ON A SOLID BARBECUE PLATE: Heat the surface, then brush it with a little oil. Brown the patties on both sides, then lower heat or move to a cooler part of the metal plate until the centre is cooked as desired. To test, pierce the centre with a small knife (the juices should run clear, not pink).

TO MICROWAVE: Before cooking, brush the upper surface of each patty with dark soy, Worcestershire, tomato or barbecue sauce. Microwave the patties one at a time on High (100% power) for 1½ minutes. Allow 2 minutes' standing time, during which time the centre of the patty should finish cooking and the surface darken. Microwaved patties will not be crusty on the outside, but not everybody considers this to be essential.

Chilli Burgers

A few minor modifications can make a relatively simple hamburger mixture into something exciting! We have spiced this recipe up to make delicious chilli burgers to suit adult tastes.

FOR 6–8 PATTIES:

2 slices firm-textured stale bread
2 Tbsp roughly chopped coriander leaves
1 small onion, roughly chopped
2 cloves garlic, roughly chopped
1 tsp ground cumin
½ tsp each chilli powder, salt and pepper
500g minced beef or lamb

In a food processor, crumb the bread until finely chopped. Add the coriander leaves and process again. Add the onion and garlic and the seasonings to the crumbs and process together until finely chopped and well combined.

Add the minced meat in golf ball-sized chunks. Process until everything is well mixed but take care not to over-process because it can make the burgers tough.

Using wet hands, shape the mixture into the required number of patties. Cook as described above.

Cajun Beany Burgers

Adding beans to a burger mixture has several advantages: it lowers their fat content and increases their fibre content at the same time. These burgers can be made in two different ways, depending on whether or not you want the beans to be obvious.

FOR 4–8 PATTIES:

1 slice stale bread or ½ cup soft breadcrumbs
½ small onion
1 clove garlic
1 x 310g can or 1 cup kidney beans, drained
400g minced beef
1 tsp each cumin, oregano and salt
½ tsp each chilli powder, thyme and pepper

If using a slice of bread, place it in a food processor and process into fine crumbs, then add the onion and garlic. Process again until finely chopped and well mixed. If you don't want the beans to be obvious, add them all now and process until they are finely chopped; otherwise add half of them only. Add the mince and seasonings, then process until well mixed. Add the reserved beans, and either stir them through the mince mixture or process again very briefly.

Working with wet hands, shape the mixture into the required number of patties. Cook as described on page 18.

Toppings, Glazes & Buns

Hamburger Toppings

You can produce different burgers every night if you place a variety of interesting toppings between a basic burger and its bun! Here are some suggestions.

- Sliced tomato, with a basil or coriander-flavoured dressing
- Sliced radishes, bean sprouts and cucumber in a slightly sweetened vinegar mixture
- Chopped red and green peppers (raw or roasted) with hot pepper sauce, with oregano or rosemary
- Grilled, sautéed or raw mushrooms with mustard and sour cream mixed to a sauce or, for special occasions, with bearnaise sauce
- Sliced gherkins or dill pickles with fresh dill or spring onions and sour cream
- Onion rings of different colours and types, crisped by soaking in cold water and then served with a little blue cheese crumbled on top
- Grilled cheese and pineapple with thinly sliced gherkins
- Sauerkraut, mild mustard and/or sour cream with caraway seeds
- Sliced cucumber with a yoghurt, mint and garlic sauce
- Sliced or mashed seasoned avocado with sour cream, sliced tomato, etc. or Guacamole (see page 75)
- Chilli beans and coriander leaves
- Tomato salsa or green salsa
- Corn salsa or fresh fruit salsa on its own or with rocket or watercress
- Grilled, large, flat brown mushrooms with pesto
- Grilled eggplant and red onion
- Sliced specialty cheeses such as blue cheese, double cream brie, or raclette

Hamburger Glazes

Patties look and taste better if their outer surfaces are glazed. Mixtures that contain sugar in any form should not be added until close to the end of the cooking time or they will burn before the patties are cooked.

Suggested glazes:

- Use tomato or barbecue sauce, soy sauce, teriyaki sauce, or Worcestershire sauce (any of these can be heated with a little butter or oil if desired).
- Mix equal parts of honey, soy sauce and thin apricot or plum jam or tart jelly with lemon or orange juice; add a little Worcestershire or soy sauce if desired.
- If you are going to cook your hamburgers in a frypan, deglaze the pan by adding a little water, fruit juice or wine, with or without some of the glaze, then swirl the mixture around the pan and turn the hamburgers in it until it coats them rather than the inside of the pan.

Hamburger Buns and Breads

The sky is the limit nowadays, as far as interesting breads are concerned. Supermarkets and specialty bakers' shops offer many different and exciting breads to hold your hamburger buns and toppings. Remember that you can make your burger smaller and thicker, wider and thinner, or elongated to suit the particular bread you want to use.

Many different kinds of flat bread are now available, too – barbecue or grill them briefly before splitting them to accommodate the burger of your choice.

And last, but certainly not least, if you have a bread machine, make and freeze your own hamburger breads and buns. Our Bread Book has many ideas.

◢ Kofta or Seekh Kebabs with Herbed Yoghurt Sauce

Seekh Kebabs, or Kofta, are traditionally made from seasoned minced lamb formed into sausage shapes, which are then skewered and barbecued or grilled. They are also delicious made with minced beef but in either case they make a good main course when served on rice or with flat bread, and a salad.

FOR 3–4 SERVINGS:

½ medium onion
2 cloves garlic
2–3cm piece fresh root ginger
500g minced lamb or beef
1 tsp each ground cumin, coriander, garam masala, dried mint and salt
½ tsp each chilli powder, ground cloves and cinnamon

HERBED YOGHURT SAUCE:

1 cup unsweetened plain yoghurt
2–3 Tbsp finely chopped fresh mint
about ¼ cup chopped coriander leaves
1 Tbsp lemon or lime juice
¼ tsp salt

9–12 skewers (if using bamboo skewers, soak them in cold water for 1 hour first to prevent them burning)

Place the onion, garlic and ginger in a food processor and process until very finely chopped or mince very finely by hand. Add the minced meat and seasonings, then process or mix by hand until well combined. Mix in the processor or by hand until the mixture is of a smooth, even consistency (thorough mixing changes the texture of the mince and ensures that it will not break up during cooking).

Divide the mixture into quarters, then into halves or thirds so you end up with either nine or 12 portions. Working with wet hands, shape each piece into a sausage shape 2–3cm thick and 10–12cm long. Spear each of these lengthwise with a skewer and make sure they are firmly moulded to the skewer by gently flattening each one between your hands.

Grill the kebabs close to the heat for 4–5 minutes on each side, or until nicely browned and no longer pink in the middle.

Mix together the ingredients for the sauce and leave to stand for at least 15 minutes in order for the flavours to blend.

Serve the kebabs with sauce as an entrée, or as the main part of a meal accompanied with rice and/or naan (or other flat bread) and a salad.

Asian-style Pork Burgers with Coleslaw

If you cook hamburgers regularly but want to make something a little different, try this delicious Asian-flavoured version. Make them any shape you like, but oval patties served in long buns make a change from the usual shape.

FOR 4 SERVINGS:

1 cup fresh breadcrumbs
250–300g minced pork
2 cloves garlic, crushed and chopped
1–2cm fresh root ginger, finely grated
1 egg
½–1 tsp minced chilli (optional)
2 tsp sesame oil
1 Tbsp Kikkoman soy sauce
½ tsp salt
2–3 Tbsp chopped coriander

Place all the ingredients in a large bowl. Working with clean wet hands, mix thoroughly. Divide the mixture into four balls, then flatten each into a longish oval shape – it doesn't matter if they're not perfect.

Barbecue or cook the burgers in a hot lightly oiled frypan, lightly browning both sides, then lower the heat and cook until the centres are firm.

Serve in lightly toasted hot dog buns or French bread with Oriental Coleslaw.

ORIENTAL COLESLAW

DRESSING:

2 Tbsp canola oil
1 Tbsp Kikkoman soy sauce
1 Tbsp sweet chilli sauce
1 Tbsp rice wine or wine vinegar
1 tsp sesame oil

SALAD:

2 cups shredded cabbage
2–3 sticks celery, thinly sliced
1 medium carrot, grated
1–2 spring onions, thinly sliced
handful of bean sprouts (optional)
chopped peanuts (optional)

To make the dressing, measure all ingredients into a screw-top jar and shake to combine.

Put the prepared vegetables in a large bowl and toss to mix, adding just enough dressing to moisten (any extra dressing will keep well in the fridge).

Sausage Burgers

This recipe stretches 450–500g sausage-meat to make up to 10 good-sized burgers that, remarkably, taste very meaty. Any leftovers taste good when cold, and are ideal for school lunches.

FOR 8–10 BURGERS:

1 egg
1 Tbsp Worcestershire sauce
1 tsp curry powder
1 onion
1 apple
2 medium potatoes, well washed
450–500g sausage-meat
oil
hamburger buns
accompaniments

Have all your ingredients at hand, especially the apple and potato, because once they have been grated they will go brown if left to stand before they are mixed and cooked.

Break the egg into a large bowl. Add the Worcestershire sauce and curry powder, then grate the onion and unpeeled apple straight into the bowl. Next grate the unpeeled potatoes, squeezing them to remove any excess liquid, before mixing them with the contents of the bowl. Add the sausage-meat and using wet hands, combine until evenly mixed. Again with wet hands, divide the mixture into the required number of patties.

Heat a little oil in a frypan and cook the patties over moderate heat for about 5 minutes per side.

Serve on toasted hamburger buns with Barbecue Bean Sauce (see page 90) and your favourite hamburger accompaniments or top with sautéed pineapple rings and serve with mashed potatoes and other vegetables.

Mountains of Meatballs

Slow-cooked Meatballs on Spaghetti

These meatballs and the sauce can be prepared when it suits you, then reheated when required. The spaghetti is best cooked a short time before serving.

FOR 4 SERVINGS:

1 small onion, roughly chopped
1 clove garlic, roughly chopped
1 cup crumbed stale bread
500g lean minced beef
1 egg
½ tsp each oregano and ground pepper
1 tsp salt

SAUCE:

2 large cloves garlic
1 x 400g can tomatoes in juice
2 Tbsp tomato paste
½ tsp each dried basil and oregano
2 Tbsp balsamic vinegar
½ tsp salt
black pepper to taste
2 Tbsp plain flour

300–400g fresh or dried pasta
1–2 Tbsp butter or oil
shaved or grated parmesan cheese to garnish

Coat the inside of the bowl of a medium-to-large slow cooker with non-stick spray.

In a food processor chop together the onion and garlic. Transfer to a bowl and add the next five ingredients and mix well.

Working with wet hands, divide the mixture into quarters, then make eight small balls from each quarter.

Heat a little oil in a large frypan and fry the meatballs in two batches until they are lightly browned on all sides. Transfer the cooked meatballs to the slow cooker and turn to HIGH.

To prepare the sauce, combine all the ingredients in a food processor and process until well mixed. Pour the sauce over the meatballs, cover and cook on HIGH for 3–4 hours, removing the lid for the last 30 minutes.

Cook the pasta in plenty of lightly salted boiling water. Drain well, toss with the butter or oil, then arrange the pasta on serving plates or a platter. Carefully spoon the meatballs and sauce over the pasta and garnish with the parmesan. Serve with a green salad and crusty bread on the side.

Moroccan Meatballs

These interesting meatballs can be ready 30 minutes after you start to prepare them, but they are even better when reheated later and simmered for 20 minutes longer.

FOR 4–6 SERVINGS:

1 large onion
2 thick slices bread
1 large egg
1 Tbsp tomato paste
1 tsp salt
⅛ tsp cayenne pepper or chilli powder
500g lean minced beef or lamb

SAUCE:

2 large onions
1–2 Tbsp oil
2 large carrots, chopped into 1cm-long slices
2 cups water
2 tsp instant chicken stock powder
1 Tbsp tomato paste
½ cup dried apricots, chopped
¼ cup brown sugar
1 tsp cinnamon
1 x 300g can chickpeas in brine

Before you make the meatballs, cut the onions for the sauce into wedges and brown in the oil in a large frypan, turning occasionally.

To make the meatballs, finely chop the onion in a food processor, then add the bread, broken into pieces, followed by the next four ingredients. Process until well mixed. Add half the minced meat, broken into small chunks, and process until evenly mixed. Add the remaining mince, also in chunks, and mix thoroughly.

Working with wet hands, divide the mixture into 12–18 balls, depending on the size you want them to be. Transfer the browned onions to a large pot or flameproof casserole, then brown the meatballs in the frypan in a little oil.

Place the browned meatballs on top of the browned onions. Add the rest of the ingredients including the brine from the chickpeas. Bring to the boil over moderate heat, then simmer for about 20 minutes, allowing about one-third of the liquid to boil away. Thicken the liquid with a little cornflour paste.

Serve on couscous when required.

Meatballs with Indonesian Sauce

These meatballs may be made small and served with dipping sauce as an appetiser, or made larger and served on rice with the sauce thinned to gravy consistency.

SERVES 6–8 AS A STARTER OR 2–3 AS A MAIN:

1 small onion, quartered
1½ thick slices bread, roughly chopped or broken
3–4 mint sprigs or basil leaves
1½ tsp instant beef or chicken stock powder or
    ¾ tsp salt
1 Tbsp lemon juice
250g minced lamb or beef

SAUCE:

2 cloves garlic, chopped
2 tsp grated fresh root ginger
1 tsp freshly ground coriander seeds (optional)
2 Tbsp each dark soy sauce and lemon juice
1 Tbsp oil
3–4 drops hot pepper sauce
¼ cup brown sugar
2 Tbsp peanut butter
¼ cup water

In a food processor chop together, the onion, bread, mint or basil, and the instant stock or salt. Add the lemon juice and minced meat and process until evenly mixed and quite smooth. Take care not to process to a paste.

Working with wet hands, shape the mixture into 24 small balls or 12 larger ones.

To microwave, arrange the meatballs evenly around the edge of the microwave turntable and cook on High (100% power) for 3–4 minutes or until they feel firm.

OR cook them in a lightly oiled non-stick frypan for 5–10 minutes, tossing to cook evenly.

To make the sauce, combine all the ingredients in a pot and cook over low heat until smooth and slightly thickened. Dilute with water to the consistency you like, then taste and adjust the seasonings as required.

If serving them as an appetiser, spear each ball with a toothpick before reheating in a microwave oven on Medium (50% power) until evenly hot, but not superheated. Serve on a shallow dish with the hot dip. When made into larger balls, they will reheat more evenly in a plastic or oven bag. Serve on rice, with the sauce thinned to gravy consistency.

Swedish Meatballs

These meatballs have a rather luxurious taste because of their accompanying rich mushroom sauce, but in fact the recipe contains only a small amount of cream.

FOR 4–5 SERVINGS:

3 slices stale rye bread
¼ cup fresh herb leaves, roughly chopped (optional)
1 medium onion, roughly chopped
¼ tsp ground allspice
½ tsp freshly grated nutmeg
1 tsp salt
freshly ground black pepper
1 large egg
400–500g minced beef, lamb or pork
milk
2 Tbsp flour

SAUCE:

250g button mushrooms, quartered
1–2 Tbsp butter
¼ cup water or stock
¼ cup cream
salt and pepper to taste
2 Tbsp finely chopped parsley or dill leaves

Break the bread into pieces and chop to crumb consistency in a food processor. Add the herbs, if using, the onion, spices and seasonings and chop with the crumbs until very fine. Add the egg and then the mince in chunks. Process until evenly mixed, adding a few drops of milk if the final mixture is not moist enough to form into balls.

Put the flour into a dry bowl. Working with wet hands, form the meat mixture into about 20 balls. Drop four or five at a time into the bowl, rotating it so the balls roll round in the flour until evenly coated. Repeat with the remaining balls, adding a little extra flour if necessary.

Heat a large non-stick frypan with a little oil and cook the balls for 5–6 minutes, jiggling the pan so they move around and brown evenly. Add the water, reduce the heat and cover the pan.

In another frypan or pot over fairly high heat, brown the mushrooms in the butter, add the water or stock, then cover and cook until the mushrooms are wilted and the water has disappeared. Tip the mushrooms into the meatball pan and set aside if not serving immediately.

When required, heat the meatballs through with a little extra water if necessary, then add the cream. Simmer for 5 minutes, adding seasonings, and enough water or stock to make a creamy glaze to coat the meatballs.

Just before serving, sprinkle with chopped parsley or dill. Serve with mashed potatoes and broccoli.

Mediterranean Meatballs in Pita Pockets

Chickpeas add an interesting flavour, texture and certain authenticity to these tasty meatballs. They also add fibre, which keeps you feeling full for longer.

FOR 4 SERVINGS:

1 medium onion, peeled
1 large clove garlic, peeled
1 x 310g can chickpeas, rinsed and drained
500g minced lamb (see page 2)
1 tsp each ground cumin and dried mint
½ tsp each cinnamon and chilli powder
½ tsp salt

SAUCE:

1 cup plain low-fat unsweetened yoghurt
2 Tbsp lemon juice
2 Tbsp tahini
¼ tsp salt

TO SERVE:

4 x 20cm wholemeal pita breads, warmed
½ lettuce, shredded
2 medium tomatoes diced
1–2 medium carrots, grated

Preheat the oven to 200°C with the rack in the middle.

Put the onion and garlic in a food processor and chop finely. Add the drained chickpeas and process until roughly chopped. Break up the mince into six to eight chunks and drop into the processor along with the spices, herbs and salt. Process in short bursts until everything is well mixed and beginning to hold together.

Remove the mixture from the bowl and divide into quarters. Working with wet hands, divide each quarter into four equal portions and shape into neat balls. Arrange the meatballs on a Teflon or baking paper-lined oven tray and bake for 12–15 minutes, turning once after 6 minutes, until golden brown.

While the meatballs cook, combine the sauce ingredients in a small bowl and prepare the accompaniments.

To serve, split the pita breads (halve them first if you like), then fill each with some shredded lettuce, chopped tomato, shredded carrot and some of the meatballs. Finish each pocket off with a spoonful or two of the sauce and serve. A simple green or cucumber salad makes an ideal accompaniment.

Slow-cooked Giant "New York-style" Meatballs ▼

These are loosely based on the meatballs that seem to feature in American TV programmes – particularly in meatball sandwiches (known as subs) that feature enormous, sliced meatballs. Making a smaller number of big meatballs makes shaping them much quicker, but you can make smaller ones if you want.

FOR 4–6 SERVINGS:

3 slices bread, roughly torn
400g minced pork (see page 2)
400g beef mince
2 cloves garlic, crushed, peeled and chopped
½ tsp dried marjoram
½ tsp dried oregano
½ tsp salt
black pepper to taste

SAUCE:

2 cloves garlic, crushed and peeled
2 x 400g cans diced tomatoes in juice
2 Tbsp tomato paste
2 Tbsp flour
½ tsp dried basil
½ tsp salt
black pepper to taste
½–1 cup grated cheese to top (optional)

Turn the slow cooker on to HIGH and coat the inside of the bowl with non-stick spray.

Place the bread in a food processor and chop into fine crumbs. Tip the crumbs into a large bowl, add the remaining meatball ingredients and mix until evenly combined.

Working with wet hands, divide the mince mixture into quarters, then divide each quarter into two or three equal-sized pieces (depending on how many meatballs you want to make) and shape each portion into a round ball. Arrange the balls in the slow cooker bowl.

To make the sauce, place all the sauce ingredients, except the cheese, in the food processor, and process until smooth. Pour the sauce over the meatballs, then turn the slow cooker to LOW and cook for 8–9 hours. Turn the meatballs and stir the sauce gently a couple of times during cooking if you are passing. About 30 minutes before serving, switch the cooker to HIGH, stir the sauce gently, then sprinkle with the grated cheese, if using.

Serve over pasta, accompanied with lightly cooked vegetables or a green salad. Leftovers make good hot or cold sandwiches.

Thai-style Curried Meatballs

These meatballs are simmered in a creamy Thai-style curry sauce and the results are deliciously different from their more familiar Italian-style cousins. Serve over rice for a quick and delicious meal.

FOR 4 SERVINGS:

500g lean minced beef (see page 2)
2 cloves garlic, crushed, peeled and finely chopped
1 Tbsp sweet chilli sauce
1 tsp red curry paste
½ tsp salt
2 Tbsp canola or olive oil
1 medium onion, diced
2 Tbsp red curry paste
¾ cup coconut cream
½ cup hot water
3–4 fresh or dried kaffir lime leaves
1 Tbsp fish sauce
1 medium carrot, julienned
1 cup small broccoli florets or frozen peas or beans

Place the mince in a large bowl. Add the garlic, chilli sauce, curry paste and salt. Working with wet hands, mix or stir until well combined. Divide the mixture into quarters, then into six to eight portions and shape into even-sized balls.

Heat the oil in a large, non-stick frypan. Add the meatballs and cook, shaking the pan frequently to prevent sticking and to keep the balls round until golden brown on all sides. Remove the meatballs from the pan with a fish slice and set aside.

Add the onion to the pan and cook, stirring frequently, until soft. Stir in the second measure of curry paste and cook, stirring continuously, for 1–2 minutes longer, then add the coconut cream, hot water and lime leaves. Stir thoroughly and bring to the boil, then add the meatballs and the fish sauce. Allow the mixture to boil again, then reduce the heat and simmer gently for 5 minutes.

Add the carrot and green vegetables of your choice to the pan, stir gently and simmer for a few minutes longer until the vegetables are just cooked.

Serve over steamed rice, with a simple green salad on the side if desired.

Hedgehog Meatballs

When cooked, these little meatballs look as if they have spikes all over them. Cook them in a pressure cooker for extra speed, in the oven (especially if it is on for something else), or in the microwave which will turn itself off. Each method has its own advantages.

FOR 4 SERVINGS:

SAUCE:

100g mushrooms, quartered
1 onion, chopped
1 green pepper, chopped
1x 440g can tomato soup
½ cup water

MEATBALLS:

500g minced lamb or beef
1 onion, very finely chopped
½ cup uncooked long grain white rice
1 tsp chopped fresh thyme, optional
1 tsp each oregano and paprika
2 tsp dark soy sauce

The three suggested cooking methods produce slightly different results.

Pressure cooked and microwaved meatballs sometimes break up during cooking. If you brown the meatballs (in a non-stick pan) before cooking them, this is unlikely to

happen. Meatballs that are mixed well tend to be firmer and also break up less.

To bake, put the quartered mushrooms, chopped onion, coarsely cut pepper, soup and water into a casserole dish.

Mix the remaining ingredients thoroughly by hand, then shape into 16 meatballs. Place in dish with sauce ingredients.

Cover tightly and bake at 180°C for 45 minutes.

To microwave, place all the sauce ingredients except the water in a large, shallow, round or oval dish. Arrange meatballs in one layer in the sauce. Cover with a lid or cling film.

Cook on High (100% power) for 5 minutes, then on Medium (70% power) for 20 minutes or 50% power for 30 minutes. (These times are for a 650 watt microwave oven.)

If the liquid seems very thin, thicken with 2 teaspoons of cornflour mixed to a thin paste with water, then leave to stand for 5 minutes before serving.

To pressure cook, put all the sauce ingredients into the pressure cooker and bring to the boil. Mix together the remaining ingredients and form into eight or 10 larger meatballs. Place these in the hot sauce. Bring up to pressure, then cook at high pressure for 10 minutes.

Japanese Meatballs

Invited to someone's home for a Japanese dinner, Alison found these meatballs that were served so delicious that she accepted the host's kind offer of showing her how to make them. Both Alison and Simon are sure that you will enjoy them, too.

FOR 3–4 SERVINGS:

500g minced beef, lamb or chicken
2 eggs
2 Tbsp cornflour
1–2 Tbsp cold water

BROTH:

2 cups water
2 tsp instant chicken stock powder
1 tsp sugar
3 Tbsp Kikkoman soy sauce
1 Tbsp vegetable oil
2–3 spring onions

Mix the mince with the eggs in a medium-sized bowl. Mix together the cornflour and cold water and stir through the beef mixture. Set aside to stand while you make the broth.

To make the broth, combine the first five ingredients in a pot or frypan with a lid and large enough to hold the meatballs in one layer, and heat until gently simmering.

Divide the beef mixture into even-sized portions, then using two wet dessertspoons shape into 12–16 balls. (If the mixture is too soft to work with, add up to 2 teaspoons of extra cornflour, mixed with a very small amount of cold water.)

Drop the soft meatballs carefully into the simmering broth – it doesn't matter if they flatten slightly. Cover and leave to simmer for 10 minutes.

While the meatballs cook, chop the spring onions, both the white and the green leaves. Sprinkle over the meatballs in the broth after 8 or 9 minutes.

Serve the meatballs in bowls with the broth, or serve the meatballs on rice with some of the cooking liquid, thickened with a little extra cornflour paste.

VARIATION: When making the broth, replace the instant stock powder and water with home-made chicken stock.

Savoury Forcemeat Balls

A roast chicken for a festive occasion goes much further when you serve it with these savoury forcemeat balls. Make the forcemeat balls without the chicken for an everyday family meal.

FOR 20 BALLS:

1 Tbsp butter or oil
1 large onion, finely chopped
450–500g sausage-meat
1 x 440g can cream-style corn
1 egg, lightly beaten
1 tsp oregano
1 tsp garlic salt
1 tsp celery salt
1 cup fine dry breadcrumbs
1 cup water
½ cup tomato paste

Preheat the oven to 170°C.

Heat the butter or oil in a large frypan and cook the onion over moderate heat until transparent.

Transfer the onion to a bowl and mix with the next seven ingredients. Use your hands to make sure all ingredients are thoroughly combined.

Mix the water and tomato paste in a shallow baking dish or roasting pan that will hold 20 balls in one layer.

Working with wet hands form the sausage-meat mixture into 20 balls and place them in the tomato mixture in the baking dish.

Bake, uncovered, for about 40 minutes, turning halfway through the cooking time so that the meatballs have an attractive rosy colour.

Serve hot with roast chicken or serve forcemeat balls as a meal by themselves alongside several vegetables or a salad.

NOTE: Use ½ teaspoon salt in place of 1 teaspoon garlic salt or celery salt if preferred.

Fruited Forcemeat Balls

Fruit-flavoured forcemeat balls make an interesting accompaniment for roast chicken or turkey. They may be cooked the day before and reheated when needed. The mixture can also be used to stuff chicken or turkey.

FOR 20 BALLS:

1 Tbsp butter or oil
1 onion, finely chopped
¼–½ cup chopped dried apricots, apples or prunes, or a mixture
¼–½ cup white wine or water
2 thick slices stale bread
450–500g sausage-meat
¼ cup finely chopped fresh herbs or ½ tsp dried thyme
½ tsp salt
pepper to taste
½ cup fine dry breadcrumbs for coating

Heat the butter or oil in a large frypan and gently cook the onion until transparent. Add the dried fruit and the wine or water. Cook for a further 2–3 minutes until the liquid is absorbed, then remove from the heat.

Crumble the bread in a food processor if available, and add to the pan with the sausage-meat, herbs, and salt and pepper to taste. Mix well to combine all the ingredients.

Working with wet hands, form the mixture into 20 balls. Gently roll the balls in the dry breadcrumbs, taking care to retain their shape.

Cook for 30 minutes alongside a roast chicken or turkey in the oven or cook in a covered frypan over a medium heat for 15–20 minutes, shaking the pan every 2–3 minutes until the balls are golden brown and cooked right through.

"Stretched" Sausages

This combination of sausages, browned onions and apples is very satisfying. It came about one cold night when a method had to be devised to make a few sausages go further – it soon proved to be a good and inexpensive way to keep out winter chills.

FOR 4 SERVINGS:

3 fairly large onions
a little butter or oil
6–8 sausages (about 500g)
3 green-skinned apples
2 Tbsp brown sugar
2 Tbsp wine vinegar
salt to taste
about ¼ cup sweet Thai chilli sauce
¼ cup chopped parsley

Cut the onions into wedges, and slowly cook them in a large, non-stick frypan in the smallest amount of butter or oil they need to stop them sticking until golden brown.

Slit each sausage, end to end, and hold under a cold tap to peel away the skin. Break each skinned sausage into three or four even-sized pieces, and roll each into a small ball. Brown the sausage balls evenly in another frypan, pouring off any resulting fat.

Quarter and core the apples. Cut each quarter into three or four wedges and add to the pan with the partly cooked onions. When the onions are evenly browned, and the apples slightly browned, add the brown sugar, vinegar, and salt to taste.

Stir the cooked sausage balls into the apple and onion mixture. If you want more sauce, add about half a cup of water, chicken stock or wine, then thicken the mixture with a little cornflour paste, and adjust the seasonings to taste. Keep warm.

A few minutes before serving, stir half the sweet chilli sauce through the sausage mixture, then drizzle the rest over the mixture for extra colour. Sprinkle generously with chopped parsley just before serving.

VARIATION: If the mixture is too large for your frypan, combine the onion and sausage mixtures in a roasting pan or large baking dish.

Frypan Favourites
with Mince & Sausages

Spicy Indian Mince & Rice

This is a delicious one-pan mince and rice meal. Although the list of ingredients may look a little long due to the spices used, it really is a simple dish to prepare.

FOR 4 SERVINGS:

2–3 Tbsp oil
1 large onion, finely chopped
2 cloves garlic, chopped
2 tsp each curry powder, garam masala and ground ginger
½ tsp each chilli powder, whole cloves and ground cinnamon
1 tsp salt
1 tsp whole black peppercorns
2 bay leaves
3–4 whole cardamoms, crushed (optional)
400–500g minced lamb or beef
1 cup long grain or basmati rice
1 x 400g can chopped tomatoes in juice
2 cups chicken or beef stock
¼ cup each toasted whole or slivered almonds and currants
1–2 Tbsp chopped coriander leaves (optional)

Heat the oil in a very large frypan (an electric frypan is ideal). Add the chopped onion and garlic and cook, stirring frequently, for about 5 minutes or until the onion begins to brown. Add all the seasonings and cook for 1–2 minutes further, then stir in the mince. Continue to cook, stirring frequently, to break up any lumps until the mince has lost its pink colour, then add the rice, the tomatoes in their juice and the stock. Break up the tomatoes and bring the mixture to the boil, then reduce the heat to a gentle simmer. Cover and cook, stirring occasionally, for about 15 minutes, or until the rice is cooked.

Brown the almonds and puff up the currants by heating them in a little oil in a small pot or frypan. Stir them into the mixture with the chopped coriander leaves just before serving. Serve with naan bread and side dishes of cubed tomatoes, cucumber etc.

For a slow-cooked version of this recipe see page 51 in Simon and Alison Holst's 100 Great Ways to use Slow Cookers & Crockpots.

Spicy Pork with Peanut & Noodles

This is a meal in its own right. Quick to prepare, it can be served warm or at room temperature or even chilled if you have time to make it in advance.

FOR 2–3 SERVINGS:

100–150g bean thread or fine rice noodles
1 Tbsp canola oil
1 medium onion, diced
2 cloves garlic, crushed and chopped
400g minced pork
1 Tbsp red curry paste
1 Tbsp fish sauce
1 cup green beans, cut into 3–4cm lengths
1 medium carrot, peeled and finely julienned
10–15cm cucumber, deseeded and sliced
½ cup peanuts, roughly chopped
2–4 Tbsp roughly chopped mint
2–4 Tbsp roughly chopped coriander

DRESSING:

2 Tbsp lemon juice
1 Tbsp fish sauce
1 Tbsp light soy sauce
2 Tbsp water
1 tsp sugar
1 tsp finely chopped red chilli

Place the noodles in a large bowl, cover with boiling water and leave to stand for about 5 minutes until softened through, then drain.

While the noodles soak, heat the oil in a large frypan. Add the onion and garlic and cook for 2–3 minutes, stirring occasionally, until softened. Stir in the pork and curry paste and cook for a further 4–5 minutes, stirring frequently to break up any lumps until the pork is lightly browned. Stir in the fish sauce and green beans, cook for about 1 minute further then remove from the heat.

Put the drained noodles in a large bowl. Add the carrot, cucumber and most of the peanuts, reserving the rest to use for garnishing. Add the pork mixture and toss to mix.

Make the dressing by combining all the ingredients and stirring until the sugar has dissolved.

Drizzle the dressing over the salad mixture, add the coriander and mint and toss gently together until evenly mixed. Garnish with the remaining peanuts just before serving.

Stuffed Peppers ▼

We add Middle Eastern flavourings to mince and rice when we make these tasty, colourful, stuffed peppers. Prepare them ahead and produce them for a delicious, interesting summer meal for friends.

FOR 4 SERVINGS:

4 large peppers of mixed colours
3 medium onions
2 cloves garlic
3 Tbsp oil
250g minced lamb or beef (see page 2)
1 cup brown or white long-grain rice
½ cup pine nuts or chopped almonds
½ cup currants
¼ cup each chopped mint and parsley
½ tsp each ground allspice, nutmeg and cinnamon
1 tsp salt
1 x 400g can chopped tomatoes in juice
8 young grape leaves, if available

Halve the peppers lengthwise. Remove and discard all seeds and pith.

Finely chop two of the onions and the garlic and cook in 1 tablespoon of the oil in a large frypan until the onion is transparent. Add the minced lamb or beef and the rice and cook for 1–2 minutes further. Add 2 cups of water, cover, and simmer for about 30 minutes for brown rice, or about

15 minutes for white rice, adding extra water if the mixture looks dry before the rice is cooked.

While the rice cooks, stand the prepared peppers in boiling water for 5 minutes, then drain and discard the water.

Brown the pine nuts or almonds lightly in 1 tablespoon of oil in another frypan. Add the currants and cook until they have plumped up.

Stir the nuts and currants with the mint, parsley, spices and salt into the meat and cooked rice mixture.

Lightly brown the remaining onion in the last tablespoon of oil using the frypan or baking dish in which the peppers will cook. Add the tomatoes and juice.

Firmly pack the stuffing into the peppers until the tops are rounded. Arrange the stuffed peppers on the tomato mixture in the frypan or baking dish, ensuring that the stuffing is not in contact with the tomatoes. Cover the pan or dish and simmer very gently for 20–30 minutes until the peppers are tender and the tomato mixture thickened. OR cover with lightly buttered foil and bake at 180–200°C for 30–45 minutes, checking that the tomato mixture does not dry out, in which case add some extra liquid.

Serve hot, warm or at room temperature, alone or with a salad and crusty bread.

Macaroni Mix-Up

Here is a tasty one-pan dinner, easy enough for a learner cook to make for the family's dinner on a cold day, and just the thing for anyone who doesn't like clearing up and washing lots of dishes afterwards.

FOR 4–5 SERVINGS:

1 Tbsp oil
500g minced beef (see page 2)
1 tsp oregano
1½ tsp salt
2 tsp sugar
2 cups uncooked macaroni
4 cups boiling water
½ cup tomato paste
3 cups frozen peas or frozen mixed vegetables

In a large preferably non-stick frypan heat the oil and cook the mince over high heat until it has lost its pinkness, stirring continuously and breaking up any lumps as it cooks. Add the oregano, salt and sugar, then stir the uncooked macaroni into the hot mince, followed by the boiling water.

Cook, covered, for 10 minutes, stirring once or twice to make sure the mixture keeps bubbling gently, but is not sticking to the bottom. Stir in the tomato paste and the frozen vegetables, turn up the heat until the mixture starts to boil again, then lower it, replace the lid, and cook gently for a further 10 minutes, adding more water if it looks dry before the macaroni and vegetables are tender.

Serve in bowls sprinkled with grated cheese or chopped parsley if desired.

VARIATION: Use fresh carrots and celery instead of frozen vegetables. Before you start cooking, cut the vegetables into 5mm cubes until you have 3 cupfuls altogether, and add them to the mince when you add the macaroni. If you have some broccoli, cut the stems and the tops into little pieces and add them when you add the tomato paste.

Sang Chow Bow (Lettuce Leaf Parcels)

Crisp lettuce leaves stuffed with this flavourful pork mixture are irresistible. They can be put together in advance or they can be assembled by diners at the table.

FOR 4 SERVINGS:

1–2 Tbsp canola oil
2–3 cloves garlic, crushed, peeled and chopped
1cm piece fresh root ginger, grated
500g minced pork or chicken (see page 2)
100–150g mushrooms, chopped
½–1 tsp minced chilli (optional)
1 Tbsp rice wine or sherry
1 Tbsp oyster sauce
1 Tbsp hoisin sauce
1–2 Tbsp Kikkoman soy sauce
¼ cup chopped fresh basil, mint or coriander (or a mixture)
1 iceberg or 2 cos lettuces
1–2 medium carrots, grated
1–2 cups bean sprouts

Heat 1 tablespoon of the oil in a large non-stick frypan, add the garlic, ginger and minced meat and cook, stirring frequently, until the pork is lightly browned (add the extra oil if the mixture looks too dry). Add the mushrooms and chilli and cook for a further 3–5 minutes.

Add the next four ingredients. Stir to mix, then reduce the heat and simmer gently for 8–10 minutes. Remove from the heat and stir in the chopped herbs. Leave the mince mixture to cool while you separate the lettuce/s into individual leaves.

Divide the mixture between four small dishes or serve in one large bowl surrounded with whole lettuce leaves. Serve the grated carrot and bean sprouts in separate bowls if preferred. To eat, place some bean sprouts, a little carrot and a small quantity of mince mixture onto a lettuce leaf, roll it up if you like, or use the leaf as an edible spoon.

Serve accompanied with steamed rice if you feel the need for something extra. The rice can be added to the parcels or eaten on its own.

Slow-cooked One-pot Dinner

This popular and well-balanced dinner involves no last-minute work. Start it cooking just before the children get out of school, organise everyone's after-school activities, then serve the meal in bowls when it's time to eat, maybe 2½–3 hours later. We suggest you choose fairly solid, medium to large-sized dried pasta shapes as the more delicate pasta pieces may collapse during cooking.

FOR 5–6 SERVINGS:

1–2 tsp canola or olive oil
1 large onion, chopped
2 cloves garlic, chopped
500g minced beef (see page 2)
1 tsp dried oregano
about 3 stalks celery, sliced
3 medium carrots, diced
1 x 350g can whole-kernel corn, drained, liquid reserved
1 x 400g can concentrated tomato soup
1 tsp salt
2 cups hot liquid (see below)
about 2 cups large macaroni or spirals, etc.
1 cup frozen peas
chopped parsley

Coat the inside of the bowl of a medium-large slow cooker with non-stick spray and turn to HIGH.

Heat the oil in a large frypan. Add the chopped onion and garlic, turn in the oil, and brown lightly. Add the minced beef in golf ball-sized pieces, then brown it with the onion over fairly high heat, breaking it up as it cooks. Stir in the oregano.

Add the prepared celery and carrots, then the drained corn along with the soup and the salt. Adjust the heat so the mixture simmers.

Add enough boiling water to the corn liquid to make it up to 2 cups, and stir into the pan.

Tip the dry pasta into the slow cooker, then pour in the contents of the hot pan, trying not to disturb the layer of pasta. Cover and cook on HIGH for 2 hours, then carefully turn and mix the contents, checking that the pasta is cooked through.

While the pasta is cooking, allow the frozen peas to thaw at room temperature. After 2 hours, stir the thawed peas into the pasta mixture and cook for about 30 minutes longer. Serve immediately – or within the next half an hour – sprinkled with chopped parsley.

Cook-in-a-bowl Dinner for One

This recipe will help you make a really easy and nutritious meat and vegetable dinner, ready to eat in 15 minutes – perfect for a child's early dinner or a solo TV dinner.

FOR 1 SERVING:

100g minced beef or lamb
½ onion
1 Tbsp tomato soup powder (about ¼ packet)
½ tsp soy sauce, preferably dark
pinch of paprika, oregano or thyme (optional)
1 cup boiling water
1 cup frozen vegetables
¼ cup small pasta shapes, e.g. macaroni, shells, orzo or
     ½ cup small lasagne noodles

In a small, lidded microwave serving bowl, mix together the minced meat, chopped onion, soup powder, soy sauce and flavourings, if using. Pour the boiling water over and stir to mix.

Add the frozen vegetables and the pasta. Stir so that the pasta is covered by the liquid, then cover. Cook at High (100% power) for 12 minutes, then leave to stand for 2–5 minutes before stirring, tasting and adjusting the seasoning. At this stage you can add extra flavours such as hot sauce, chilli sauce, sesame oil, chopped fresh herbs, spring onions, coriander leaves, etc.

For convenience and ease, eat your meal from the dish in which it has been cooked.

VARIATIONS: For a large serving, double the quantities and cook for 18–20 minutes.

To make an easy dinner for four, multiply all the ingredients by four. Put everything in a 2 litre lidded microwave dish, following the directions above. Cover and cook on High (100% power) for 30–35 minutes, then allow 5 minutes' standing time before serving.

Thirty-minute Bolognese

This sauce may not be all that close to the original Italian version, but it is still very good.

FOR 4–6 SERVINGS:

2 Tbsp olive oil
1 medium onion, diced
2 cloves garlic, chopped
1 medium carrot, finely diced
1 stick celery, thinly sliced
400–500g lean minced beef
½ tsp dried basil
½ tsp dried marjoram
1 x 400g can whole or diced tomatoes in juice
1x 300g can tomato purée
½–1 tsp salt
black pepper to taste
400–500g spaghetti, fettuccine, or other long pasta
1–2 Tbsp olive oil or butter
chopped parsley and/or grated parmesan cheese to garnish

Heat the oil in a large frypan. Add the onion and garlic and cook for 2–3 minutes, stirring frequently, until the onion is soft.

Stir in the carrot and celery and cook for 1 minute further, then add the beef. Cook, stirring frequently, until the beef has lost its pink colour. Add the herbs, tomatoes and tomato purée. Allow the mixture to boil, then reduce the heat to a gentle simmer and cover. Simmer gently for 10–15 minutes, stirring occasionally, while you cook the pasta (if the sauce begins to look dry add a quarter of a cup of pasta water or wine).

Drain the cooked pasta and toss it with the oil or butter, then arrange on individual plates or a platter. Spoon the sauce over the pasta and top with some chopped parsley and/or grated parmesan.

Serve accompanied by a salad or vegetables and crusty bread.

"Buttons & Bows" Frypan Dinner ▼

When you have had a long and tiring day, a well-balanced family dinner that can be cooked in half an hour in one pan seems a great idea. If you don't already have a large non-stick frypan with a lid, we suggest you get one.

FOR 4–5 SERVINGS:

2 tsp oil
1 large onion, chopped
1 tsp chopped garlic
500g minced beef or lamb
3 medium carrots
3 cups water
150g bow-shaped pasta
½ tsp salt
4 medium zucchini
1 x 430g can concentrated chicken soup
2–3 Tbsp chopped parsley or grated cheese (optional)

Heat the oil in a large frypan. Add the onion, garlic and the minced beef or lamb and brown slightly, stirring to break up the mince.

Cut the carrots into slices about 5mm thick (these comprise the red "buttons"). Add to the pan with the water and bring to the boil. Add the pasta and the salt, cover and simmer for 15 minutes.

Slice the zucchini (the green "buttons") a little thicker than the carrots, and stir them into the mixture in the pan. Cover and cook for 3–5 minutes until the pasta and zucchini are just tender.

Stir in the soup, then add the parsley or herbs and bring to the boil. Turn off and leave to stand for 5 minutes.

Serve in bowls, sprinkling each serving with chopped parsley or a little grated cheese if desired.

VARIATIONS: Use tomato, pumpkin or mushroom soup instead of the chicken soup if desired.

For a richer, creamy sauce, add ¼ cup cream along with the soup.

Replace the zucchini with green beans or broccoli, as long as you don't mind doing without the green "buttons".

"Home Alone" Special

Here is a recipe for any hungry person who wants an easy, filling 15-minute meal to eat in front of the television set. It is equally useful to feed to a couple of kids before the baby-sitter arrives and you rush out the door.

FOR 1 LARGE OR 2 MEDIUM SERVINGS:

250g sausage-meat or 4 sausages
1 tsp minced garlic
½ tsp oregano
1 x 425g can savoury tomatoes
1 cup water
1½ cups pasta spirals
¼ tsp salt
½ tsp sugar
1 cup frozen peas

Thaw the sausage-meat or the sausages in the microwave if necessary. Microwave on Medium (50%) power for 2 minutes.

If using sausages, cut through the sausage skins lengthwise, hold under a cold tap and peel away skins. Cut the sausage-meat or sausages into about 12 chunks, then brown in a medium-sized, non-stick frypan with a spoonful of minced garlic and the oregano.

Add half the contents of the can of tomatoes and all the water to the pan. When it starts to boil, stir in the uncooked pasta, cover, and cook for 10 minutes, turning once or twice during this time.

When the pasta is nearly cooked, add the salt, sugar, and the frozen peas. Mix to break up the peas, add a little extra water if the mixture looks dry, cover and cook for 4 minutes. Pour the remaining tomatoes over the mixture, and leave for a few minutes until they warm through.

Serve in one large bowl or two bowls with a crisp green salad on the side.

NOTE: If you keep a tube of sausage meat and peas in the freezer, a jar of minced garlic in the fridge, and pasta and a can of savoury tomatoes in your cupboard, this quick meal may be made at any time. Teach everybody in your house how to make it.

Easy Sausage & Macaroni

This recipe requires few ingredients, little time and next to no energy and as such is just the thing for an easy family dinner at the end of a busy day. What's more it will probably be a hot favourite with your children.

FOR 4 SERVINGS:

450–500g sausages or sausage-meat
1 large onion, chopped
1 x 400g can whole tomatoes in juice
1 cup water
½ tsp oregano
½ tsp salt
1 tsp brown sugar
1 small macaroni shapes
chopped parsley or grated parmesan cheese (optional)

Split the skins of sausages. With wet hands, remove the meat and form it into eight patties, or form the sausage-meat into eight patties.

Brown the patties on both sides in a large non-stick pan with a lid.

Add the onion and cook for 1–2 minutes, then add the tomatoes in their juice and the water. Stir in the oregano, salt, and sugar and break up the tomatoes.

When the liquid boils sprinkle in the macaroni, stir to mix well, then cover tightly and leave to simmer very gently until the macaroni is tender and the liquid absorbed, about 15 minutes.

Stir the mixture carefully, sprinkle with chopped parsley or grated parmesan cheese if using, and serve immediately on its own or with a green salad.

Ferhoodled Sausage ▶

Ferhoodled is a wonderful Pennsylvanian Dutch word meaning "all mixed up". In this recipe sausage patties are all mixed up with rice and vegetables in a one-pan dinner. You prepare the next ingredient while the previous one cooks – really easy!

FOR 4 SERVINGS:

250g plain or seasoned sausage-meat (see page 85)
2 onions, finely chopped
1 green pepper, roughly chopped
2 stalks celery, roughly chopped
1 large carrot, roughly chopped
1 cup long-grain rice
1 tsp each oregano, thyme and ground cumin
3 cups chicken stock or 3 cups water + 2 tsp instant
    stock powder
1 bay leaf (optional)
chopped parsley

Working with wet hands, form the sausage-meat into 12–16 small patties.

Brown the patties in a large lidded frypan. Add the chopped onions and cook until transparent, browning lightly. Add the prepared vegetables, then stir in the rice and the herbs and cook until the rice is translucent. Add the chicken stock and the bay leaf.

Cover and simmer for 15 minutes or until the rice is cooked and the water absorbed. Check several times, adding extra water during cooking if the mixture looks dry before the rice is cooked.

Adjust seasoning, adding salt if necessary. Sprinkle generously with chopped parsley and serve on its own or with a green salad or coleslaw.

VARIATION: Leave out the green pepper and add 1 cup of frozen peas after the rice has cooked for 10 minutes.

Sausage & Kumara Dinner

This tasty mixture may be cooked in a frypan or in a casserole in the oven. Once you have everything in the dish you can relax with your feet up or get on with something else until serving time.

FOR 4 GENEROUS SERVINGS:

800g kumara
500g plain or seasoned sausage-meat (see page 85)
salt and pepper (optional)
1 large onion
2 stalks celery
1 large green-skinned apple
¾ cup chicken stock or ¾ cup of water mixed with 1 tsp
    instant chicken stock powder
1 cup orange juice
2 Tbsp brown sugar
½ tsp mixed spice
4 tsp cornflour
¼ cup cold water
chopped parsley

Put the whole unpeeled kumara in a covered pot or in a microwave oven and cook until just tender. Season the sausage-meat if desired, then working with wet hands form it into 12–16 patties.

Brown the patties on both sides in a large frypan, discarding any fat. Remove the patties from the pan and set aside briefly.

Chop the onion, celery and unpeeled apple into 1cm cubes and place them in the pan in which the patties were cooked or in a large, fairly shallow casserole dish.

Peel the skin from the kumara and cut the flesh into 1cm cubes. Scatter over the uncooked vegetables in the pan and place the patties on top. Pour the chicken stock into the pan and add the orange juice. Mix the brown sugar and mixed spice and sprinkle over the contents of the pan.

Cover and simmer for 20 minutes, or bake at 180°C for 1¼ hours, until the vegetables are tender. Turn carefully once or twice if you are nearby.

Mix the cornflour with the water and stir in enough to thicken the juices in the pan or dish. Serve in shallow bowls, sprinkled with chopped parsley.

Slow-cooked Sausage Cassoulet

This may not be particularly authentic, but it is delicious, nonetheless.

FOR 4 SERVINGS:

1 Tbsp canola or olive oil
1 medium onion, quartered and sliced
about 150g chorizo or other smoked sausages, sliced
1 x 400g can whole or diced tomatoes in juice
2 x 400g cans cannellini beans, rinsed and drained
2 Tbsp tomato paste
½ tsp dried sage
½ tsp dried marjoram
500g pork sausages
½–1 tsp salt
pepper to taste

Heat the oil in a large pan. Add the onion and the sliced chorizo and cook, stirring occasionally for about 5 minutes or until the onion is soft.

Coat the slow cooker bowl with non-stick spray, then tip in the tomatoes (breaking up whole tomatoes if using). Add the beans, tomato paste and herbs, and stir gently until evenly mixed.

Prick each pork sausages with a fork in several places then nestle them into the bean mixture. Turn the cooker on to LOW, cover and cook for 8–9 hours.

Shortly before serving, lift the sausages from the beans and cut them into 1–2cm thick slices. Stir the sliced chorizo back into the bowl, and season to taste with salt and pepper.

Serve in bowls, with chunks of crusty French bread and a salad on the side.

Saturday Sausages

Over the years we have made, and our respective families have eaten with enjoyment, several versions of this recipe. This frypan version cooks in the shortest time. Instructions for a baked version are also provided.

FOR 4 SERVINGS:

500g precooked sausages
oil
2 onions
2 green-skinned apples
1 tsp each ground cumin and oregano with ¼ tsp chilli powder or ½ tsp dried thyme or ½ tsp crumbled dried sage (optional)
1 x 440g can baked or chilli beans
about ½ cup water, beer or wine
chopped parsley (optional)

Peel the skins from the sausages and slice each one diagonally into 5–6 pieces.

Brown the sausage pieces in a large non-stick frypan over moderate heat, adding a little oil if necessary, then remove from the pan and set aside briefly.

Halve the onions from top to bottom, then again, from top to bottom, slice them into wedge shapes. Brown in the pan in a little extra oil if necessary, then add the cored apples, each cut into 8–12 wedges.

When the apple and onion have browned add seasonings if using. Return the sausage pieces to the pan and add the beans and liquid of choice. Simmer for 5–10 minutes, stirring occasionally.

Sprinkle with chopped parsley if using, and serve on toasted split hamburger buns, rice or pasta, or on its own.

VARIATION: For baked Saturday Sausages combine all the ingredients, without browning, in a well-sprayed casserole dish with a cover. Add the empty bean can full of liquid, rather than ½ cup. Cover tightly, with a layer of foil under the lid if necessary, and bake at 180°C for about 1 hour or at 150°C for about 2 hours.

Slow-cooked Sausage & Mushroom Casserole ▼

Sausages cooked like this are transformed into very popular comfort food. We like the chunks of browned mushroom in this casserole but you could use smaller, lighter coloured canned mushrooms, if desired.

FOR 4 SERVINGS:

8 sausages
1 large onion
6 flat mushrooms, quartered
1 cup hot water
1 x 35g packet mushroom soup
¼ cup sherry or orange juice
6 medium potatoes
chopped parsley

Turn a 4-litre capacity slow cooker onto LOW and coat the inside of the bowl with non-stick spray.

Leave the sausages as they are or twist then halve them to make a total of 16 shorter sausages. Brown lightly in a non-stick frypan, then transfer them to the prepared slow cooker.

Chop the onion and brown with the quartered mushrooms in the frypan, adding a little oil if necessary. Add the browned vegetables to the sausages in the slow cooker.

Combine the hot water with the mushroom soup mix in a jug or bowl. Add the sherry or orange juice and pour over the sausage mixture.

Scrub or peel the potatoes and cut in half crosswise. Put them into the slow cooker with the cut surfaces against the sides of the bowl (it is more important for the potatoes than the sausages to be submerged in the liquid).

Cook on LOW for 6–8 hours, stirring gently and repositioning the sausages after about 5 hours, if possible. The mixture thickens quite a lot as it cooks, but you can thicken it a little more with a cornflour or arrowroot paste, if desired. Sprinkle with chopped parsley before serving. Serve with peas, cabbage or a salad.

VARIATIONS: About half an hour before serving, stir 2–3 chopped tomatoes through the mixture.

Make this recipe using the meat from skinned sausages formed into patties. To skin the sausages, split sausage skins end-to-end with a sharp knife and hold under a cold tap. The skins will then lift off easily and cleanly.

Slow-cooked Pork Sausages & Pineapple with Rice

It's worth experimenting with different sausages until you find some that slow cook well, then use them for all your slow cooker sausage recipes. While browning them first may seem fiddly, we have found that they nearly always look and taste better for this extra step.

FOR 4 SERVINGS:

canola or olive oil
8 good quality pork sausages
2 medium onions
¾ cup brown rice
1 or 2 peppers, preferably red and orange
1–1½ cups sliced celery
1 x 425g can pineapple pieces, juice reserved
2 tsp chicken or green herb instant stock powder or
    1 tsp salt
1 Tbsp brown sugar

Coat the inside of the bowl of a medium-to-large slow cooker with non-stick spray.

In a large frypan heat just enough oil to film the inside base over moderate heat. Add the sausages and brown evenly, turning and pricking them as they cook. Remove from heat and set aside.

Halve, then peel the onions. Cut into chunky pieces or slivers, as desired, and brown in the remaining oil in the pan, turning frequently. Add the rice to the pan, stir until lightly coated with oil, then transfer the mixture to a slow cooker.

Chop the peppers into fairly small, chunky pieces and add to the slow cooker with the sliced celery and drained pineapple. Add to the reserved pineapple juice enough water to make the liquid up to 1½ cups. Stir in the instant stock and the brown sugar. Pour the liquid over the rice and vegetables and stir to mix.

Lay the sausages on top of the rice mixture. Cover and cook on HIGH for 4 hours or LOW for 7–8 hours.

Serve with quickly cooked green vegetables or a green salad or coleslaw. (Refrigerate leftover sausages and rice for later microwaving.)

NOTE: Don't be put off by brown rice. It's perfect for this recipe because you won't even notice that it isn't white, and it doesn't overcook as white rice would when cooked for this length of time.

Slow-cooked Curried Sausage Balls with Beans

One of our favourite and easiest recipes in 100 Great Ways To Use Slow Cookers & Crockpots is made with sausages, apples and tomatoes. This new mixture is more highly seasoned and includes baked beans, too. We ladle the mixture from the slow cooker into bowls, exactly as it is, without any rice, etc. We always make a large quantity because it is a good meal for six (or eight if you use the third can of beans) or it can be reheated for a second meal for a smaller number of people. Vary the seasonings to suit yourself. It is as good gently seasoned as it is when more interestingly spiced.

FOR 6–8 SERVINGS:

2 tsp ground cumin
1 tsp smoked or plain paprika
2 x 400g cans diced apple
2 or 3 x 400g cans baked beans
1 x 400g can whole tomatoes in juice
2 x 500g tubes sausage-meat
4 tsp curry powder, mild or hot as you prefer
4 Tbsp brown sugar
2-3 tsp arrowroot, potato flour or cornflour
½–1 cup chopped parsley

Spray the inside of the bowl of a 5.5 litre slow cooker with non-stick spray.

Mix together the cumin and the paprika.

Spread the diced apple in the cooker, then sprinkle with half the cumin mixture. Top with a layer of baked beans, including any liquid. Repeat these layers using the remaining apple, spices and baked beans. Cut the canned tomatoes in half then use them, along with their juice, to make a final layer on top of the beans.

Cut down the length of each tube of sausage meat with a sharp knife or scissors, then hold them, one at a time, under a gently running cold tap so the plastic peels off easily. Cut each length of sausage-meat into 12 even pieces, then working with wet hands form each piece into a ball.

Mix together the curry powder and brown sugar and sprinkle quarter of it into a round, flat-bottomed container. Roll six balls at a time in the curry mixture to coat, then transfer them to the top of the tomato layer in the slow cooker. Repeat this procedure three times until you have 24 coated balls in the slow cooker.

Cook on LOW for 8–9 hours or HIGH for 4 hours, then gently stir the mixture before thickening it with a little arrowroot or cornflour mixed to a paste with 3–4 tablespoons cold water. Leave for a few minutes until the sauce thickens, then stir the chopped parsley through the mixture. Check and adjust the seasonings as desired.

When serving the mixture, divide the meatballs evenly between bowls.

VARIATIONS: Change the amount of any ingredient to suit your taste or situation.

Always refrigerate leftovers. Reheat them in a microwave oven or in the slow cooker when required.

Sausage & Mushroom Patties ▶

This really quick and easy recipe is a great standby when you want food on the table 10 minutes after you come in the door.

....

FOR 3–4 SERVINGS:

450–500g sausage-meat
1 x 24g packet savoury mushroom sauce mix
1 cup water
3–4 Tbsp finely chopped parsley or mixed fresh herbs

....

Heat a large non-stick (preferably electric) frypan.

Cut down the length of the tube of sausage-meat with a sharp knife or scissors, then hold it under a gently running cold tap so the plastic peels off easily. Slice the sausage-meat into 16–20 rounds, then working with wet hands flatten and shape them fairly evenly. Put them into the hot pan, close together, to brown underneath, then turn them to brown the other side.

Turn down the heat. Cut the top off the packet of sauce. Open it to form a pouch, and holding it securely fill nearly to the top with the water. Stir with a teaspoon to mix the contents, then tip it over the patties. Turn the patties in the sauce after it has thickened and simmer for 2–3 minutes, adding extra liquid if you want more sauce.

Sprinkle generously with finely chopped parsley or other fresh herbs and serve immediately, on rice or fresh pasta, or with mashed potatoes. Peas and baby carrots go well alongside.

VARIATIONS: Add 1 teaspoon finely chopped garlic and 1 large flat brown mushroom, cut into 5mm cubes, to the browned patties. Cook over fairly high heat, stirring often, until the mushroom softens. Replace ¼ cup of the water with sherry, and add 1 teaspoon each of wine vinegar and soy sauce.

Slow-cooked Braised Sausages with Lentils

There is something very comforting about this combination of sausages and lentils – it conjures up images of sitting round a cosy fire eating on a cold winter's night.

....

FOR 4 SERVINGS:

1 Tbsp olive or canola oil
8 beef or pork sausages
1 medium onion, finely diced
2 cloves garlic, chopped
2 medium carrots, finely diced
2 sticks celery, diced
2–3 sprigs fresh thyme (or 1 tsp dried)
2 bay leaves
2 x 400g cans brown lentils, rinsed and drained
½ cup chicken stock
½ cup dry white wine
½ –1 tsp salt
pepper to taste

....

Heat the oil in a large frypan, add the pricked sausages and brown lightly on one side.

While the sausages brown, coat the inside of a slow cooker bowl with non-stick spray. Add the vegetables and herbs, stir to combine, then gently stir in the drained lentils. Transfer the sausages to the slow cooker and nestle them into the lentil mixture browned side up, then pour in the stock and wine.

Cover with the lid and cook on LOW for 8–9 hours.

Just before serving, lift out the sausages and set aside to keep warm. Season the lentil and vegetable mixture with salt and pepper to taste. If the mixture is very wet, turn the machine to HIGH and cook, uncovered, for a further 30 minutes.

To serve, spoon the lentils into shallow bowls and top with a couple of sausages. Some bread to mop up juices, and a simple salad, make ideal accompaniments.

Sausage Stir-fry

Delicious, tender-crisp, colourful vegetables teamed with precooked sausages make a very quickly prepared and nutritious meal.

FOR 4 SERVINGS:

1 Tbsp oil
1 tsp sesame oil
3 cloves garlic, finely chopped
2 tsp grated fresh root ginger
500g precooked sausages, skinned and sliced
8 cups sliced colourful and quick-cooking fresh
    vegetables, e.g. cabbage, broccoli, cauliflower,
    zucchini, red and green peppers, mushrooms,
    asparagus, green beans, and celery
½ cup chicken stock or 1 tsp instant chicken stock
    powder + ½ cup water
1 tsp cornflour
2 Tbsp brown sugar
2 Tbsp light soy sauce
2 Tbsp sherry

Heat the two oils in a large frypan or wok. Add the garlic and ginger and cook over high heat for 1 minute. Add the sliced sausages and stir-fry until the sausages have browned, then remove from the pan and set aside.

Reheat the pan and add the prepared vegetables with a little extra oil if necessary. Stir-fry until the vegetables are barely tender. Add the chicken stock to wilt and steam the vegetables as they cook, without adding any more oil. Return the browned sausages to the pan.

Mix together the cornflour, brown sugar, soy sauce and sherry and pour over the vegetables and sausages. Reheat, stirring constantly, until the mixture is glazed.

Serve immediately over cooked noodles or rice.

NOTE: For best results when you stir-fry use high heat all the time. A heavy-bottomed frypan or wok gives best results.

Curried Pineapple Patties

Put some rice on to cook before you start this, and you will have a tasty meal with very little effort! With a tube of sausage-meat in the freezer, and pineapple and rice in your cupboard, you are never stuck for a quick, easy meal.

FOR 4 SERVINGS:

450–500g sausage-meat
2 tsp curry powder
2 tsp flour
1 tsp minced garlic
1 x 225g can pineapple rings in juice
1 Tbsp soy sauce
2–3 spring onions, finely chopped

Heat a large non-stick (preferably electric) frypan.

Working with wet hands, form the sausage-meat into 16–20 flattened patties. Put the patties in the hot pan, close together, to brown underneath, then turn them to brown the other side.

While the patties are browning, mix the curry powder and flour together. Transfer to a sieve and shake the mixture evenly over the uncooked side of the patties. Using tongs, turn the patties over and add the garlic to the pan and shake to disperse evenly.

Cut the pineapple rings into small slices. Tip the pineapple, juice, and soy sauce into the pan before the garlic browns.

When the juice has thickened, turn the patties to coat the other side with the pineapple glaze.

Sprinkle the patties with the chopped spring onion. Serve on rice or pasta, or with mashed potatoes. Beans, broccoli or frozen peas go well alongside.

NOTE: If you are starting with a tube of frozen sausage-meat, cut the metal fastener off the tube, then microwave the tube on High (100% power) for 2 minutes. Remove the plastic casing under the cold tap, and slice the roll while it is partly frozen.

Winter Sausages

If we have tamarillos in the house, we always use them for this recipe because they go so well with sausages. When they are out of season, you can make this recipe using a can of peeled tomatoes instead, in which case you won't need to add so much juice. This recipe may be made ahead and reheated.

FOR 4 SERVINGS:

8 sausages
1 large onion, chopped
2–3 cloves garlic, chopped
vegetable oil
4 tamarillos
1 cup orange, tomato or other fruit juice
¼ cup brown sugar
½ tsp salt
1 Tbsp tomato paste
Tabasco sauce to taste

Brown the sausages in a large heavy pot, pan or iron casserole, turning to colour evenly. Add the onion and garlic, with a little oil, if necessary, and cook until lightly browned, stirring occasionally.

Peel and chop the tamarillos into chunky pieces and add, with the remaining ingredients, to the sausages.

Cover and simmer for about 20 minutes until the liquid is of gravy consistency. If it is too thin, boil it down or thicken it with a little cornflour paste.

Serve with plainly cooked pasta, rice, or mashed potatoes, and pan-cooked cabbage, and you have a really good family meal for a cold night.

NOTE: To remove the skins from tamarillos, spear the fruit with a fork and hold it over a gas flame, turning so the skin is evenly heated, then run under the cold tap before peeling off the skin. Alternatively, pour boiling water over the fruit, then cool as above.

VARIATION: Instead of wine or fruit juice, you may prefer to use 2 tablespoons of wine vinegar or lemon juice, made up to 1 cup with water.

Sweet & Sour Sausages

We're always surprised at the number of children who list sweet and sour as one of their all-time favourite flavours. This recipe is easy enough for children to make after they have watched and helped you a couple of times.

FOR 4 SERVINGS:

8 sausages
oil or butter
¼ cup brown sugar, firmly packed
1 Tbsp cornflour
¼ cup cider vinegar
2 tsp soy sauce
1 x 225g can pineapple pieces in juice

Prick the sausages and cook in a frypan in a small amount of oil or butter over moderate heat, turning frequently, until they are evenly browned.

While the sausages cook, make the sauce in a medium-sized pot. Mix the brown sugar thoroughly with the cornflour, then stir in the vinegar, soy sauce and the juice from the pineapple. Bring the sauce to the boil, stirring continuously. As soon as it is thick and clear, turn off the heat.

Drain the oil from the sausages. When they are cool enough to handle, slice them diagonally and return them to the pan with the sauce and the pineapple pieces. Bring to the boil and simmer for 5 minutes.

Serve on rice. A crisp salad makes a nice accompaniment.

VARIATIONS: Use precooked sausages if you prefer. Slice them diagonally, then brown in a large frypan. Cut a red and a green pepper into thumbnail-sized pieces. Add to the browned sausages and cook for 2–3 minutes before adding the sauce (see above). Add 1–3 tablespoons of sweet Thai chilli sauce to the thickened sauce.

Kiwi Curried Sausages

These are the curried sausages that most New Zealanders of a certain age will remember fondly from their childhood. Feel free to add extra ingredients – such as coconut, chutney etc. – that your own mother may have used.

FOR 4 SERVINGS:

8 sausages
1 onion, chopped
1 apple, diced
2–3 tsp curry powder
1 cup sultanas
1 cup water
1 tsp instant chicken stock powder
2 Tbsp apricot or plum jam
1 Tbsp wine vinegar
1 tsp cornflour

Brown the sausages gently in a large frypan or pot. Add the onion and cook until lightly browned. Add the apple and the curry powder. Cook for 3–4 minutes, stirring to coat the sausages, onion and apple.

Add the remaining ingredients, including any of your own special additions, except the cornflour and stir well to combine. Cover and cook over a low heat for 20–30 minutes.

Mix the cornflour with a little water to make a thin paste. Stir into the sausage mixture and reheat, stirring, until the mixture thickens slightly.

Serve with rice or mashed potatoes and a variety of fresh vegetables.

VARIATIONS: Add 1 tablespoon of Worcestershire sauce.

If you have no jam handy, use 1 tablespoon of brown sugar instead.

Spicy Sausages

If you keep a packet of precooked sausages in your freezer, replacing them each time you use them, you know you can put a meal on the table in just a few minutes.

FOR 4 SERVINGS:

about 500g precooked sausages
about 2 tsp oil
2 rashers bacon
1 medium onion
¼ cup tomato or barbecue sauce
2 tsp prepared mustard
about ¼ cup water
chopped parsley

If necessary, thaw the sausages still in their packet or in a plastic bag on Defrost (30% power) in a microwave oven until they are soft enough to slice. Peel off the skin and cut each into about six diagonal slices.

Heat the oil in a large frypan. Cook the slices over moderate heat, turning them at intervals so all the cut surfaces brown.

While the sausages are browning, cut the rind from the bacon and chop the rashers into 1cm pieces. Peel and chop the onion finely. Add the bacon and onion to the browned sausages and cook until the onions have browned slightly. Stir in the tomato or barbecue sauce, mustard and water. Bring to the boil, turn the sausage slices to coat with the glaze, sprinkle generously with chopped parsley and serve.

VARIATION: You may like to try this recipe with some of the flavoured sausages that are now readily available, e.g. chorizo or spicy Italian. Gently cook the raw sausages in a little water in a covered pan until they are firm, then drain off any fat which has accumulated during cooking. Slice sausages diagonally and proceed as above.

Slow-cooked Curried Sausage Patties ▶

This mixture may be easy and inexpensive, but it is also very popular and tasty. What's more, it makes a surprisingly large amount, expanding as it cooks. We like this mixture served on brown rice, previously cooked in the slow cooker then frozen or refrigerated, with green beans or a green salad.

FOR 4 SERVINGS:

500g sausage-meat or skinned sausages
2 tsp curry powder
2 Tbsp dark brown sugar
2 Tbsp flour, preferably wholemeal
1 x 400g can diced apple or 1 x 350g can apple sauce or
   2 large apples, grated
salt and pepper to taste
ground cumin (optional)
1–2 cups chopped ripe red tomatoes or 1 x 400g can
   chopped tomatoes
chopped parsley

Coat the inside of the bowl of a 3–4 litre capacity slow cooker with non-stick spray and turn to HIGH.

To skin the sausages, cut down the length of each with a sharp knife or scissors, then hold under a gently running cold tap so the casing peels off easily. Working with wet hands, form the sausage-meat into eight balls.

Measure the curry powder, sugar and flour into a round flat-bottomed bowl or dish, mixing well with dry fingers or a whisk.

Drop three or four of the sausage-meat balls at a time into the bowl and rotate the bowl to coat all surfaces of the balls. Transfer the coated balls to the slow cooker.

Arrange the apple over the balls, sprinkle with the remaining curry mixture and the other seasonings, then spread the chopped tomatoes on top.

Cover with the lid and cook on HIGH for 3–4 hours or on LOW for 6–8 hours. Turn the contents gently at least once to combine them, then sprinkle with chopped parsley just before serving. Serve on or with white or brown rice with a green cooked vegetable or a side salad.

South-of-the-Border Sausages

This spicy corn and sausage sauce is almost as good on rice as it is on pasta. If you are cooking for people who do not like hot food, just leave out the chilli powder. The other flavourings add flavour, not hotness!

FOR 4–6 SERVINGS:

500g precooked sausages, sliced diagonally
1 tsp minced garlic
1 onion, chopped into thumbnail-sized chunks
1 green, yellow or orange pepper, chopped into
   thumbnail-sized chunks
1 red pepper, chopped into thumbnail-sized chunks
1 tsp each oregano and ground cumin
¼ –½ tsp chilli powder
1–2 tsp oil
1 cup chicken stock or 1 cup water + ¾ tsp instant
   chicken stock powder

SAUCE:
2 Tbsp butter
2 Tbsp flour
1 cup milk
1 x 310g can whole kernel corn
salt and sugar to taste
chopped parsley or coriander leaves

In a large non-stick frypan cook the sliced sausages over medium heat until lightly browned. As they cook, stir in the minced garlic, and the onion and peppers.

Sprinkle the spices over the mixture as it cooks. Add the oil only if no fat comes out of the sausages. After 3–4 minutes add the chicken stock. Simmer for 3–4 minutes until the vegetables are tender-crisp.

Make the sauce in a small pot or microwave dish. Melt the butter, stir in the flour, then add the milk and heat, stirring often, until the sauce thickens.

Drain off and keep the liquid from the canned corn, then combine the corn, white sauce and sausage mixture. Thin down with some of the corn liquid if too thick, then taste and add enough salt and sugar to bring out the flavours, if necessary.

Serve over cooked rice or pasta, sprinkled with parsley or coriander leaves.

Perfect Pies
& Packages

with Mince & Sausages

Filo Lamb Packages

These little crispy, golden filo packages are absolutely irresistible. By keeping the parcels small, you don't need to precook the lamb filling, which means they're also quick to make.

Sumac is a red wine-coloured, slightly crystalline-looking Middle Eastern seasoning. It has a fruity, tangy flavour that makes a nice addition to this recipe if you have it, but it can be omitted without any dire effects.

FOR 4 SERVINGS:

1 Tbsp olive oil
1 medium onion, diced
2 cloves garlic, chopped
¼ cup pine nuts
½ cup currants
400g minced lamb
2 tsp cumin
2 tsp sumac (optional)
½ tsp cinnamon
1 large egg
¼ cup chopped parsley
½ tsp salt
black pepper to taste
8–10 sheets filo pastry
2 Tbsp olive oil or melted butter

Preheat the oven to 170°C.

Heat the oil in a medium-sized frypan. Add the onion and garlic and cook, stirring frequently, for about 5 minutes until the onion is soft. Stir in the pine nuts and currants and cook for 2–3 minutes longer, or until the pine nuts are lightly browned and the currants have puffed up.

Combine the mince, spices, egg and parsley in a large bowl, add the cooked onion mixture and stir until everything is well combined. Add salt and pepper to taste, then mix again to combine.

Lay a sheet of filo pastry on a clean, dry surface. Lightly brush one side with oil or melted butter, then fold the sheet in half lengthwise. Place quarter of a cup of the lamb mixture near one end (avoid being over generous or the packages will be hard to shape and may burst during cooking), then diagonally fold one corner over the filling to make a pointy end. Fold the pointy end and the filling up to make the end square again. Continue folding until you are left with a triangular package. Brush the outside with a little more oil or butter, then place the package on a non-stick sprayed or teflon-lined baking sheet. Repeat to use all the filling and filo sheets.

Bake for 15 minutes, reducing the heat a little if they look like they're browning too much (but don't take the packages out too soon because the filling has to cook through).

Serve with rice or plain couscous and a green or tomato salad.

Filo Lamb Samosas

Although samosas are traditionally made with a special crust, we make our popular version by wrapping the spicy filling in filo pastry. They are best served the same day they are made as the pastry softens if it stands too long.

FOR 12 SAMOSAS:

250g minced lamb
1 onion, finely chopped
1 tsp grated fresh root ginger
½ tsp chilli powder
½ tsp turmeric
1 x 400g can Indian-style tomatoes or whole tomatoes in
    juice
1 cup frozen peas
1 tsp garam masala
2 Tbsp chopped coriander leaves, if available
1 Tbsp cornflour

12 sheets filo pastry
melted butter or oil

Combine the minced lamb and onion in a preheated frypan and cook, stirring frequently, until the mince is no longer pink. Stir in the ginger, chilli powder and turmeric as the meat cooks. Add the tomatoes in their juice and cook, uncovered, until almost dry. Stir in the peas, garam masala and chopped coriander leaves, and cook for a further 2 minutes.

Thicken with cornflour mixed to a thin paste with water; this will stop the filo pastry going soggy later. Set the mixture aside to cool.

Preheat the oven to 200°C.

Layer three sheets of filo pastry each brushed with a little melted butter or oil on top of each other and cut crosswise into four strips. Working with one strip at a time, put a twelfth of the filling mixture at the top of the strip, then fold the pastry over it so the top touches the side, forming a triangle. Keep folding in triangles until the filling is completely enclosed by the pastry and the whole strip is folded up. Repeat with the remaining filo pastry and filling to make a total of 12 samosas.

Place the samosas on a non-stick sprayed or teflon-lined baking sheet and bake for 8–10 minutes until evenly browned.

Serve warm or hot, reheating them if necessary.

Patricia's Pork Pie ▶

So quick and easy to make, and absolutely delicious served hot, warm, or cold, this pie is perfect for a picnic or packed lunch.

FOR 4–6 SERVINGS:

400g savoury short or crusty pastry, thawed
3 thick slices wholegrain bread
2 eggs, lightly beaten
1 large onion, roughly chopped
6 fresh sage leaves, chopped, or ½ tsp dried sage
about ¼ cup chopped parsley
1 tsp salt
2 Tbsp sherry (optional)
400–500g minced pork

Preheat the oven to 200°C.

Cut the block of pastry in half crosswise. Working on a lightly floured surface with a floured rolling pin, roll each half out on a floured board to form two 30–35cm squares. Set aside while you make the filling.

Break the bread into chunky pieces, then process to crumbs in a food processor. Set the crumbs aside.

In the bowl of the food processor combine the eggs (reserving about 1 tablespoonful to use as glaze), onion, sage, parsley, salt and sherry, if using, and process until the onion is finely chopped. Add the crumbs and minced pork, broken up into several chunks, then process in short bursts until everything is evenly mixed.

Put one square of pastry on a baking paper or Teflon-lined baking sheet, and spread the pork mixture in the centre. Moisten the uncovered pastry around the filling with cold water, and place the other sheet on top, pressing it down around the filling. Cut a dozen or so air vents over the filling.

Evenly trim the pastry edges, fold about 1cm under, then crimp or flute the edges. Brush with the reserved egg mixed with a teaspoon of water. If desired, cut the trimmings into shapes and arrange them on top of the pie, then brush with the remaining egg glaze. Bake for 15 minutes, then at 180°C for a further 30 minutes.

Spring Rolls

Everyone loves spring rolls, and as the wrappers can be found in the frozen foods sections of most larger supermarkets or specialty Asian food stores these days, why not have a go at making them yourself? If you don't like the idea of deep-frying the rolls, brush them with oil and bake in a very hot oven.

FOR 8–12 ROLLS (3–4 SERVINGS):

1 Tbsp canola oil
2 cloves garlic, crushed and chopped
2 Tbsp chopped fresh root ginger
250g pork mince
150g cooked and peeled prawns
1 medium carrot, peeled and grated
1 cup thinly sliced cabbage
1 x 110g can sliced bamboo shoots
3–4 spring onions, thinly sliced
2 Tbsp oyster sauce
1 Tbsp soy sauce
1 tsp sugar
2–3 tsp cornflour
2 Tbsp cold water
8–12 square spring roll wrappers, thawed
canola or other vegetable oil to fry or brush

Heat the first measure of oil in a large non-stick frypan. Add the garlic, ginger and pork mince.

Cook, stirring frequently to break up any lumps, for about 5 minutes or until the pork mince has lost its pink colour, then remove the pan from the heat.

Tip the pork mixture into a large bowl and add the prawns, carrot, cabbage, bamboo shoots and spring onions. Stir to combine, then add the oyster sauce, soy sauce and sugar and mix thoroughly.

Mix the cornflour and water together and set aside.

Working with one wrapper at a time, place it on a clean dry board with one corner pointing towards you. Place 3–4 tablespoons of filling to form a line just below the halfway mark. Don't be too generous or they will be hard to roll and may burst during cooking. Fold the bottom corner of the wrapper up so it covers the filling, brush the exposed parts of the wrapper with the cornflour and water mixture, then fold the two edge corners in to make an envelope-shaped package. Starting from the bottom, roll up the package to form a cylinder, then brush the flap with a little more cornflour-water mixture to seal if required. Repeat this process until the desired number of wrappers has been filled.

Heat 3–4cm of oil over medium-high heat in a wok or pot and fry two or three rolls at a time, turning occasionally, for 4–5 minutes or until golden brown, then drain on paper towels. OR arrange the rolls on a teflon or baking paper-lined oven sheet. Generously brush the rolls with oil and bake at 225°C for 15 minutes.

Serve with steamed rice, and Asian vegetables such as bok choy, broccolini, or sesame cabbage.

Pieburgers ▲

This American recipe is easier to make than regular meat pies and is popular with all age groups. The filling is not precooked, the pastry is very tasty, and when cooked the pieburgers can be frozen for future school lunches, picnics and unexpected callers.

CRUST:
1 quantity cheese pastry (see page 58)
milk

FILLING:
1 egg, lightly beaten
500g minced beef
1 x 25g packet mushroom sauce or 1 x 30g packet
   French onion soup
¼ cup tomato sauce
2 Tbsp flour
lightly toasted sesame seeds (optional)

Make the cheese pastry following the instructions on page 58. Roll out the chilled pastry into two thin squares, each about 30–35cm. (Use edge pieces of pastry to patch any areas that are not quite big enough, sticking them on with a little water.)

Set half the beaten egg mixture aside. Combine the other half with the rest of the filling ingredients except the sesame seeds in a mixing bowl or food processor and mix.

Preheat the oven to 200°C.

Divide the filling into nine equal portions, then roll out each portion into a ball.

Brush one square of pastry lightly with a little milk. Using your fingernail or the back of a knife blade, lightly mark out three rows of three equal-sized squares (making nine squares altogether). Place a ball of filling on each square, then slightly flatten it. Roll the other square of pastry round the rolling pin to avoid stretching it, then lay it on top so all the balls are covered. Use the rolling pin and your fingers to press the two layers of pastry together between and around the balls of filling. Cut an air vent in the top of each. Cut the pastry into nine squares using a knife or serrated cutting wheel.

Brush the pieburgers with the reserved beaten egg. If desired, reroll the pastry off-cuts, then cut them into strips and use them to decorate the glazed tops.

Carefully transfer the pieburgers onto an oven sheet covered with baking paper or a Teflon liner. Sprinkle with lightly toasted sesame seeds, if desired. Bake for about 30 minutes or until golden brown. Reduce the temperature after 15–20 minutes if they brown too quickly.

Serve hot, warm, reheated or cold. Refrigerate for up to 2 days or wrap individually and freeze up to 3 months.

VARIATION: Make 16 small pieburgers.

Picnic Pie

Sausages make excellent additions to "portable" picnic pies. Use frankfurters, precooked sausages or luncheon sausage, with vegetables for colour and texture. Large shallow pies cook faster than small deep ones, and are easier to eat, too.

FOR 8–12 SERVINGS:

400–500g flaky pastry
2–4 medium cooked potatoes
2 cups cooked peas
6 frankfurters or cooked sausages
¼ cup chopped mint or other fresh herbs
6 eggs
½ tsp salt
1 x 400g can whole tomatoes in juice

Preheat the oven to 220°C.

Roll out a bit more than half of the pastry very thinly and use it to line a 23 x 35cm sponge roll tin, allowing an overhang. Roll out the remaining pastry equally thinly and set aside.

Slice the potatoes into the pastry-lined tin, then spread half the peas around them. Slice the frankfurters or sausages into chunky, small pieces and add them to the tin. Sprinkle with the chopped herbs.

Beat the eggs one at a time with a fork, just enough to break the yolks, and pour over the filling, reserving 1 tablespoon to glaze the pastry. Add the remaining peas to the pie and sprinkle with salt. Drain the canned tomatoes, then slice them. Drain again and arrange evenly over pie filling.

Spread the thinly rolled pastry top over the filling. The pastry from the bottom crust should be large enough to overlap the top crust by about 2cm. Trim evenly if necessary, dampen the edges with water and gently press down over the edge of the top crust. Brush the surface with the reserved egg and pierce about 12 times over the top crust.

Bake for 15 minutes until golden brown, then bake at 150°C for a further 15 minutes.

Serve, warm, reheated or cold, cut into rectangular pieces, with a salad, bread rolls, etc. to suit the occasion.

Uncooked Fillings for Pies

Using minced beef or lamb as the main ingredient, you can make many different kinds of pie fillings. Leftovers from numerous recipes in this book will make a few little pies for school lunches, while delicious uncooked fillings make larger scale pie production easy.

ARABIAN LAMB FILLING (MAKES 8–10 LITTLE PIES)

1 large onion
1½ tsp salt
½–1 cup loosely packed parsley leaves
2 Tbsp fine dry breadcrumbs
½ tsp each chilli powder and allspice
¼ cup toasted pine nuts (optional)
3 Tbsp lemon juice
1 Tbsp tomato paste
about 500g minced lamb

Roughly chop the onion and put into a food processor bowl with the next five ingredients, including the pine nuts, if using. Process in bursts until everything is very finely chopped, then add the lemon juice and tomato paste, and process again to mix. Add the minced lamb, broken into six even-sized chunks and process until blended. Use the filling to make little pies of your choice.

FOR PIEBURGERS: Make some short pastry following the recipe on page 58 and then follow the directions for Pieburgers on page 56.

FOR PASTIES: Cut thinly rolled short pastry in 10cm rounds, and shape them into pasties following the recipe on page 58.

FOR LAMB TRIANGLES: Put a little filling in the centre of 10cm rounds of thinly rolled short pastry, brush the edges with beaten egg, and lift the edges up to the centre in three places, pinching them together to make small triangular pies. Brush the outsides with more egg and bake at 200°C for about 20 minutes until golden. (The sides usually shrink a little during cooking, leaving some of the filling visible. This looks good!)

OTHER FILLINGS:

The following recipes may be modified to make pie fillings in the same way as the Pieburger and Arabian Lamb Pie fillings:

Swedish Meatballs, see page 24 (use only 1½ slices of rye bread)

Meatballs with Indonesian Sauce, see page 24 (use only 1 thin slice of bread)

Moroccan Meatballs, see page 23 (use only 1 slice of bread)

American Meat Loaf, see page 12 (use ¼ cup dry breadcrumbs)

Curried Meat Loaf, see page 14 (use only ½ cup rolled oats)

Tomato-topped Meat Loaf, see page 11 (use only ¼ cup rolled oats)

Pastry for Pies

Pies are always popular. The combination of a minced beef, lamb, pork or chicken filling and a good pastry crust can make an excellent pie – as long as you get the pastry crust right. Here are some of our favourite pastry recipes.

Short Pastry

Short pastry is much cheaper than bought pastry and can be made in less time than it takes to thaw frozen pastry. It is especially easy to make if you have a food processor.

It makes a better lower pie crust than either flaky or puff pastry, which do not brown as well and do not finish up with such good texture because they contain more fat.

Short pastry is also good for the upper crust too, especially when brushed with egg before it is baked, although it is not as flaky as upper crusts made with flaky or puff pastry.

FOR 1 LARGE MEAT PIE OR 6 DOUBLE-CRUST 10CM MEAT PIES:

2 cups flour
125–150g cold butter
½ cup cold water
2 tsp lemon juice (optional)

1 egg, lightly beaten with 1 Tbsp water

BY HAND: Sift the flour into a bowl. Cut the butter into about nine cubes and rub into the flour (using a pastry blender, two knives or your fingers) until the mixture looks like rolled oats. Add the lemon juice to half the cold water, and have the rest of the water on hand.

Add the lemon-water to the flour in a thin stream while you toss the flour with a fork. Add just enough of the plain water to make a dough wet enough to stick together when you press it with your fingers.

IN A FOOD PROCESSOR: Measure the flour into the bowl fitted with the metal chopping blade. Add the cold butter, cut into about nine cubes. Do not process until you start adding the lemon-water in a thin stream, then process in short bursts, using the pulse button. Over-mixing makes pastry tough. Add some of the plain water in the same way, stopping and testing the mixture, which will probably still look dry, but should be damp enough to hold together when you press it with your fingers.

Whether made by hand or food processor, form pastry into a ball and refrigerate for at least 5 minutes before rolling out.

FOR A 23–25 CM DOUBLE CRUST PIE: Preheat the oven to 200°C. Divide the pastry in half. On a lightly floured board roll out one half to form a circle 3–5cm larger than the pie dish. Ease the pastry into the dish, then add the filling. Brush the rim with the beaten egg before covering with the remaining pastry rolled out to the size of the pie dish. Press the edges together then trim with a sharp knife before crimping the edges with your fingers or press with a fork. Cut vents in the top and brush with the remaining

beaten egg. Bake for about 1 hour. If the pie browns too quickly, reduce the temperature to 180°C after 20–30 minutes. Remove from the pie dish while still warm and cool on a rack.

FOR SMALL PIES: Preheat the oven to 200°C. On a lightly floured board roll out the pastry very thinly to measure about 35–40cm across. To make the top or upper crusts, cut the tops a little bigger than the actual pie dishes and set aside while you make the bases (it doesn't matter if you piece together the bottoms from various bits of pastry as it won't show). Cut out a piece of thinly rolled pastry to fit the pie dish. Press and stretch it to get rid of "pleats" round the top, then trim off unwanted edges. Repeat to line five more pie dishes, rerolling scraps of pastry if necessary. Spoon in the filling so pies are three-quarters full, leaving the top of the pastry sides clear. Brush with a little beaten egg (see previous recipe), then put the tops on, firmly pressing the edges onto the egged part, using a fork if desired. Brush the top crusts with the remaining beaten egg etc. and cut a hole in the top of each for steam to escape. Bake for 20–30 minutes. Take out of the pie dishes while hot, or quite warm, and leave to cool on a rack.

Cheese Pastry

This pastry has a better colour and flavour than short pastry. It makes wonderful Pieburgers (see page 56) and pasties. Use it for pies that are baked on flat oven sheets rather than in pie dishes.

2 cups flour
125g very cold butter
1 cup grated tasty cheese
about ½ cup cold water
2 tsp lemon juice

BY HAND: Sift the flour into a large bowl. Cut or grate the butter into the flour until the mixture resembles rolled oats. Add the cheese and toss to mix. Add the liquid as for hand-made short pastry then refrigerate for at least 5 minutes or until required.

IN A FOOD PROCESSOR: Measure the flour into the bowl. Add the cubed cold butter and the grated cheese. Mix as for food-processor short pastry (see above), stopping when the mixture holds together when pressed against the side of the bowl. Refrigerate for at least 5 minutes or until required.

Pasties

Cut saucer-sized circles in some short or cheese pastry. Put cooked or uncooked filling in the centre of each circle (don't use too much), dampen the edge with beaten egg and water, then fold in half to make a semi-circle shape. Press the edges together, decorate if desired, brush with egg and cut one or more air holes in each. Bake at 200°C for 20–30 minutes until golden brown.

Jane's Sausage Pie

This practical family pie is good served hot or cold. Vary the amount of curry powder according to your family's taste.

FOR 6 SERVINGS:

½ cup rice
400g flaky pastry
2 medium apples
2 onions
1 egg, beaten
1 Tbsp curry powder
1 Tbsp Worcestershire sauce
1 Tbsp tomato sauce
1 Tbsp chopped parsley
450–500g sausage-meat

Preheat the oven to 200°C.

Cook the rice in 1½ cups of lightly salted boiling water until tender. Drain. Roll out a little more than half the pastry very thinly and use it to line the bottom of a 23cm square cake tin with sides at least 3cm high, bringing the pastry up the sides of the tin and allowing some to overhang. Roll out the remaining pastry in a smaller square to fit the top of the pie, and set aside.

Peel the apples and onions and chop very finely or grate coarsely into a large bowl. Add the cooked rice and the remaining ingredients and mix thoroughly. (If you have a food processor chop together the peeled apple and onion, add the egg, seasonings, then the sausage-meat in chunks and the cooked rice. Using the pulse button, process in bursts without over-mixing.)

Lightly press the filling into the pastry-lined tin, top with the rolled-out pastry, trimming off any excess, and seal the edges. Prick the top with a fork in several places.

Bake for about 1 hour at 200°C until the pastry is golden brown, and the filling feels firm when pressed.

Serve hot with a salad for an easy summer meal, cut into small pieces and serve as finger food, or serve cold for an outdoor meal or picnic.

Empanadas

Empanadas are little pies, that are now commonly eaten as fast food in Central America. The fillings vary in content and spiciness – here is our delicious variation.

MAKES 8:

PASTRY:

3 cups plain flour
½ tsp salt
½ cup oil
½ cup yoghurt
about ¼ cup water

FILLING:

¼ cup raisins or sultanas
2 Tbsp rum, brandy, sherry or lemon juice
2 eggs
1 medium onion, finely chopped
2 cloves garlic, finely chopped
250–300g minced lamb or beef
2 Tbsp oil
2 tsp ground cumin
½ tsp each paprika and cinnamon
¼ tsp chilli powder (optional)
¼ cup chopped green or black olives
1 Tbsp tomato paste
2 Tbsp white wine, lemon or lime juice
2–3 Tbsp chopped parsley
about ¼ tsp salt

To make the pastry, measure the flour, salt, and oil into the bowl of a food processor. Process in short bursts until the mixture looks like fine breadcrumbs. Add the yoghurt and process in a few more bursts. Add the water, 1 tablespoon at a time, processing briefly and testing to see if the mixture will press together to form a dough between each addition (take care not to over-mix as this will toughen the dough). Transfer the dough ball to a plastic bag and refrigerate while you make the filling.

Steep the raisins in the rum, brandy, sherry or lemon juice. Hard-boil the eggs for 8–10 minutes, then cool and peel.

Meanwhile, cook the onion, garlic and mince in the oil in a large frypan, stirring frequently, until the meat has lost its pink colour. Add the seasonings, followed by the olives, tomato paste and wine or juice. Reduce the heat and cook, stirring occasionally, for 5 minutes then remove from the heat. Chop the hard-boiled eggs and add them along with the soaked raisins, and any remaining soaking liquid, to the meat mixture in the pan. Add salt to taste.

Preheat the oven to 180°C.

Divide the chilled dough into eight pieces. Shape each piece into a ball and return all but one to the fridge. Roll out the reserved ball on a floured surface until it measures 15cm across. Place about quarter of a cup of the filling in the middle, then moisten the edges with a little water and fold the dough in half, making a half moon shape. Seal the edges using your fingers or the tines of a fork. Repeat with the remaining dough balls to make eight empanadas.

Arrange the pies on a lightly oiled or Teflon-covered baking sheet, then brush with oil. Bake for 25–30 minutes or until golden brown.

Serve warm, or at room temperature, with your favourite chilli sauce or salsa.

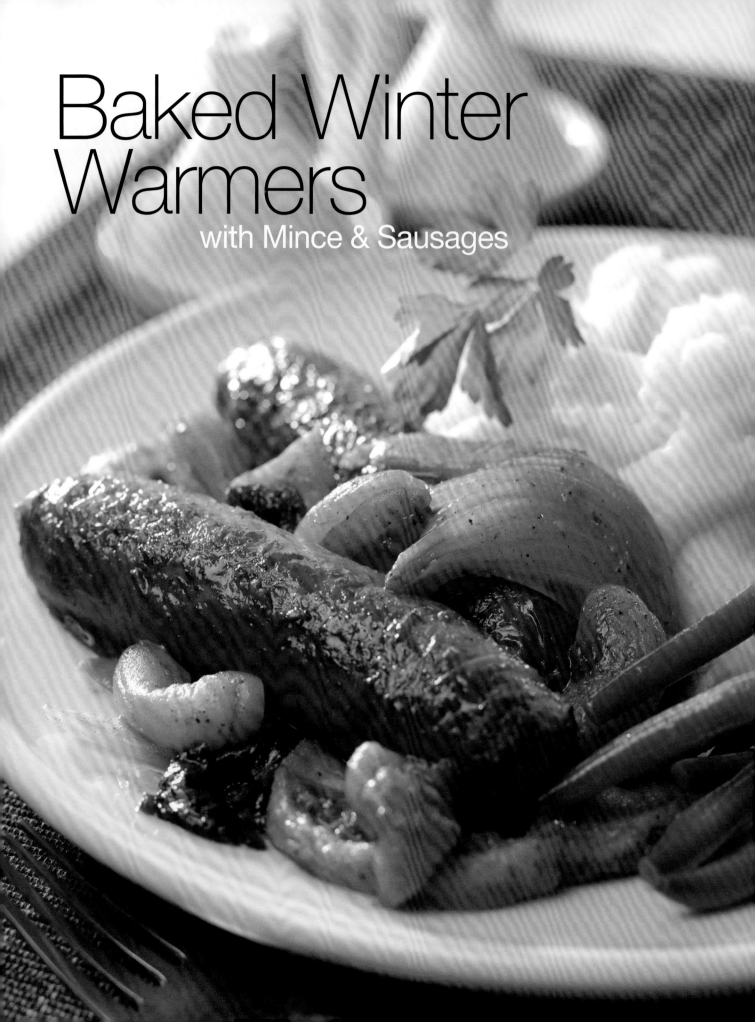

Baked Winter Warmers

with Mince & Sausages

Sultan's Sausages

These sausages are simmered in a well-spiced fruity sauce that turns them into something really special. You may like to make this recipe with some of the gourmet sausages that are now readily available. You can also make this ahead and reheat it when required.

FOR 4 SERVINGS:

8 sausages
1 small onion
1 tsp minced garlic
oil
1 tsp grated fresh root ginger
1 tsp grated orange rind
½ cup orange juice
¼ tsp chilli powder (optional)
½ cup white wine
1 cup chicken stock or 1 cup water + 1 tsp instant
    chicken stock
8 dried apple rings, halved
8 dried apricots, halved
8 prunes, halved
½ tsp each ground allspice and cinnamon
2 tsp brown sugar
1 Tbsp sour cream
salt and pepper to taste

Cook the sausages in a large heavy pot, frypan, or iron casserole, turning to colour evenly. Add the onion, cut into wedges, and the garlic with a dribble of oil if necessary and cook until lightly browned, stirring occasionally.

Add the remaining ingredients except the sour cream, salt and pepper. Cover and cook over a low heat for about 20–30 minutes. Remove from the heat and stir in the sour cream. Season to taste.

Serve with couscous cooked in chicken stock, rice or mashed or baked potatoes and with a lettuce, tomato and cucumber salad.

Slow-cooked Babotie

Alison was given the recipe for this mild curry baked under an eggy crust when she was a student. Like most recipes, it has changed a little over the years and we've now found that it translates well to the slow cooker. You can use pretty much any type of bread.

FOR 4 SERVINGS:

2 slices stale bread
1 cup milk
1 large onion
1 Granny Smith or Braeburn apple, peeled
1 Tbsp butter or oil
2–3 tsp curry powder, according to taste
500g minced beef
½–1 tsp salt
¼ cup currants or sultanas
2 Tbsp brown sugar or jam
2 Tbsp lemon juice or wine vinegar
2 eggs
2 Tbsp parmesan cheese (optional)

Coat the inside of the bowl of a medium-to-large slow cooker with non-stick spray.

Break the bread slices into several pieces. Place in a small bowl, cover with the milk and leave to soften.

Finely chop the onion and apple. Heat the butter in a large frypan, then add the apple and onion and cook over moderate heat, stirring occasionally, until lightly browned and softened. Stir in the curry powder, cook for a few minutes longer, then stir in the mince. Raise the heat and cook until the meat is no longer pink. Stir in the salt, brown sugar or jam, dried fruit and lemon juice, then remove from the heat.

Drain the soaked bread, reserving the milk. Add one egg to the softened bread, and mix well with a fork until evenly combined. Stir the bread mixture evenly through the partly cooled mince mixture, then press it evenly into the slow cooker. Turn it to HIGH, cover and cook for 3 hours.

When the cooking time is up, add the second egg to the reserved milk and beat with a fork to mix well. Pour over the meat to cover, then sprinkle with the parmesan cheese, if using. Cover and cook on HIGH for 1 hour, with the lid ajar for the final 20–30 minutes.

Serve with a green salad and bread rolls, or with mashed potatoes and green beans or broccoli.

Cornbread-Crusted Chilli

We love the smell of this wonderful comfort food wafting through the house. It could be described as a "South Western" or "Tex-Mex" version of Shepherd's Pie.

FOR ABOUT 6 SERVINGS:

2 Tbsp oil
2 onions, chopped
600g minced beef or lamb
½–1 tsp chilli powder
1 tsp each oregano, ground cumin and paprika
1 x 400g can whole tomatoes in juice
1 x 440g can baked beans

CORNBREAD TOPPING:

50g butter, melted
1 onion, chopped
½ cup sour cream
¼ cup milk or water
1 x 225g can creamed corn
1 egg
1 cup yellow cornmeal *
1 tsp each baking powder and salt
1 cup grated tasty cheese

* Use cornmeal of the same consistency or coarseness as semolina.

Preheat the oven to 180°C.

Heat the oil in a large frypan and lightly but evenly brown the chopped onion. Add the minced meat and cook over high heat, stirring frequently to break up the pieces, until the mince is no longer pink. Add the chilli powder (use the smaller amount for a mild chilli flavour), oregano, cumin and paprika, then cook for about 1 minute longer. Stir in the tomatoes and baked beans, then simmer gently for about 10 minutes while you make the cornbread topping.

For the topping melt the butter in a microwave dish or pot large enough to hold all the topping ingredients. Add the chopped onion and cook until the onion turns translucent (i.e. without browning).

Remove from the heat and add the sour cream, milk or water, creamed corn and egg and mix well with a fork. Stir in the cornmeal, baking powder, salt and grated cheese.

Transfer the mince mixture to a large shallow ovenware dish. Spread the topping over it and bake, uncovered, for about 30 minutes until the topping is firm in the centre and browned on top.

Spoon onto individual plates and serve with a green salad or cooked green vegetable.

Anne's Stroganoff

This recipe was given to Alison many years ago by a Californian friend and over subsequent years we've both found it a great recipe to make ahead and serve when we entertain families with children. Come to think about it, we can't remember a single child who hasn't enjoyed it!

FOR 8 SERVINGS:

250g small lasagne noodles or other pasta shapes
50g butter
2 large onions, chopped
2 cloves garlic, chopped
about 300g button mushrooms, quartered
1kg minced beef or lamb
1 x 35g packet mushroom soup mix
2–3 tsp instant beef or chicken stock powder
2 cups water or ½ cup white wine + 1½ cups water
2 Tbsp tomato paste
1 x 250g carton regular or light sour cream
about ¼ cup grated parmesan cheese

Cook the pasta in plenty of boiling salted water until barely tender. Drain, rinse with cold water to stop over-cooking and spread in a large, shallow, lightly sprayed ovenware dish.

While the pasta cooks, melt the butter in a large frypan and cook the onion and garlic and mushrooms until the onions are transparent. Remove from the pan, then cook the mince until it has lost all its pinkness. Stir in the mushroom soup mix and the instant beef stock powder. Add the water (or wine and water) and stir until the mixture boils. Simmer for 5 minutes, then stir in the cooked onion mixture, the tomato paste and sour cream. Spoon over the pasta. Sprinkle with parmesan cheese, cover and refrigerate until required.

To reheat, bake, covered, at 180°C for 20 minutes, then uncovered for another 20 minutes, or until the mixture has heated right through and is bubbling around the edges.

Serve with a crisp green salad.

VARIATION: To make half this recipe, use one packet of soup and leave out the instant stock. Halve all the other ingredients.

Cottage Pie

This recipe isn't exactly highbrow, but it makes a delicious cottage pie – with a twist! It can be cooked in a slow cooker or, if you prefer, it can be baked traditionally in the oven. To get it ready the day before, prepare it up to the point it is ready to place in the slow cooker or oven, then refrigerate it until required. While this recipe can be doubled, do check that your slow cooker – and the container in which the pie will cook – is large enough.

FOR 2–3 SERVINGS:

600–700g floury or all-purpose potatoes
1 onion
1–2 carrots
1 stalk celery
250g minced beef
1 Tbsp flour
1 Tbsp tomato concentrate
1 Tbsp Worcestershire sauce
½ cup stock or 1 tsp instant stock powder dissolved in ½ cup water
2 tsp butter
milk as required
¼ cup grated cheese
pinch of ground paprika (optional)

Peel and quarter the potatoes. Cook, covered, in lightly salted water until tender.

Process the onion, carrot and celery in a food processor until finely chopped or grate by hand. Put the prepared vegetables and mince into a large non-stick frypan. Brown the mixture, stirring regularly, adding a little oil if necessary to avoid it sticking. Stir in the flour, tomato concentrate, Worcestershire sauce and stock, and bring to the boil. Take the mixture off the heat and spoon it into a non-stick sprayed dish.

Drain the cooked potato and mash with the butter. Beat with a fork, adding enough milk to make a smooth, creamy mixture. Spread over the top of the meat and vegetable mixture, swirling the surface attractively. Sprinkle with the grated cheese and add a little paprika for extra colour if desired.

SLOW COOKER: Place the prepared cottage pie in its container in the slow cooker. Add enough cool water to come 1cm up the side of the container. Cover and cook on LOW for 8–10 hours.

OVEN BAKE: Place in a preheated 180°C oven and bake for 30–40 minutes.

Serve with a green salad or lightly cooked vegetables.

Sausage Braid

The plaited pastry coating on this sausage meat really dresses it up! You can serve it hot, but we think it is better cold.

FOR 4 SERVINGS:

400–500g flaky pastry
450–500g sausage-meat
1 onion, finely chopped
2 cups cooked, drained vegetables, chopped into small cubes *
1 tsp curry powder
2 tsp instant chicken stock or 1 tsp salt
pinch of cayenne pepper
2 Tbsp finely chopped fresh herbs
1 egg

* Use a mixture of leftover cooked vegetables, or canned vegetables such as whole kernel corn.

Preheat the oven to 220°C.

Roll out the pastry to form a 45cm square, then transfer to a sheet of baking paper that will later be put in a sponge roll tin. Using the back of a knife, lightly mark it lengthwise into thirds. Cut the two outside thirds into 12 strips (the pastry will look rather like a stylised fern leaf).

In a large bowl mix the sausage-meat, onion, vegetables, seasonings and herbs. Beat the egg, reserving 2 teaspoonfuls for glaze, then add the rest to the sausage mixture. Mix by hand until the sausage-meat is well combined with the other ingredients.

Spread the filling down the centre third of the pastry. Starting at the far end, fold a strip from one side over the filling, at a slight angle, then one from the other side. Continue until the whole of the filling is hidden by the strips that appear to be plaited. Glaze the top with the reserved beaten egg and bake for 15 minutes until the pastry is golden brown, then at 180°C for 10–15 minutes longer.

Serve with a selection of salad vegetables.

Devilled Sausages

This is one of our favourite sausage recipes. Having made it regularly over the years, with minor changes at times, we know that our respective families happily eat it on a regular basis.

FOR 4–6 SERVINGS:

8–12 sausages
¼ cup brown sugar
1 level Tbsp cornflour
1 level tsp dry mustard
1 level tsp celery salt
¼ tsp salt
1 Tbsp soy sauce
1 Tbsp wine vinegar
2 Tbsp tomato paste
1 cup water
1 large onion
1–2 green-skinned apples, cored but unpeeled

Preheat the oven to 180°C.

Separate the sausages and set aside until required. In an ovenware dish or a small roasting pan in which the sausages will fit in one layer, mix the sugar, cornflour, mustard, celery salt and salt. Add the liquids and stir until smooth.

Chop the onion and the unpeeled apple into 1cm cubes and stir into the mixture.

Place the sausages in one layer in the pan, cover tightly with a lid or foil, and bake for 1 hour, turning the sausages in the sauce once or twice during this time.

Stir in half a cup of extra liquid (water, beer or wine) before serving if the sauce is thicker than desired.

Serve on rice or with potatoes and peas.

VARIATIONS: A teaspoon of ground cumin, added with the mustard, is delicious. And if you don't have any tomato paste, omit it, the vinegar and the brown sugar and replace them with ¼ cup tomato sauce. Add more sauce at the end of the cooking time if the sauce is not tangy enough.

FOR A QUICK ALTERNATIVE: Cook the devilled sausages in a large covered frypan for 20–30 minutes, after browning the sausages first.

Toad in the Hole

Properly made, this mixture consists of sausage patties (i.e. the "toads") partly buried in light, crisp and crunchy well-risen Yorkshire pudding batter. It makes a wonderful spring dinner when served with a mixed green salad. However, the secret is to get the batter just right, which involves aerating the flour by beating it. If you follow our recipe to the letter we are confident you'll get a good result!

(see page 85)

FOR 4 SERVINGS:

2 large eggs
1 brimming cup milk
2 cups flour (see method)
¼ tsp salt
450–500g plain or seasoned sausage-meat (see page 85)

Preheat the oven to 190°C.

Mix the egg and milk in a medium-sized bowl. In a separate bowl vigorously beat the flour using a whisk or fork before measuring it. Then, without shaking or packing it in any way, spoon it lightly into the same sized cup as you plan to use to measure the milk. Without shaking the cup, level off the top, then remove and discard 1 level tablespoon of flour. Repeat so that you have 2 cups of flour less 2 level tablespoons. Tip the measured flour into the egg and milk mixture and beat until smooth. Stir in the salt. Leave to stand.

Shape the sausage-meat into 16 patties and place in a high-sided 23cm square baking or cake pan coated with non-stick spray.

Bake the sausages for 10 minutes (without using the fan), then remove from the oven. Stir the batter briefly and quickly pour it over the sausages in the hot tin. Bake at the same temperature for about 40 minutes until the crust has risen (unevenly) around the "toads" and is crisp, golden-brown, and set (don't worry if it rises unevenly; this is normal).

VARIATION: Add 1 tablespoon of grated parmesan cheese to the batter.

NOTE: The batter is risen by steam, and does not contain baking powder etc. It rises better in small, deep-sided tins.

Savoury Sausages with Pineapple

Here is a good, down-to-earth casserole that can be prepared with the minimum of mess and cooked with little attention. It fills the house with the most inviting aromas, making it especially welcoming on a cold night.

FOR 4–6 SERVINGS:

8–12 sausages
1 level Tbsp cornflour
2 level Tbsp brown sugar
1 Tbsp mixed mustard
½ cup tomato sauce
1½ Tbsp dark soy sauce
½ tsp dried sage
1 x 400g can pineapple chunks in syrup
1 large onion, chopped
1 red pepper, chopped (optional)
1 green pepper or 2 stalks of celery, chopped

Select a casserole dish or roasting pan that will hold the sausages in one layer.

Stir together the cornflour and sugar, then add the next four ingredients and stir again.

Drain the liquid from the pineapple, make it up to 1 cup with water, and stir it into the casserole dish. Add the chopped vegetables. Top with the sausages, each pricked about eight times to prevent them bursting.

Cover tightly with a lid or foil and put in a cold oven. Cook for 1–1½ hours at 180–200°C until the sausages are cooked and the liquid in the dish is clear and thick. Stir once or twice during cooking if possible. Add a little hot water if the casserole lid is not tight-fitting and the sauce thickens too much.

Stir the pineapple pieces through the cooked casserole and allow them to heat through before serving on rice or with mashed potatoes.

Layered & Baked
with Mince & Sausages

Lazy Lasagne

We are very proud of this very easy lasagne, which Alison created, and which requires absolutely no precooking. We know that many thousands of families have enjoyed it since it was first published.

FOR 4–6 SERVINGS:

500g minced beef or lamb
2 cloves garlic, chopped
1 tsp each basil and oregano
1 x 425g can tomato purée
2 Tbsp tomato paste
1 x 45g packet tomato soup mix
2 tsp instant beef stock powder or 1 tsp salt
1½ cups hot water
about 3 cups small lasagne shapes or long lasagne strips
1 cup grated tasty cheese

TOPPING:

2 tsp cornflour
1 egg
¾ cup milk
1 cup grated tasty cheese
paprika

Preheat the oven to 180°C.

Measure the first seven ingredients into a food processor or bowl. Add the hot water and process until well blended or mix with a fork and/or potato masher until everything is combined.

Spray or butter a 23cm square or 25 x 20cm rectangular ovenware dish or a suitable roasting pan or foil dish. Spread one third of the meat mixture evenly over the bottom, followed by a layer of half the lasagne noodles. Sprinkle over half of the grated cheese. Repeat this layer and cover with the remaining meat mixture (you may like to use more than a third of the meat mixture for the top layer).

Bake immediately, uncovered, for 50 minutes, or cover and microwave on High (100% power) for 30 minutes.

To make the topping, mix together the cornflour, egg, milk and cheese. Pour evenly over the cooked mixture, sprinkle with the paprika if using and bake, uncovered, at 150°C for about 10 minutes until the topping sets or microwave at 50% (Medium power) for 10 minutes.

Leave to stand 15–30 minutes before cutting into squares or rectangles. Serve immediately or refrigerate. Cut into serving–sized pieces and wrap in cling film for freezing. Reheat in a moderate oven or microwave.

Serve with a green salad and with warmed, crusty bread rolls, if you like.

NOTE: The topping does not always set well in a microwave oven. If this happens, heat it under a grill for 5–10 minutes.

Alison's Slow-cooked Lazy Lasagne

This is a variant of the above recipe. It is almost too good to be true – lasagne with no precooking, just a little assembly! Made in an oval 4.5 litre slow cooker, it will be about 4–5cm thick, but obviously the depth will vary depending on the size of the cooker you use.

FOR 4–6 SERVINGS:

2 cloves garlic, peeled and chopped
1 x 400g can whole or diced tomatoes in juice
1 x 30g packet tomato soup, or tomato and onion
    soup mix
500g minced beef
¼ cup tomato paste
1 tsp each dried basil and oregano
2 tsp instant beef stock
1 cup hot water
250g (about 3–4 cups) small lasagne shapes or long
    lasagne strips

TOPPING:

2 tsp cornflour
1 large egg
¾ cup milk, sour cream, or a mixture
1 cup grated tasty cheese
paprika (optional)

Turn the slow cooker on to HIGH to preheat and coat the bowl with non-stick spray.

Put the first eight ingredients in a food processor, then process or mix until well combined.

Spread one third of the meat mixture evenly over the bottom of the slow cooker bowl. Place half the lasagne noodles over the meat. Repeat the layering with another one third of the meat mixture, the remaining pasta, then cover with the remaining meat mixture.

For the topping, mix together the cornflour, egg, milk (and/or sour cream) and cheese. Pour into the slow cooker and sprinkle with paprika, if using. Turn the slow cooker to LOW and cook for 8–9 hours.

Lift out individual servings with a fish slice. Serve with a green salad or cooked vegetables and garlic bread.

Murphy's Moussaka ▲

This moussaka, similar to one Alison ate in a back street in Athens, always gets a thumbs up sign when we make it on a cold winter's night. Much of its appeal is the creamy cheesy layer on top.

FOR 6 SERVINGS:

750g potatoes
2 large onions
500g minced lamb or beef
2 Tbsp oil
½ tsp salt
freshly ground black pepper
1 Tbsp flour
1 x 400g can Italian-style tomatoes
¼ cup tomato paste

CHEESE SAUCE:

2 Tbsp each butter and flour
freshly ground black pepper
½ tsp freshly grated nutmeg
1 cup milk
1 cup grated tasty cheese
1 egg, beaten

Preheat the oven to at 180°C.

Scrub the unpeeled potatoes and cut into 5mm slices. If you are in a hurry, precook them in a microwave oven in a lidded microwave dish with ¼ cup of water, or simmer them in a covered pot with a little water.

Finely chop the onions and brown with the mince in the oil in a large frypan until the meat is no longer pink. Stir in the seasonings and flour, and cook briefly before adding the tomatoes and tomato paste. Heat until the mixture boils and thickens.

To make the sauce, melt the butter. Add the flour and seasonings and cook briefly, stirring continuously. Add half the milk, return to the heat and keep stirring until the sauce thickens. Add the rest of the milk and keep stirring and heating until the sauce boils and thickens again. Stir in the grated cheese, removing from the heat as soon as it melts. Beat in the egg with a fork.

Spray or butter an ovenproof dish of 10–12 cup capacity and cover the base with a third of the sliced potatoes. Cover with half the mince, another layer of potatoes, then the rest of the mince. Finish with the remaining potatoes. Press down to make a fairly flat and compact mixture. Pour the cheese sauce over the top and bake for 30 minutes. (Cover with foil if topping browns too quickly.) Check that the potato is cooked by piercing one with a sharp knife. Leave to stand for 5–10 minutes before serving.

Serve with a cooked green vegetable or salad.

NOTE: If using a large shallow dish, make double the amount of sauce.

Simon's Traditional Lasagne

This traditional lasagne has become a firm family favourite, reaching "comfort food" status. Making this version lasagne involves a few steps, but it is well worth it.

FOR 6 SERVINGS:

2 Tbsp olive oil
1 large onion, chopped
2 cloves garlic, chopped
500g minced beef or lamb
1 x 300g can tomato purée
1 400g can Italian-style seasoned tomatoes
1 tsp salt
½ tsp sugar
1 Tbsp chopped basil or 1 tsp dried basil
225–250g lasagne sheets or noodles

TOPPING:

25g butter
3 Tbsp flour
½ tsp salt
grated nutmeg and pepper to taste
2 cups milk
1½ cups grated cheese
paprika

Preheat the oven to 180°C.

Heat the oil in a large frypan and lightly brown the onion and garlic. Add the minced meat and cook, stirring frequently, until it is no longer pink. Stir in the tomato purée, tomatoes in their juice, salt, sugar and basil. Bring to the boil, then lower the heat and leave to simmer gently while you prepare the cheese sauce.

To make the cheese sauce, melt the butter in a medium-sized pot. Add the flour and seasonings and stir well over low heat for 30 seconds. Pour in half the milk and bring to the boil, stirring frequently. Add the remaining milk and bring to the boil again, still stirring, then remove from the heat and stir in 1 cup of the grated cheese.

Spread a third of the meat sauce in the bottom of a lightly oiled 20 x 30cm casserole dish. Put one layer (about a third) of the noodles over the meat. Spread the next third of the mince mixture over the layer of lasagne, then add another layer of lasagne. Repeat this process with the remaining meat and noodles, so you finish with a layer of pasta. (Don't worry if you have some noodles left over.)

Pour the cheese sauce over the top of the pasta, spreading evenly so the entire surface is covered. Sprinkle with the remaining grated cheese and dust lightly with paprika.

Bake for 30–45 minutes, then leave to stand for 15 minutes before cutting.

Serve with crunchy bread and a crisp green salad.

NOTE: Do not leave the lasagne to sit uncooked, or the pasta will turn soggy. If you want to make it in advance. bake it first and reheat when required.

Enchilada Casserole

This popular, layered one-dish dinner could be described as a Mexican lasagne. Its interesting flavour and appetising aroma will be popular with everyone who likes Mexican flavours – and it's a great way to use up broken corn chips.

FOR 4–6 SERVINGS:

1 large onion
1 large clove garlic
1 Tbsp oil
1 large red pepper (optional)
1 tsp ground cumin
½ tsp oregano
¼–½ tsp chilli powder
400–500g minced beef or lamb
1 Tbsp flour
1 x 400g can tomatoes in juice
1 x 440g can whole kernel corn
1–2 Tbsp tomato paste
2 tsp sugar
¾ tsp salt

about 150g corn chips
2 cups grated tasty cheese

Preheat the oven to 180°C.

In a large pot, cook the chopped onion and garlic in the oil over moderate heat for 3–4 minutes until the onion browns lightly. Chop the pepper into small cubes if using, and add to the onion. Stir in the cumin, oregano and chilli powder. Raise the heat, add the minced meat and cook, breaking the meat into small pieces as it browns. Stir in the flour, then the next five ingredients, using all the liquid from the cans. Simmer for about 10 minutes.

Spray an 8–10 cup capacity ovenproof dish with non-stick spray. Spread a third of the meat mixture over the bottom. Cover with half the corn chips, followed by a third of the cheese. Evenly spread half the remaining meat over the cheese, then make a layer with the rest of the corn chips. Top with the rest of the meat, and sprinkle with the remaining cheese.

Bake, uncovered, for 30 minutes, until the mixture has heated through. Leave to stand for about 5 minutes. Use a large spoon to serve from the dish.

Serve with crusty bread or rolls and a green salad, but it's also good on its own.

Moussaka

Moussaka is a traditional Greek dish, made with layers of eggplant and mince, and topped with sauce. Grill rather than fry the eggplant, and use a yoghurt-based topping. The result is delicious!

FOR 4–6 SERVINGS:

2 medium eggplants
3–4 Tbsp olive oil

MEAT SAUCE:

1 medium onion
2 cloves garlic
1 Tbsp olive oil
500g minced lamb or beef
2 Tbsp tomato paste
½ cup red wine or stock
1 Tbsp chopped fresh or 1 tsp dried oregano
2–3 Tbsp chopped fresh parsley
¼ tsp each ground allspice and cinnamon
1 tsp salt
freshly ground pepper to taste
2 Tbsp dried breadcrumbs

TOPPING:

2 cups plain unsweetened yoghurt
2 large eggs
1 cup grated tasty cheese

Preheat the oven to 200°C.

Cut the unpeeled eggplants lengthwise into 12mm thick slices. Arrange on a baking tray, brush both sides lightly with oil, then grill about 10cm from the heat, turning once until they are browned on both sides (about 5 minutes per side).

Prepare the meat sauce while the eggplant browns. Finely chop the onion and garlic. Heat the oil in a large frypan, then add the onion, garlic and mince. Cook, stirring frequently, until the mince is crumbly and beginning to brown. Stir in the tomato paste, the red wine or stock and the seasonings. Simmer over a low heat for 8–10 minutes.

Lightly oil a 20 x 30cm casserole dish, then sprinkle the bottom with the breadcrumbs. Arrange half the browned eggplant in an even layer over the bottom of the dish, followed by the evenly spread mince mixture, then layer the remaining eggplant on top.

To make the topping, whisk together the yoghurt and eggs and pour over the top of the layered eggplant and mince, then sprinkle with the grated cheese.

Bake for 15–20 minutes or until the topping is set and golden brown.

Leave to stand for about 15 minutes before serving with crunchy bread rolls and a salad.

Pastitio (Layered Mince & Pasta) Casserole

Like lasagne, this layered mince and pasta dish takes some time to prepare as the layers must be made separately before assembling the whole thing.

FOR 4–6 SERVINGS:

250g ziti (long macaroni)
¼–½ cup grated parmesan cheese
½ tsp salt
pepper and grated nutmeg to taste

MEAT SAUCE:

1 medium onion, chopped
2–3 cloves garlic, chopped
2 Tbsp olive oil
500g minced lamb or beef
½ cup beef or vegetable stock
1½ cups bought pasta sauce
2 Tbsp basil pesto
salt and pepper to taste

TOPPING:

25g butter
2 Tbsp flour
1 cup milk
¼ cup parmesan cheese
1 large egg
½ cup grated tasty cheese

Preheat the oven to 200°C.

Cook the pasta in plenty of boiling water.

To make the meat sauce, cook the onion and garlic in the oil for about 2 minutes, stirring frequently. Add the minced meat, and cook until it has lost its pink colour. Add the stock and pasta sauce and simmer for about 5 minutes. Take off the heat, add the pesto and salt and pepper to taste.

Drain the cooked pasta, then stir in the parmesan, salt, and a little pepper and grated nutmeg.

Press the pasta mixture into the bottom of an oiled 20 x 30cm casserole dish. Cover with the meat sauce, then set aside while you prepare the topping.

To prepare the topping, melt the butter in a medium-sized pot. Stir in the flour and cook for 1 minute. Pour in half the milk and bring to the boil, stirring frequently. Add the remaining milk and bring to the boil again, stirring often. Take off the heat then using a fork, beat in the grated parmesan and the egg. Pour the sauce evenly over the meat layer, and top with the grated cheese.

Bake for 15 minutes, then grill briefly to brown the top if necessary. Leave to stand for a few minutes before serving with a green salad and bread rolls.

Sausage & Potato Pie ▼

This sausage pie was entered in a competition that Alison judged some years ago. It proved so popular with everyone who tasted it that it emerged a clear winner. This variation uses sausage-meat because it is easier to manage than the sausages used in the original recipe.

FOR 4–6 SERVINGS:

6 medium potatoes
2 medium onions
1 kg sausage-meat or sausages
2 Tbsp brown sugar
2 Tbsp flour
2 tsp curry powder
1 x 400g can apples or 1 x 400g can Mexican, Italian or
    savoury tomatoes
1 Tbsp butter
freshly ground black pepper
½ cup milk
½–1 cup grated cheese

Preheat the oven to 180°C. Peel the potatoes, cut into small pieces, and cook in a pot of lightly salted water.

Cut the onions into thin wedges. Sprinkle about half the onion in a roasting pan or a large shallow baking dish. Using wet hands, form the sausage-meat into walnut-sized pieces and place on a sheet of cling film.

Mix together the brown sugar, flour and curry powder and sprinkle over the sausage meat, turning the pieces to coat all sides. Arrange the coated sausage-meat in a layer over the onion in the baking dish. Top with the rest of the onion. Spread the apples or tomatoes evenly over the sausage and onion layer.

Drain the cooked potatoes and mash them with the butter, pepper and milk. Spread the mash evenly over the sausages, swirl or roughen the top attractively, then sprinkle with the grated cheese.

Bake, uncovered, for 1 hour.

NOTE: If using whole sausages, cut the skins lengthwise, then one at a time hold them under running cold water so the skins will peel off easily.

If the canned apples seem dry, add ¼–½ cup of fruit juice, wine or beer.

Nicely Spicy

Chilli Con Carne

This non-authentic mince and bean dish is probably our most popular and practical recipe for everyday use. It uses store cupboard ingredients, is easily modified to suit a family group or flatmates, and may be easily stretched to feed unexpected guests.

FOR 6–8 SERVINGS:

2 large onions
2 Tbsp oil
2 large cloves garlic, chopped
500–700g minced lamb or beef
2 tsp paprika
2–3 tsp ground cumin
1–2 tsp oregano
½–1 tsp chilli powder
1 x 400g can Mexican-style or chopped tomatoes
up to 3 x 425g cans baked or chilli beans
1–3 Tbsp lemon juice or wine vinegar
2 or more Tbsp tomato paste
water (optional)

In a large pot or frypan, lightly but evenly brown the chopped onion in the oil. Add the garlic, mince, paprika, cumin, oregano and chilli powder and stir over a high heat until the mince is no longer pink. Stir in the tomatoes, then cover and simmer for about 15 minutes. Add as many cans of baked beans as required plus 1 tablespoon of lemon juice or vinegar for each can of beans, and as much tomato paste as you like to intensify the tomato flavour.

If necessary, thin with extra water to a pouring consistency. Cover and simmer gently for a further 10–30 minutes to blend the flavours, taking care not to let the mixture catch on the bottom after the beans are added. Taste and add extra seasonings if necessary.

Ladle the mixture over rice in bowls and serve with corn chips alongside or use for Nachos, Tostadas, Tacos or Burritos, (see pages 74 and 75) or as a baked potato topping, or in any other way that suits the situation, adding suitable toppings and accompaniments such as grated cheese, sour cream, mashed or chopped avocado, shredded lettuce, etc. if they are available.

NOTE: Combining ½ tsp chilli powder with 1 can of beans makes a reasonably hot mixture. House-brand baked beans cost less than the branded product.

Spicy Dark Chilli

This is a favourite in our house. Spoon it over rice in individual bowls and top with sour cream, chopped spring onion, grated cheese and a pile of crunchy corn chips for a casual but interesting meal. The darker the beer, the better the flavour will be.

FOR 4–6 SERVINGS:

1 large or 2 medium onions
2 large cloves garlic
1 Tbsp oil
2 tsp whole cumin seeds
1 large red or yellow pepper, cored and finely chopped
500g minced beef or lamb (see page 2)
1 tsp oregano
¼–¾ tsp chilli powder
1 x 400g can tomatoes in juice
¼ cup tomato paste
1 can beer
2 bay leaves
2 medium carrots, cut into 5mm cubes (optional)
2 stalks celery, cut into 5mm cubes (optional)
2 Tbsp cornmeal or flour
salt and sugar to taste

Finely chop the onion and garlic. Heat the oil in a large pot and gently cook the onion and garlic. Push the onion to one side of the pan and heat the cumin seeds until they brown a little and pop. Stir in the chopped pepper and the minced meat. Cook over high heat, stirring at intervals, until the meat is no longer pink, adding the oregano and chilli powder during this time. Add the tomatoes, tomato paste and beer. Cover and heat through, stirring in the bay leaves and then the carrots and celery if using.

Simmer for 1 hour, stirring occasionally, then thicken with the cornmeal or flour mixed to a paste with a little water. Season to taste (we usually add 1 teaspoon salt and 2 teaspoons white or brown sugar). Remove the bay leaves.

Serve immediately or reheat when required. Spoon over rice with toppings of sour cream (or sour cream mixed with plain yoghurt), chopped spring onions, grated cheese and chopped, canned jalapeño peppers, if desired. Serve corn chips alongside.

NOTES: If vegetables are included, this recipe makes about 5 ½ cups altogether. It refrigerates and freezes well, with leftovers being perfect for serving with nachos.

If you need to make it go further, add 1–2 cans of baked beans or drained kidney beans.

Spicy Mexican Mince

This spicy mince and bean mixture is great for making delicious nachos, tacos, tostadas and burritos. Although it is quickly made, you may like to keep some in the freezer, especially if you and your friends become addicted to it!

FOR 3–4 SERVINGS:

1 Tbsp oil
1 large red onion, chopped
2 cloves garlic, chopped
250g minced beef, pork or chicken
1 red or green pepper
½–1 tsp chilli powder
2 tsp ground cumin
1 tsp oregano
1 tsp salt
1 tsp sugar
1 x 440g can kidney beans
2 Tbsp tomato paste
about ½ cup water

Heat the oil in a large pot, add the chopped onion, garlic and minced meat and cook over fairly high heat until browned. Dice the pepper and add to the pot with the spices and cook for a further 2 minutes.

Reduce the heat, add the remaining ingredients, including the liquid from the beans, and simmer for about 15–20 minutes, stirring occasionally to prevent sticking and adding extra water during this time if necessary.

Nachos

Nachos are deservedly popular and are always received with great enthusiasm by all age groups. In their simplest form they are just corn chips with melted cheese over them, but by adding some Spicy Mexican Mince and/or other optional extras as desired, you can turn them into quite a substantial meal.

OPTIONAL EXTRAS:

diced tomatoes
diced peppers or chillis
guacamole
sour cream
chilli sauce or salsa
chopped fresh coriander leaves
chopped spring onions

Place a pile of hot and preferably quite Spicy Mexican Mince mixture (see above) in the centre of a flat heatproof plate and pile corn chips around it. Sprinkle the corn chips with grated cheese and grill or microwave them until the cheese has melted. Top the mince with a dollop of sour cream and/or guacamole plus any of the other optional additions and serve immediately.

OR: For one large platter, pile corn chips and cheese on an oven tray and grill or bake them until the cheese melts. Heap onto a large tray with a bowl of hot Spicy Mexican Mince. Serve with smaller bowls or a platter of some of the other optional ingredients.

Burritos

A burrito is the Mexican equivalent of a filled roll – a soft flour tortilla wrapped around fillings of your choice. This kind of tortilla varies quite widely in size from fairly small (about 20cm across) to quite large (about 40cm across) and can be bought packaged in several different ways. Some imported varieties come in vacuum packs, (which gives them a long shelf life) that are sold separately or as part of "dinner kits". Locally made products with a shorter shelf life are sometimes available, too. These are often found in or near the bread departments of supermarkets.

Use the same fillings as you would for tacos and tostadas and follow these steps to assemble them:

Place the tortilla on a flat surface.

Arrange the fillings in a line that runs down the centre, leaving 2cm clear at the bottom (don't be too generous with the fillings or your burrito will be difficult to roll and almost impossible to eat!)

Fold the bottom 2cm over the filling, then fold one edge in, followed by the other.

Wrap the filled burrito in a napkin, paper towel or even a piece of foil to make it easier to eat with your fingers.

NOTE: If you find soft flour tortillas hard to fold, put one or two at a time in a plastic bag and microwave them briefly until warm, but not hot.

Tacos and Tostadas

Taco shells are corn tortillas that are folded over into a U shape and fried or baked until crisp, while tostadas are simply tortillas (usually corn), cooked in the same way, but left flat. The same fillings can be used for both.

Serve everyone with their own crisp tacos or tostadas and encourage them to help themselves from bowls of fillings.

Be warned, there is no easy and/or neat way to eat tacos and tostadas. Use your fingers and accept a little mess as part of the fun!

FILLINGS:

Spicy Mexican Mince (or other chilli mixtures, see pages 73 and 74)
Grated cheese
Very finely shredded lettuce
Finely grated carrot
Optional extras as for nachos

Guacamole

This versatile sauce makes a good dip to serve with corn chips or use it to make nachos, tacos, tostadas or burritos really special.

Mash, or chop in a food processor the flesh from a ripe avocado with the juice from 1 lemon and 1 minced clove of garlic (optional). Add 1–2 finely chopped spring onions and a finely chopped tomato for colour, if desired. Season to taste with salt, freshly ground black pepper, hot pepper sauce, a little sugar, ground cumin, and chopped fresh coriander leaves.

Cover with cling wrap if not using immediately or it will brown on standing.

75

Thai-style Chicken & Noodle Salad ▶

Quick to prepare, this main meal salad makes a great meal on a warm evening.

FOR 3–4 SERVINGS:

250–300g fine egg noodles
3 Tbsp canola oil
2 cloves garlic, chopped
1–2 Tbsp grated fresh root ginger
450g minced chicken
1 tsp Thai red curry paste
1 tsp minced red chilli, fresh or bottled
¼ cup basil leaves (optional)
1 Tbsp fish sauce
1 Tbsp light soy sauce
1 tsp sugar
juice of 2 lemons
4 cups mesclun
¼ cup chopped peanuts to garnish

Cook the noodles according to the instructions on the packet in plenty of lightly salted boiling water. Rinse with cold water, then drain well and return to the cooking pot. Add 1 tablespoon of the oil and gently toss to coat.

Heat the remaining oil in a large frypan. Add the garlic and ginger and cook for about 1 minute, then add the chicken, curry paste and chilli. Cook, stirring frequently to break up any large lumps, for about 5 minutes or until lightly browned.

Stir in the basil leaves if using, then the fish and soy sauces, sugar and half the lemon juice. Cook for a further 2–3 minutes, stirring occasionally, then remove from the heat.

Scatter the mesclun over a large platter, spoon over the noodles and top with the chicken. Sprinkle with the remaining lemon juice and the peanuts and serve.

Thai-Style Red Curry

In the past, we have made red curries using chicken mince. Since it is not always readily available, however, we decided to experiment and try minced beef. We were very pleased with the results, finding it just as good – if not better – made this way.

FOR 4 SERVINGS:

1 medium onion
2 cloves garlic
2 Tbsp oil
2–3 Tbsp Thai red curry paste*
2–3 kaffir lime leaves, soaked if dried, then chopped (optional)
500g lean minced beef (see page 2)
1 x 400g can coconut cream or 1 cup coconut cream + 1 cup chicken or beef stock
¼ cup crunchy peanut butter
up to ½ cup water, if required
2 Tbsp fish sauce
½–1 tsp each salt and sugar
2–3 Tbsp chopped fresh coriander leaves
1–2 cups sliced or diced vegetables, e.g. zucchini, cauliflower or broccoli florets etc.
chopped coriander or spring onion and chopped roasted peanuts to garnish (optional)

* Red curry paste comes in a variety of strengths and hotness, depending on the brand. If you are new to Thai cooking, or are using a different paste from your usual one, err on the side of caution.

Quarter the onion lengthwise, then cut into thin slices. Chop the garlic. Heat the oil in a large frypan, add the onion and garlic and cook, stirring frequently until the onion is soft. Stir in the red curry paste and lime leaves, if using, and cook for about 1 minute longer, then add the beef mince. Continue to cook, stirring frequently and breaking up any lumps of mince, until the mince has lost its pink colour. Pour in the coconut cream or coconut cream and stock and stir in the peanut butter. Reduce the heat to a simmer and cook for 6–8 minutes, stirring occasionally. If the mixture looks too dry during this time, add the extra water. Stir in the remaining seasonings and the prepared vegetables, then cook until the vegetables are just tender.

Serve on rice garnished with a little extra chopped coriander and/or some chopped roasted peanuts if desired.

Braised Eggplant with Pork

Simon first tasted this dish in San Francisco as part of a take-out buffet enjoyed with friends. After several attempts, he came up with a version that compares very favourably with the original. Since this recipe was published, a number of readers have written to us saying how much they love his recipe.

FOR 2–3 SERVINGS:

2 small eggplants
4 Tbsp canola oil
2 large cloves garlic, chopped
½ medium onion, diced
150–200g minced pork
2 Tbsp rice wine or sherry
1 tsp cornflour
1 Tbsp dark soy sauce
½ cup water
1 tsp sesame oil
½ tsp instant chicken stock powder
¼ tsp sugar
¼–½ tsp salt
1–2 Tbsp chopped fresh coriander

Top and tail the eggplants and cut them lengthwise into quarters, then halve each quarter lengthwise. Cut the wedges into pieces about 5cm long.

Heat 2 tablespoons of the oil in a large non-stick frypan or wok, and add half the eggplant pieces. Cook for about 5 minutes, turning once or twice, until the cut surfaces are golden brown. Remove from the pan and set aside, add 1 tablespoon of the oil and brown the remaining eggplant in the same way, then remove from the pan.

Heat the remaining canola oil in the same pan and cook the garlic and onion, stirring frequently, until soft and beginning to brown. Add the minced pork and stir-fry until the pork looks opaque. Sprinkle in the rice wine or sherry and continue to cook until it has mostly evaporated. Mix the cornflour to a paste with the soy sauce in a small bowl, then stir in the water, sesame oil, instant stock powder, and sugar.

Stir the browned eggplant into the pork, then add the soy-water mixture and simmer for 5–10 minutes, stirring occasionally, until the eggplant is very tender. Season to taste with salt.

Garnish with the chopped coriander and serve with steamed rice.

Tex-Mex Squares

These squares are interesting, different, and tasty, the type of thing we like to feed to young people who want a substantial snack or meal, rather like pizza.

FOR 4–6 SERVINGS:

TOPPING:
400–500g minced beef or lamb
2 tsp ground cumin
1 tsp oregano
1 tsp each onion and garlic salt
1 tsp sugar
½–1 tsp chilli powder
2 Tbsp tomato paste
1 x 440g can kidney beans
1½ cups grated tasty cheese

CRUST:
1½ cups self-raising flour
about ¾ cup milk

Preheat the oven to 200°C.

Brown the minced meat in a large pot or frypan, adding the flavourings in the order listed as the mince cooks. When the meat is no longer pink, stir in the tomato paste, followed by the contents of the can of kidney beans. Stir over low heat until everything is mixed, then leave to simmer while you prepare the crust.

To make the crust, measure the self-raising flour into a medium-sized bowl. Add most of the milk. Stir to make a dough about the consistency of cake batter, adding more milk if necessary. Thinly spread the batter to coat the bottom of a 20–23cm square low-sided oiled baking pan with a non-stick finish. Spread the hot mince mixture over the uncooked flour mixture, cover lightly with a piece of baking paper and cook for 20–30 minutes until the dough in the centre looks cooked when you push a knife into it.

Remove from the oven and immediately spread with the grated cheese.

Serve hot or warm, cut into 4–6 pieces.

This goes well with a salad made by mixing a finely cubed tomato with 1 cup of shredded lettuce, 1 chopped spring onion and 2–3 tablespoons of chopped coriander leaves. Sprinkle with salt and toss. Divide the salad between the squares, spooning it on top. Drop some sour cream on top of the salad and add a few drops of hot sauce if desired.

NOTE: Although the mixture in the pot may seem very spicy, it is much milder when cooked and served.

Spiced Lamb with Tomatoes & Peas ▼

Lovers of spicy food are sure to enjoy the way that Indian spices turn this minced lamb into something really special in merely half an hour! You can also make it with minced beef – it may not be traditional, but it still tastes great.

FOR 4 SERVINGS:

1 onion, roughly chopped
1 Tbsp chopped fresh root ginger
3–4 cloves garlic, roughly chopped
2–3 Tbsp oil
1 tsp each cumin and coriander seeds, crushed
½ tsp each chilli powder and turmeric
500g minced lamb (see page 2)
1 x 400g can tomatoes in juice
½ cup plain unsweetened yoghurt
1 tsp salt
1 Tbsp garam masala
2 Tbsp lemon juice
1 fresh green chilli, thinly sliced (optional)
¼ cup chopped coriander leaves
2 cups peas, fresh or frozen

Put the onion, ginger, and garlic into a food processor and chop finely.

Heat the oil in a large non-stick frypan over medium-high heat. Add the onion mixture and stir-fry until the mixture begins to brown. Stir in the crushed cumin and coriander seeds, then the chilli powder and turmeric. Cook for 1 minute longer, stirring frequently, then add the minced lamb. Cook over high heat, stirring occasionally to break up any lumps, until the meat has lost its pink colour, then add the tomatoes and their liquid, breaking up the tomatoes with a spoon, followed by the yoghurt. Bring to the boil, and cook for 10–15 minutes until the mixture thickens.

Stir in the salt, garam masala, lemon juice, green chilli if using, coriander and peas. Bring back to the boil, then cover and cook for a further 5 minutes.

Serve on basmati rice, alone, or with naan or other flat bread and a selection of chutneys and pickles if you like.

Summery Sausage Ideas

Clare's Terrine Slow-cooked

Although this recipe contains quite a high proportion of sausage-meat, the finished pâté has a lovely soft texture and does not look or taste as if it contains sausage-meat. When chilled, it is firm enough to slice, but is spreadable at warm room temperature.

FOR ABOUT 8 SERVINGS:

350g chicken livers
1 egg
¼ cup sherry
2-3 cloves garlic, chopped
1 tsp salt
½ tsp freshly grated nutmeg
1 Tbsp coarsely chopped fresh sage leaves
1 Tbsp coarsely chopped fresh thyme leaves
¼ tsp ground cloves
½–1 tsp freshly ground black pepper
500g sausage-meat
about 250g thinly sliced bacon or chicken bacon

You will need a medium to large oval slow cooker that will hold a 6-cup capacity loaf tin.

Rinse the chicken livers in a bowl of cold water then halve, discarding any fibrous bits. Transfer the rinsed and halved livers to a food processor and add the next nine ingredients. Process until smooth, then add the sausage-meat in golf ball-sized pieces and process again until smooth.

Coat the inside of the loaf tin with non-stick spray and line the long sides with bacon strips, leaving long ends to fold over the top of the terrine if you like. Spoon the processed mixture onto the bacon in the loaf tin. Fold the bacon ends over the top, then cover tightly with foil.

Place the terrine on two metal jar lids in the slow cooker, pour in enough bath-temperature water to come halfway up the sides, then cover and cook on HIGH for 2–3 hours or until the centre of the terrine feels firm when pressed through the foil.

Turn off the cooker and remove the loaf tin. If you want a flat-topped terrine, cover with a piece of heavy, foil-covered card, then stand several cans on top to flatten the surface. Allow to cool, then refrigerate for up to three days. When ready to serve unmould the terrine so its bottom is uppermost, and slice as required.

Serve sliced, on a platter, garnished with baby tomatoes, gherkins and lettuce leaves, etc.

Accompany with slices of interesting crusty bread.

NOTE: Use leaves from a full-grown sage plant for best flavour. If fresh herbs are not available, use 1 teaspoon each of dried sage and thyme.

VARIATIONS: Arrange the bacon strips on top, rather than using them to line the tin.

Don't press the top flat after cooking, but serve it rounded-side up, like a loaf of bread.

If preferred, use the filling from pork sausages instead of sausage meat.

Country Terrine

This terrine cooks quickly and tastes very good, but it is not an exciting mixture to work with when it is raw. Don't let this put you off though, because the end result is worthwhile!

FOR 8–12 SERVINGS:

300g lamb's liver
1 egg
¼ cup sherry
1 tsp minced garlic
½ tsp salt
1 tsp fresh thyme
¼ tsp grated nutmeg
¼ tsp dried sage
⅛ tsp ground cloves
300g sausage-meat
2–4 thin bacon rashers

Trim and cut the liver into small cubes. Purée in a food processor or blender until smooth, then add the egg, sherry and seasonings. Process to mix, then add the sausage-meat in several pieces and process again until mixed.

Line the long sides and bottom of a medium to large loaf tin with baking paper and place the bacon rashers crosswise on the bottom and up the sides. Pour the meat mixture into the bacon-lined tin. Stand the tin in a larger pan holding enough water to come halfway up the sides of the loaf tin. Cover with a strip of baking paper or foil and bake at 160°C for 1–1½ hours or until firm in the centre.

Remove from the oven and allow the terrine to cool in the tin. To flatten the bulge, place a sheet of foil over the tin while the terrine is cooling, then cover with a board. Place several fairly heavy cans on the board. When cold, turn upside down so the bacon-covered side is uppermost.

Serve with radishes, tomatoes, gherkins or other pickles and salad vegetables on crisp bread rolls or toast.

Scotch Eggs

Scotch Eggs are popular with everybody, and may be cooked in different ways. Microwaving is the easiest of these. Overcooking, or too high a heat, can cause splitting, whatever method you use.

SERVES 4:

4 hard-boiled eggs
2 thick slices stale bread, crumbed
1 Tbsp tomato sauce
2 tsp dark soy sauce
½ tsp curry powder
450–500g sausage-meat
1 cup dry breadcrumbs

TO MICROWAVE: Shell the hard-boiled eggs. Mix together the next five ingredients thoroughly, then working with wet hands divide the mixture into four portions. Wrap each portion around an egg, pinching together the joins. Coat with the breadcrumbs. Place the prepared eggs, one at a time, on a folded paper towel and microwave on High (100% power) for 1 minute. Turn it over and cook for 1 minute further or until the coating feels firm.

TO BAKE: Make as above, then bake, uncovered, in a shallow baking dish at 180°C for 20–30 minutes until the sausage-meat is firm.

TO DEEP-FRY: Make as above. Heat a small pot with enough oil to cover the eggs, then carefully place the eggs, one at a time, in the hot oil and cook without letting the oil smoke for about 10 minutes or until the coating is firm right through.

Alison's Favourite Sausage Salad

Almost any cooked sausage (or a combination of sausage and potato) tastes great when mixed with this dressing. Try it with sliced leftover barbecued sausages, frankfurters, or your favourite precooked deli sausages.

FOR 1 CUP DRESSING:

¼ cup wholegrain mustard
2 Tbsp brown sugar
2 Tbsp wine vinegar
1 tsp dry mustard
1 large clove garlic, roughly chopped
1 Tbsp roughly chopped parsley
1 Tbsp roughly chopped chives or spring onions
1 Tbsp chopped coriander leaves (optional)
½ cup olive or other oil
¼ cup warm water

This dressing is best made in a food processor or blender. Measure the first four ingredients into the bowl of the machine. If the mustard you use is sweet, start with half the amount of brown sugar. Add the garlic, parsley and chives or spring onions. The coriander leaves add a lovely flavour, but are not essential. With the motor running, add the oil slowly then add the water. Taste and add extra sugar if required. The finished dressing should be of a thickness somewhere between mayonnaise and French dressing. Use immediately or refrigerate in a covered container, but bring to room temperature before using.

To make the salad, slice the desired number of cold cooked sausages about 5 mm thick, toss in enough dressing to coat and serve immediately. OR leave to stand in the dressing to flavour the sausage, then toss with a little more just before serving.

VARIATION: Toss the coated sausage slices through a bed of prepared salad vegetables as a warm weather main meal.

Try it mixed with warm, sliced new potatoes, too, coating both potatoes and sausage with the dressing.

Sausage Barbecuing Basics

In all probability, a sausage was the first barbecued food most of us ever tasted!

Well-regulated heat is very important if you want to produce a good barbecued sausage. Nobody wants sausages which are charred on the outside and raw in the middle, yet many barbecued sausages finish up like this. There are several ways of coping with this problem. Start with uncooked sausages of regular thickness, turn the heat to low, and move and rotate the sausages regularly so that they heat through slowly, and the centres cook before the outsides darken too much.

Choose long 'skinny' sausages instead of thicker ones - they cook through faster~ requiring half to three-quarters of the cooking time needed by regular sausages.

You can also buy precooked sausages or precook your own before you take them outside to barbecue. In the precooking process, the important thing is to cook the centre of the sausages. The outside will brown well on the barbecue later.

Barbecue your sausages on a solid plate or on a grilling rack - both give good results. For ease in turning a large number of small sausages over a rack, put them in a double-sided wire basket.

Avoid fatty uncooked sausages since they tend to drip and produce a lot of fat which burns and chars the surface of the sausages. Precooked sausages generally produce much less fat as they brown and heat through.

Remember that all sausages were not created equal! There are many types of sausage available these days. Some are unmemorable but inexpensive, and need good sauces, relishes, breads and salads to turn them into an interesting meal, while at the other end of the sausage market are 'designer' sausages that you can serve to anyone with pride.

Make your own
Sausages

Home-made Sausages

It's fun to make your own gourmet sausages occasionally! Why not try a recipe from one of the following pages. Even though the results can be quite exciting, we highly recommend that you read this page before you start. Remember that home-made sausages which contain too little fat can be dry with a sawdust texture. For this reason we recommend using fairly fatty pork as a base.

Sausage ingredients may be minced:

- in an old-fashioned hand-turned mincer
- in an electric mixer with a grinding attachment
- in a food processor, using the metal chopping blade (excellent results can be achieved by chopping partly frozen meat, a small amount at a time, unless your food processor instructions forbid it).

Extra mixing, after the meat is chopped, will make the mixture stick together better. And a good consistency can be achieved by thinning very thick mixtures with extra water, wine, etc, while very soft mixtures can be firmed up with extra breadcrumbs.

Sausage meat cooks very well as patties, which are easy to prepare at home. Some patties stick together well without any additional ingredients while others are better with a coating of fine dry breadcrumbs, in some cases preceded by a coating of egg.

Buy sausage skins from any butcher who makes his own sausages but be aware that the skins tend to be salted and will need soaking for at least 2 hours. A little added vinegar makes them more transparent.

To make sausages, run some cold water through a metre or so of soaked sausage skin. Thread the length of skin onto the outside of the neck of a large inverted funnel with a 1–2 cm wide neck and tie a knot in one end. Turn the funnel right way up and push the sausage mixture through the funnel into the prepared skin. As you push the sausage meat into the funnel ease the skin off the outside. Ease the filling so it is distributed loosely but evenly along the length of the skin. Twist the skin at intervals to form the desired length of sausage and remove any air bubbles by pricking the skin with a sharp needle. Refrigerate for up to 3 days or freeze.

Cook over moderate heat to prevent excessive shrinkage of skins.

> To make plain unseasoned sausage-meat more interesting and flavourful you can add seasonings such as those used in Spiced beef sausages page 86, and Spicy Mexican sausages page 87.

Aberdeen Sausage

This old recipe makes a type of home-made luncheon sausage that is good for picnics and school lunches. Alison first tasted it about 60 years ago, and was really impressed – it was the first home-made sausage she had ever seen or tried.

FOR A 500g SAUSAGE:

3 rashers bacon
1 small onion
1 tsp finely chopped garlic
1 Tbsp Worcestershire sauce
1 Tbsp tomato sauce
1 tsp sugar
½ tsp salt or 1 tsp anchovy essence
2–4 Tbsp chopped fresh herbs
1 large egg
2 thick slices stale bread, crumbled
250g beef mince
fine dry breadcrumbs for coating

Although this sausage mixture is good when made in the food processor, you may choose to mix everything by hand, as long as you chop the bacon very finely first.

Cut off and discard the rind from the bacon. Finely chop the bacon and onion, then add the next six ingredients and mix well. Add the egg and crumbled bread if using a food processor or mix the egg and bread together to soften and break up the bread, then stir it into the bacon and onion mixture by hand. Mix in the minced beef until all ingredients are combined.

Test the flavours by cooking a small spoonful in a hot frypan. Add more salt, pepper or anchovy sauce as desired.

Working with wet hands, form the uncooked mixture into a 20cm long roll. Place carefully in an unpunctured oven bag, then tie the mouth of the bag with string, or seal the sausage in a double-layered foil package, or put it in a loaf tin and cover with foil. Stand on a rack in a large covered pot with boiling water around it and simmer for 2 hours.

When cold, turn out onto a piece of cling film and coat as evenly as you can with the dry breadcrumbs. Refrigerate overnight, then unwrap and slice.

Herbed Lamb Sausages

These home-made gourmet sausages use inexpensive lamb flap (sometimes sold as lamb breast or lamb fingers) to make a tasty, light-coloured mixture which may be cooked as patties or used as a filling for sausage casings. The chopped fresh herbs will show up as green flecks and add to their appeal.

FOR 4 SERVINGS:

250g meat from a lamb flap
250g shoulder or belly pork
1 onion, chopped
2 Tbsp lemon juice
1½ tsp salt
1½ tsp sugar
½–1 tsp whole coriander seeds
freshly ground black pepper
½ tsp grated orange rind
2 tsp Tabasco sauce
about ½ cup fine dry breadcrumbs
1–2 Tbsp finely chopped fresh herbs

Cut off and discard the outer skin or rind from the meat, then cut into 1cm cubes. Include some fat, either from the lamb or the pork. Place the cubes in a plastic bag and press the contents into a thin rectangular block. Freeze until very cold and ideally partly frozen.

Mix together in a large bowl all the remaining ingredients except the fresh herbs, grinding the coriander seeds before adding them to the mixture.

Break up the partly frozen block of meat and mix with the measured ingredients. Using a food processor, chop about one quarter at a time until a smooth paste is formed. You may need to add up to 1 tablespoonful of extra liquid such as water or white wine to each batch to achieve the right consistency. Remove each batch from the machine before processing the next, then combine all the meat in a bowl, before adding the chopped herbs.

Flatten a tablespoon of the mixture in a heated non-stick fry pan and brown on each side. Taste to judge if you need to adjust any seasonings such as salt. Working with wet hands, form the mixture into patties that can then be coated with beaten egg then breadcrumbs or put into sausage casings (see page 85).

Refrigerate and cook within 3 days or freeze.

Spiced Beef Sausages

These home-made sausages have an interesting spicy flavour which you can vary to get the intensity you like. Try replacing some of the beef with venison to make trendy venison sausages!

FOR ABOUT 6 SERVINGS:

250g shoulder or belly pork
500g minced beef or venison
¼ cup dry breadcrumbs
1½ tsp salt
½ cup port, sherry or beer
¼–½ tsp whole allspice berries
½–1 tsp coriander seeds
1 tsp black peppercorns
2–3 small dried chillis
½–1 tsp freshly grated nutmeg
1 onion, chopped
1 tsp minced garlic

If the beef or venison is very lean, then the pork should be fairly fatty. Discard any pork rind and bone. Cut the pork into 1cm cubes, place the cubes in a plastic bag and press the contents into a thin rectangular block. Freeze until very cold and ideally partly frozen.

Mix the minced beef or venison in a large bowl with the breadcrumbs, salt and the alcohol of your choice. Finely grind the next four flavourings and mix with the nutmeg. Mix half, three-quarters or all of the spice mixture with the mince mixture, depending on how spicy you want the sausages to be.

Break up the partly frozen block of pork and mix with the onion and garlic. Food process in three batches until very finely chopped, mixing each batch with a third of the red meat mixture after it is chopped. If you want a smoother-textured sausage, mix well in the food processor.

Flatten a tablespoon of the mixture in a heated non-stick fry pan and brown on each side. Taste to judge if you need to adjust the seasonings. Working with wet hands, form the mixture into patties or put into sausage casings (see page 85).

Refrigerate and cook within 3 days, or freeze for later use.

Spicy Mexican (Chorizo) Sausages

For years we were frustrated by recipes that called for chorizo sausages which were unobtainable until relatively recently. And even though they are now widely available, as often as not we still make our own. Since chorizo recipes vary widely, it will not matter if you make a few additions and omissions to suit yourself. You need quite fatty pork to make this recipe so do not choose lean pork or discard all the pork fat.

FOR 4 OR MORE SERVINGS:

500g shoulder or belly pork
2 tsp paprika
1½ tsp salt
1 tsp cayenne pepper or chilli powder
1 tsp oregano
1 tsp ground cumin
½ tsp ground coriander seeds
½ tsp black pepper
pinch of ground cloves
¼ cup water
2 Tbsp cider or white vinegar
2 tsp minced garlic

Remove and discard any pork rind, then cut the pork and fat into 1cm cubes. Place the cubes in a plastic bag and press the contents into a thin rectangular block. Freeze until very cold and ideally partly frozen.

In a small container mix the seasonings with the water, vinegar and chopped garlic.

Break up the block of partly frozen pork. Process in three batches until finely chopped, mixing in part of the seasoning mix to each batch, then combine all three batches and stir to mix.

Flatten a tablespoon of the mixture in a heated non-stick fry pan and brown on each side. Taste to judge if you need to adjust any seasonings such as salt. Working with wet hands, form the mixture into round flattened patties or put into sausage casings (see page 85).

Refrigerate for 3–4 days or freeze until required.

Hot Diggity Dogs

To our way of thinking a hot dog is some sort of sausage, served hot or warm, contained in a roll, or folded bread, or a batter coating, and it is definitely meant to be eaten "on the go".

Basic Hot Dogs

If using frankfurters or saveloys, gently simmer the required number in enough water to cover until they have heated through. Alternatively, barbecue or grill sausages slowly, not too close to the heat, turning them at intervals, so they cook right through before their skins burn.

If time is limited, or young diners are impatient, use "skinny sausages", or buy precooked sausages, or precook them yourself, in which case you can use a fiercer heat and cook them for a shorter time if they are precooked.

Split bread rolls, and toast lightly on both sides on the barbecue.

Serve with mustard, tomato, barbecue or chilli sauce, relish, horseradish, cheese, fried onions, pickled cucumbers etc. according to taste. Wrap securely to prevent leaks and drips, especially if they are to be eaten indoors by young children!

Microwaved Hot Dogs

The great advantage of microwaving hot dogs is that you can prepare them ahead. Put the required number of cold frankfurters, with their trimmings, into cold split rolls, wrap them in napkins, and microwave them one or two at a time, as and when required.

Heating time will depend on the size of the sausage and the roll. As a guide, allow 45–90 seconds on High (100%) power per assembled hot dog. The frankfurter should be hot but not split, and the roll warm.

Slow-cooked Hot Dogs

Want to have a snack waiting when hungry teenagers bring friends home after school or at the weekend?

Put the required number of frankfurters (straight from the fridge) in split rolls, adding grated cheese, tomato sauce (ketchup) etc. if desired. Wrap each filled roll in foil, crimping the edges so they won't come unwrapped, and put them in a slow cooker on LOW.

They will be ready after 1½–2 hours, but will be fine if left for another hour or so.

Gourmet Hot Dogs with Sauerkraut

Good quality frankfurters with sauerkraut in chewy, preferably sourdough, rolls are on our short list of "foods to die for". Simmer the required number of frankfurters in beer or water until heated through. Rinse and drain the sauerkraut, if necessary. Add the sauerkraut to a frypan with some caraway seeds along with a little beer and warm through.

Warm the split bun on a barbecue or grill or warm briefly in an oven.

Serve without any other additions, except perhaps a little mustard.

NOTE: If you do not make your own sauerkraut and it is not available from the deli counter at your supermarket, try Edgell's canned variety.

Mini Hot Dogs

Mini Hot Dogs are a very popular snack for family members of all ages and make a few savaloys go a long way. While you cannot taste the flavourings in the batter, the savaloys seem extra tasty!

FOR 4 SERVINGS:

oil
4 savaloys
1 egg
½ cup milk
1 cup self-raising flour
½ tsp curry powder
½ tsp dry mustard
½ tsp paprika

Heat 1cm of oil in a frypan.

Run a sharp knife down the length of each savaloy, then peel off the skin. Cut each savaloy diagonally into 5 or 6 slices. Push an ice-block stick into the side of each slice, lollipop style.

Break the egg into a medium-sized bowl. Add the milk and beat with a fork. Add the self-raising flour and the seasonings. Stir to mix (do not over-mix or the hot dogs will be tough). The mixture should look lumpy after you finish mixing. Hold the bowl at an angle and turn the hot dogs in the mixture, one at a time, to coat them.

Put each hot dog flat in the hot oil. Using tongs, turn when golden brown, picking them up by the side of the savaloy, not the stick. Cook the other side, then drain on paper towels and serve straight away with tomato sauce.

NOTE: Reheat under a grill if necessary.

Sauces and Salsas
to Serve with Sausages and Hamburgers

Sauces for Sausages and Hamburgers

Interesting sauces will make all the difference to plain barbecued or grilled sausages and hamburgers. Serve a selection, with different flavours and textures, so your friends have a choice.

Barbecue Bean Sauce

FOR ABOUT 12 SERVINGS:

2 medium onions, chopped
2 cloves garlic, finely chopped
1 Tbsp oil
1 x 440g can baked beans
¼ cup tomato paste
¼ cup brown sugar
2 Tbsp mixed mustard
1 Tbsp Worcestershire sauce
2 Tbsp cider vinegar
water or beer for thinning

Lightly brown the onion and garlic in the oil in a large pot. Add the remaining ingredients and simmer for 10 minutes, stirring often. Thin with water or beer if desired. Spoon over burgers and barbecued sausages.

Refrigerate for up to 1 week.

Sage and Apple Sauce

FOR ABOUT 6 SERVINGS:

1 onion, chopped
2 Tbsp butter
2 large apples, peeled and sliced
1 Tbsp chopped fresh sage
2 Tbsp apple juice, white wine or water
2–3 tsp sugar
salt and pepper

Cook the onion in the butter over moderate heat until golden brown. Add the apple, sage, the liquid of your choice, and sugar. Cover and cook until the apple is tender. Mash or purée, then season with salt and pepper to taste. Serve warm or hot with barbecued sausages, sausage loaf, etc.

Refrigerate for up to 3 days.

Satay Sauce

FOR ABOUT 6 SERVINGS:

½ cup chopped roasted peanuts
2 tsp chopped fresh root ginger
1 Tbsp brown sugar
2 cloves garlic
juice of 1 lemon
2 Tbsp light soy sauce
3–4 drops Tabasco sauce
1 cup coconut milk

In a food processor or blender, finely chop the first four ingredients together, then add the next three ingredients and enough coconut milk to make a thin sauce. Heat until boiling, thinning if necessary.

Serve hot. Refrigerate up to 2–3 days.

Salsas for Sausages

An uncooked salsa is a cross between a salad and a relish. Salsas are refreshing and interesting, combining the flavour and sweetness of the fruit or tomato with the hotness of chilli and the distinctive flavour of the herb used.

Kiwifruit Salsa

FOR ABOUT 6 SERVINGS:

4 ripe kiwifruit, chopped or sliced
¼ cup finely sliced spring onion or shallots
¼ red pepper, chopped
1 clove garlic, finely chopped
½ cup basil leaves, finely chopped
¼ tsp finely chopped red or green chilli or 1 tsp Tabasco sauce
1 tsp ground cumin
¼ cup lime juice
¼ tsp salt

Combine all the ingredients, tossing gently together so the kiwifruit keeps its shape. Refrigerate for up to 24 hours.

Mango Salsa

FOR ABOUT 6 SERVINGS:

2 cups diced or sliced ripe mango
2–3 Tbsp lime juice
2 Tbsp finely chopped coriander leaves or fresh mint
¼–½ tsp finely chopped fresh green chilli or 1 tsp Tabasco sauce
½ tsp salt

Combine all the ingredients, tossing gently so the mango keeps its shape. Refrigerate for up to 24 hours.

VARIATION: Use ripe peaches, nectarines, or pawpaw instead of the mango.

Fresh Tomato Salsa

FOR ABOUT 6 SERVINGS:

500g ripe tomatoes
½ red onion
2–3 Tbsp chopped parsley, chives, coriander leaf or fresh basil
1 Tbsp chopped jalapeño peppers
1 tsp minced garlic
1 tsp ground cumin
1 tsp oregano
2 Tbsp wine vinegar
1½ tsp salt
2 tsp sugar

Finely chop the first five ingredients, by hand or with a food processor. Gently mix in the remaining ingredients. Leave for at least 30 minutes before using. Refrigerate for up to 4 days.

Index – Mince & Sausages

Popular
potatoes

100 Easy & Delicious Recipes by **Simon & Alison Holst**

Before You Start Cooking!

In this book you will often find potatoes are referred to by size.

A small new potato weighs about 50g. Allow 2–3 per serving

A medium-sized potato weighs about 125–150g

A large potato e.g. for baking weighs 200–250g

We have suggested using different potato types (waxy or new, all purpose or floury) in these recipes – you may (of course) use different types, but be aware this may affect the end result. Look on pages 100–101 for more information on potato varieties.

In potato cookery, you seldom need to be precise about weights, but the sizes and weights above will give you an indication.

If you use a baking dish bigger than that specified, the contents may cook more quickly. In a smaller dish, cooking time will probably be a little longer.

When parsley is specified, use fresh parsley, otherwise use fresh herbs when they are specified, and dried herbs at other times.

When coconut cream is used in a recipe, use standard or low fat canned coconut cream. (Freeze leftovers in small containers for later use.)

We have used microwave ovens of 700–750 Watts. If your microwave is of higher wattage, it will require a shorter cooking time. Use our times as a guide only.

For best results use standard metric measuring cups and spoons when you use these recipes. 1 metric cup holds 250ml. 1 tablespoon holds 15ml. 1 teaspoon holds 5ml. All of our cup and spoon measures are level unless otherwise stated.

Large amounts of butter are given by weight. Butter packs usually have 50g or 100g markings on the pack. 1 Tbsp butter weighs 15g.

Abbreviations used:

cm	centimeter	g	grams
°C	Celsius	tsp	teaspoon
ml	millilitre	Tbsp	tablespoon

Acknowledgements

We would like to thank the following for their assistance:

Horticulture NZ

Crop and Food Research

Glenda Gourley

Dennis Greville

Alison's Pantry

Bennicks Poultry Farm

About This Book

Everybody loves potatoes! We hope that this book will show you just how versatile potatoes can be. It contains over one hundred tasty and interesting potato recipes and includes all our favourites!

We think that our recipes will prove to you that potatoes are not only great value for money, but that they can be cooked (and enjoyed!) successfully by anyone, from inexperienced young starter cooks to busy mothers and fathers, or by experienced gourmets!

While we've tried to give some interesting ideas from around the world, you will also find that most of our recipes require only relatively few ingredients, many which you are likely to have on hand.

You can buy potatoes all year round, in small bags or large sacks, or you can grow your own potatoes in your garden if you have the space and the inclination. (We can't think of anything nicer than new potatoes cooked with a mint sprig, a few minutes after they are dug!) Do take time to read the details about potato varieties and their characteristics on pages 100 and 101, so you will be able to choose the potatoes which are best for your purpose.

Potatoes are good for you too! Alison has always remembered an interesting fact provided by the New Zealand Potato Board, when she worked for them many years ago. The message was that, if necessary, you can survive on nothing but potatoes, as long as you sit in the sun while you eat them! She also remembers that the two biggest fund-raising demonstrations she ever did (both to over 850 people!), one just north of Auckland and the other in Invercargill, were based around a variety of obviously very popular potato dishes!

'Popular Potatoes' has new and recent recipes from Simon and Alison, lots of new photographs and includes most of the recipes in 'Alison Holst's Best Potato Recipes', which is now out of print, but sold over 100,000 copies.

We hope you will enjoy these recipes as much as we do!

Simon & Alison Holst

POTATO CONTENTS

Handy tips and facts

Look out for me and other spuddies through this book – we've got handy tips and facts to share about potatoes.

The Not So Humble Potato...

It seems it's quite easy to take the poor old potato more than a little for granted. However, if you're willing to take a little time to scratch (perhaps that should be dig in the case of potatoes!) below the surface a number of interesting facts come to light, and by taking the time to read a few basics, you may be able to enhance your enjoyment (and diet!).

It seems that potatoes are among the quiet achievers – did you know that they're the world's fourth largest food crop? Or that they are grown in more countries than any other crop except maize?

Closer to home the statistics also make interesting reading. New Zealand produces over 250,000 tonnes of fresh potatoes a year, and over 97% of the population eat them – this must put them in a fairly elite category of foods. In fact, 54% of New Zealanders eat potatoes four times a week, which might help account for the approximately 65kg we eat per person, per year (globally this puts us ahead of the US at 61kg/year but some way behind the UK at 105kg/year).

Potatoes and nutrition

As most people know, potatoes are an excellent source of carbohydrate (the body's preferred fuel source), and in their natural state are virtually fat free. But did you know that Kiwis actually get around 30% of their vitamin C from potatoes? Or that they are a valuable source of B group vitamins, particularly B6, thiamin and niacin and are a good source of fibre? As if that's not enough, they also contain some iron and magnesium. No wonder potatoes count towards your "5 plus a day" servings of fruit and vegetables!

Remember that while potatoes themselves are not fattening, some cooking and preparation methods are! Deep frying chips and/or roasting potatoes swimming in fat or oil will change them to a high fat food, which should be eaten in small quantities only!

Potatoes have so much flavour and nutrients in, or just under their skins, it's a pity to throw it away! (A microwaved or baked potato in its skin contains more fibre than two slices of wholemeal bread!) Instead of peeling them, try rubbing washed potatoes with "green scratchies" (otherwise known as rectangular green plastic scouring pads or pot scrubs). Not only is this quicker and easier than peeling, it removes the stubborn dirt, leaving most of the skin intact – and you finish up with more potato for your money.

Treated like this, you will find you can leave the skin on potatoes used for roasting, boiling, or in salads! (You can even mash potatoes with their skin on – then you can be trendy and call them "smashed" potatoes, but these aren't really quite the same as good old mash!)

If you MUST peel potatoes, use a sharp potato peeler in preference to a vegetable knife. A peeler removes a thinner layer than the knife does, saving money as well as nutrients. If you are going to peel them, do so just before you are going to cook them – if you leave them exposed to air some of the nutrients will oxidise (causing discolouration) and covering them in water to prevent this means some of the nutrients will be leeched out.

To retain maximum nutrients when boiling potatoes, keep the pieces large and don't use more water than you need. Always have a lid on the pot.

What to look for when buying potatoes

Try to choose potatoes that haven't got any cuts, bruises, green patches or shoots. Remember however, that although it's tempting to choose a smooth looking potato over a misshapen one, and assume that it is a better product, this is not necessarily the case. Some varieties have skins which are rougher and/or have more eyes in them. A potato does not have to look good to cook brilliantly!

For best results it more important to select the right potato for the job! The texture of a cooked potato varies with the variety, the time of the year (season) and the soil and climatic conditions it was grown in. Unless you are an expert, you are unlikely to be able to determine all of these factors just by looking at the potato. Thankfully, to make life easier, most bags of potatoes are labelled with both the variety, and how they are best used.

They may be marked as most suitable for 'boiling', 'salads', 'mashing', 'wedges' or 'baking', for example. This is largely determined by their cooked texture – in general a potato is either 'floury' (best for mashing, roasting or baking), or 'waxy' (great for eating boiled or in salads) or all purpose (somewhere in between floury and waxy, and generally suitable for most cooking methods).

Why are potatoes sometimes different?

Different varieties of potatoes do tend to fall into broad categories of waxy, floury or all purpose, however, to complicate things a little, this can also be affected by the time of the year (season) the potato is planted and harvested, the soil and the weather. For example, an Ilam Hardy harvested early in the season (October) is quite waxy. However if the potatoes are left to mature longer before harvesting the Ilam Hardy becomes a good general-purpose potato, whilst if left even longer, towards the end of the season when a lot more of the natural sugars have converted to starch, it tends to be floury. This is the difference between "New" or "Main crop" potatoes you will sometimes hear about. To further complicate the issue, not all potato varieties show such a range of characteristics.

Weather, climate and soil also have a dramatic effect on the cooking performance of a potato. For example, a Southland grown Nadine may be very waxy whilst a Pukekohe grown Nadine may be only slightly waxy. The flavour is also influenced.

How to store your potatoes

For best results, store potatoes in a well ventilated, cool, dark place. Don't put them in the fridge as the flavour changes will be noticeable (the starch will begin to convert into sugar). Always remove them from any plastic packaging (this helps prevent sweating), unless it is a 'Greenguard' bag, which is manufactured specifically for potatoes. A heavy paper bag or cardboard box makes a good storage container.

Remember, place them gently in your storage area – although they may seem tough, they bruise easily if you drop them or treat them roughly, so for best flavour and less waste, look after them.

When potatoes are exposed to light they can develop a green colour resulting in chlorophyll formation in the surface layers. Associated with this is the formation of a toxic alkaloid, solanine. The amount of green pigment depends on the intensity of the light, length of exposure and age of potato. New potatoes are really susceptible to greening. Some varieties have quite a yellow flesh so don't confuse this with greening. If you do purchase potatoes with lots of greening, return them to your retailer. If there are small amounts of greening simply peel or scrape away the greening and use the potato normally.

Natural dirt and dust on potatoes can help to keep them fresher so it is best not to wash them until you are ready to cook them – or if you buy ready washed, buy small quantities regularly.

Different types of potatoes

These potatoes have been cooked in exactly the same way, but notice their different textures.

Waxy
most 'early' new season varieties

These potatoes tend to be waxy and are ideal for boiling, salads, casseroles, soups.

Draga

Waxy/floury

These potatoes tend to be general-purpose making them suitable for most end uses.

Rua

Floury

These potatoes tend to be floury and are ideal for mashing, wedges, chips, roasting, baking.

Ilam Hardy

Be sure to use a potato best suited to your cooking method.

Some potatoes are less floury or less waxy than others. These potatoes fall into the area of 'general-purpose' and will tend to perform more tasks, although perhaps with not as good results as the ones which clearly fall into the floury or waxy category.

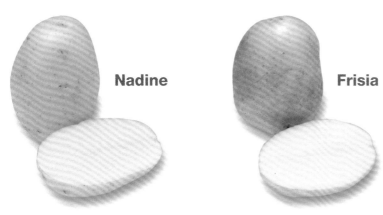

Nadine

Frisia

And limited or localised supplies of Jersey Bennie, Liseta, Red King Edward, Tiffany.

Desiree

Karaka

Moonlight

And limited or localised supplies of Red Ruby, Rocket, Maris Anchor.

Red Rascal

Agria

Fianna

And limited or localised supplies of White Delight.

Souper
Potatoes

Potatoes make wonderful soups! When they are cooked then puréed in stock, they make a smooth and creamy soup, and when the cooked, cubed potatoes are left in small pieces throughout a soup or chowder, they have just the right texture – not too firm, and not too soft. Enjoy our soups, then try making your own specialties, adding different vegetables and seasonings!

Corn, Ham & Potato Chowder

A big bowl of this thick, creamy soup, packed with corn, other vegetables and ham, makes a satisfying meal on a cold day. By working efficiently and using a few short cuts, you can have it on the table in 20 minutes.

FOR 3–4 LARGE SERVINGS:

1 Tbsp oil
½–1 tsp minced or finely chopped garlic
1 large onion, peeled and halved
1 medium carrot, scrubbed
2 cups hot water
2 medium–large (about 300g) all purpose or floury potatoes, scrubbed
1 leek or 2 tender celery stalks, optional
2–3 tsp instant chicken or bacon stock powder
50g butter
¼ cup flour
2 cups milk
2 tsp basil pesto, optional
1 x 440g can cream-style corn
100–200g chunky ham pieces
chopped parsley and chives

In a large pot over moderate heat, heat the oil and garlic while you chop the onion into 7mm cubes. Stir the prepared onion into the oil and keep cooking the mixture while you chop the carrot into 5mm cubes. Add the hot water, then the prepared carrot. While the mixture simmers, cut the potatoes into 7mm cubes and thinly slice the celery or leek if using. Add the vegetables and the stock powder to the pot, cover and leave the vegetables to finish cooking while you make the sauce.

Melt the butter in a medium–large pot. Stir in the flour and heat until it bubbles, without letting it brown. Add the milk, half a cup at a time, stirring constantly and bringing to the boil before the next addition. When it boils after the last measure of milk is added, remove the pot from the heat and stir in the pesto, if using, and the corn.

Finely chop the ham chunks, then as soon as the potato and carrot are tender, tip the sauce and the ham and parsley into the large pot with the vegetables. Stir to mix thoroughly, and cook for a few minutes to heat through, without actually letting the mixture boil. Serve in large bowls with warmed crusty bread or rolls.

VARIATIONS: To make Corn and Bacon Chowder, leave out the ham, but brown 2–4 chopped bacon rashers in the oil before adding the garlic and chopped onion. To save time, replace the onion, carrot and celery with 4 cups frozen vegetables.

Leek & Potato Soup

This is a delicately flavoured, smooth, creamy and filling winter soup that uses inexpensive winter vegetables. While our version is not traditional, it is quick and easy to make without the bother of white sauce. The amount of cream you use is up to your taste and your conscience!

FOR 4–6 SERVINGS:

50g butter
1 clove garlic, crushed
3 medium leeks, white and pale green parts only, finely sliced
3 medium (400–450g) all purpose or floury potatoes
4 cups water
3 tsp instant chicken stock
1 tsp instant green herb stock
1 tsp sugar
about ¼ cup cream
salt, pepper and hot sauce to taste
extra cream and chopped chives or ground paprika to garnish, optional

Melt the butter in a large pot. Chop the garlic and add the leeks. Cover and gently cook for about 10 minutes. Take care not to let the vegetables brown at all during this stage.

Peel and thinly slice the potatoes, then chop the slices into quarters. Add to the pot along with the water, both stock powders and the sugar. Simmer for about 10 minutes until both the leeks and potatoes are just tender. (Overcooking will spoil the fresh flavour of the vegetables.)

Blend or process the vegetable mixture until smooth and creamy or, if you want a chunky soup, mash with a potato masher. Return to the pot and stir in the cream, then taste before adding the seasonings.

Reheat gently and serve immediately or reheat when required. Swirl a little runny cream on top of each bowl of soup, or top each bowl with a spoonful of lightly whipped cream. Sprinkle with chopped chives or paprika if desired.

NOTE: Sometimes leeks come with dirt between their layers of leaves. If you cut each leek in half lengthwise, then hold it under a running tap cut side up, you should be able to get rid of most of the soil before you chop them crosswise.

Chunky Shrimp & Potato Chowder

This delicious, chunky chowder is one of Alison's favourite soups. Keep a can of shrimps in your store cupboard so you can make it at short notice as a satisfying meal for unexpected guests. You can also double the quantities of everything – as long as you have a large enough pot!

FOR 4–6 SERVINGS:

25g butter
2 medium onions, chopped
1 cup sliced celery, optional
1 cup hot water
1 tsp instant green herb stock powder
1 tsp instant chicken stock powder
3 medium (450g) all purpose or floury potatoes, scrubbed and cut into 1cm cubes
about 1 cup frozen mixed vegetables or peas
1 x 200g can shrimps
2 cups milk
about 2 Tbsp cornflour
chopped parsley and a pinch of paprika to garnish

Gently heat the butter in a large pot. Add the onions – and celery if using – and cook, covered, until tender but not browned. Add the water, stock powders, and the potatoes.

Cover and simmer for 15 minutes or until the potatoes are tender, adding the frozen vegetables three-quarters of the way through so they will be cooked at the same time as the potatoes.

Add the shrimps and the liquid from the can (unless it is dark in colour and very strongly flavoured) and the milk. Bring the mixture to the boil. Thicken with the cornflour which has been mixed with a little water to form a paste. Taste and adjust the seasonings as required.

Serve in large bowls for lunch or dinner, garnished with parsley and paprika, with toast or bread rolls alongside.

VARIATIONS:

Add a spoonful of lightly whipped cream for special occasions.

For Chunky Salmon & Potato Chowder, replace the shrimps with canned salmon. Break the salmon into smallish chunks, removing and discarding the bones and any dark skin. Use all the salmon liquid in the chowder.

Potato, Garlic & Thyme Soup

This simple soup, made from basic ingredients, is particularly delicious if made with good stock. Always season the soup carefully before serving it. Home-grown thyme from your garden has a stronger flavour than very young thyme plants, so you will need to use larger quantities if you use the young, hothouse variety. Add smaller amounts of dried thyme instead, if you like.

FOR 4 SERVINGS:

1 large onion
3 large cloves garlic
1 Tbsp butter
1 Tbsp canola or olive oil
500g floury potatoes
1 Tbsp fresh thyme leaves, chopped
3 cups chicken or vegetable stock
seasoning to taste
¼ cup cream or Greek-style yoghurt, plus extra to garnish
fresh thyme leaves and ground paprika to garnish

Peel and halve the onion, then chop finely. Cut off the root ends of the garlic cloves, bang them with the bottom of a bottle to loosen the skins, then chop finely. Put the prepared onion and garlic in a medium pot with the butter and oil and cook over low to moderate heat, covered, until the onion is clear but not browned.

Meantime, thinly peel the potatoes, then chop into 1cm cubes. Add to the pot with the thyme, then stir in the chicken or vegetable stock (or use the same volume of water plus 4 teaspoons instant chicken or vegetable stock). Simmer for 15 minutes until the potatoes are tender.

Purée the mixture in a food processor, mouli fitted with a fine blade or a wand. Taste and season if necessary, then stir in the cream.

Just before serving, reheat, but do not boil. Serve in bowls, topped with a swirl of cream or Greek yoghurt, a few thyme leaves, and a sprinkling of paprika.

NOTE: Greek yoghurt has a less tangy flavour than plain yoghurt, which can overwhelm the other flavours in this soup.

 Don't feel you should always peel potatoes – rub off any rough bits using a "green scratchy", and eat the skins too – the skins are particularly tasty and fibre-rich!

Fish Chowder

Fish chowder makes an excellent meal at any time of the year. This version is light enough to serve during summer, but is also warm and comforting on a cold winter's evening.

FOR 3–4 SERVINGS:

1 Tbsp olive oil
25g butter
1 medium onion, diced
100g bacon, diced
2 sticks celery, thinly sliced
2 medium (300g) all purpose or floury potatoes, cut into
    1cm cubes
1 medium carrot, finely diced
2½ cups milk
½ tsp garlic salt
500g fish fillets, cubed
1 Tbsp chopped fresh dill, optional
1 Tbsp cornflour
salt and pepper to taste
chopped fresh dill or parsley to garnish

Heat the oil and butter together in a large pot. Add the onion and cook until the onion softens. Add the bacon, celery, potato and carrot to the pot and cook, stirring frequently to prevent browning, for about 5 minutes.

Add 2 cups of the milk and the garlic salt and simmer for about 10 minutes or until the potato is just tender, then add the cubed fish – and dill if using. Mix the remaining milk with the cornflour to form a paste and add to the pot. Bring the chowder to the boil, then reduce the heat and simmer for 5 minutes.

Season to taste, then ladle into large bowls, garnish with chopped herbs and serve accompanied with crusty garlic bread.

NOTE: To make easy garlic bread for 4, mix 2 tablespoons of olive oil or melted butter with a finely chopped clove of fresh garlic. Lightly brush both sides of 4 thick, diagonally sliced lengths of French bread with the garlic mixture. Grill, turning once, until both sides are golden brown (watch closely to prevent burning).

Cool Potato
Salads

Using new potatoes or waxy potato varieties, you can make really interesting salads right through the year! Potato salads are substantial enough to be served as the main part of lunch, and are also excellent served in warm weather with barbecues, steaks or cold meat, as the main meal of the day. Potato salads travel well in packed lunches too, and they are a real boon for family cooks who like a salad that can be made ahead, then refrigerated.

Salad Niçoise

This salad makes a wonderful hot weather lunch or a light evening meal course. It always looks best if you arrange the ingredients, one at a time, on individual dinner plates.

FOR 2 SERVINGS:

2 large eggs
4–6 small new or waxy potatoes
100–150g green beans
mixed lettuce leaves, including small cos lettuce leaves
2 medium or 8–10 baby tomatoes
10cm telegraph cucumber
1 x 185–200g can tuna
2–4 spring onions, diagonally sliced
4–6 anchovy fillets, whole or chopped
8–12 black olives, whole or sliced

DRESSING:

2 Tbsp lemon juice
6 Tbsp olive oil
1 tsp Dijon mustard
¼ tsp salt

Hard-boil the eggs and cook the potatoes and beans until just tender at least 30 minutes before serving time. Cool the potatoes and beans in cold water, then drain and set aside.

While the vegetables are cooking, chop the remaining ingredients as required.

Just before you are ready to serve, arrange the lettuce leaves on two dinner plates so that the tips are close to the edge of the plates and the stems are towards the centre. Thickly slice the potatoes and beans if required and peel and quarter the eggs. Slice the tomatoes if using medium ones. Cut the cucumber in half lengthwise, scoop out the seeds with a teaspoon, then cut in crosswise slices.

Arrange the prepared salad vegetables on the lettuce. Drain and flake the tuna, and spoon over the salad. Top with the spring onion, anchovies and olives.

Just before serving, combine the dressing ingredients in a screw-topped jar and drizzle over the plates. Serve with French or garlic bread.

NOTE: Vary the quantities of any of the ingredients to suit yourself.

Sausage & Potato Salad with Mustard Dressing

New potatoes and sliced precooked sausages taste really good when you mix them with this dressing! Make the salad with your favourite precooked specialty deli sausages, with frankfurters, or even leftover fried or barbecued sausages. You will end up with more dressing than you need, but you can refrigerate it for later use.

FOR 4 SERVINGS:

about 300g new or waxy potatoes

DRESSING:

¼ cup wholegrain mustard
2 Tbsp brown sugar
2 Tbsp wine vinegar
1 large clove garlic, roughly chopped
1 Tbsp roughly chopped parsley
1 Tbsp roughly chopped chives or spring onions
1 Tbsp chopped fresh coriander, optional
½ cup olive or canola oil
¼ cup warm water

200–300g cooked sausages
4–6 gherkins, optional
2–4 pickled onions, optional
about 2 cups coarsely chopped crisp lettuce

Scrape the potatoes, cutting them in half if they are large and place in a pot with just enough lightly salted water to cover and simmer for about 20 minutes or until they are

tender (test with a sharp knife). Remove the pot from the heat and leave the potatoes to stand in the water for 5 minutes.

Make the dressing next. Measure the first three ingredients into the bowl of a food processor or into a blender. Add the garlic, parsley and chives. With the motor running, slowly add the oil, followed by the water. Taste and add extra sugar if required. The consistency of the finished dressing should be between that of mayonnaise and French dressing.

Drain and slice the warm potatoes, then gently toss them in enough dressing to coat. Cut the sausages into slices about 5mm thick and separately toss them in enough dressing to coat. Leave to stand for a few minutes so the dressing will flavour the sausages.

Gently mix together the prepared sausages and potatoes. Finely slice or chop the gherkins and pickled onions if using, and add to the salad.

Serve the salad on a bed of chopped lettuce on individual plates or shallow bowls.

NOTE: If the wholegrain mustard you use is sweet, start with half the amount of brown sugar.

For extra colour, add some tomato wedges to the salad just before serving.

Use the dressing immediately or refrigerate in a covered container, but bring to room temperature before using.

American Potato Salad

This is a wonderful salad if you make it with good mayonnaise. Make it the day you are going to serve it and refrigerate it promptly.

FOR 2–3 SERVINGS:

2 cups cooked, cubed new or waxy potatoes
1 Tbsp wine vinegar
1 Tbsp olive oil
1 spring onion, finely chopped
2 Tbsp chopped parsley
¼ cup traditional mayonnaise or Best Foods Mayonnaise
½–1 large hard-boiled egg, peeled and chopped
extra chopped parsley

Put the cubed potatoes in a plastic bag, then add the vinegar and the oil. Mix gently, without breaking up the potatoes.

Mix together in a shallow bowl the next three ingredients, then add the potato mixture and the egg and fold through.

Just before serving, sprinkle with a little extra parsley.

Cover and refrigerate until ready to serve.

Traditional Mayonnaise

Home-made mayonnaise is just as good as, if not better than, the best quality bought mayonnaise, and costs a fraction of the price.

FOR ABOUT 2 CUPS:

2 large eggs
½ cup white wine vinegar
1 tsp salt
1 tsp sugar
1–2 tsp mixed mustard
1–2 garlic cloves, crushed, optional
fresh or dried herbs to taste, optional
1½–2 cups canola oil

Put the metal chopping blade in the food processor. Add the first five ingredients. Process to mix. With the machine on, add the oil in a thin stream through the tube in the lid.

The mixture will keep getting thicker as more oil is added, so stop adding oil as soon as the mayonnaise is the thickness you like it to be.

If you are adding the optional ingredients, add them after you have added a cup of the oil.

If you have added the optional ingredients, it is best to leave the mayonnaise to stand for a while until the flavours intensify, before using any of it. Cover and refrigerate in a jar for up to 3 weeks. (Don't leave your jar of homemade mayonnaise standing round in a warm kitchen – always keep it in the refrigerator.)

NOTES: You can also make this mayonnaise in a blender or small food processor. If you do this, halve the quantities.

Don't leave out the mustard as it helps the mayonnaise become thick and smooth.

Cumin Potato Salad

It is surprisingly quick and easy to make interesting salad dressings yourself from scratch. Try this zingy dressing to add zest to a salad made from lovely, waxy new potatoes – be sure to use freshly ground cumin.

MAKES ABOUT 1 CUP:

1 Tbsp onion pulp (see below)
½ cup olive oil
½ cup white wine vinegar
2 tsp ground cumin
¾ tsp salt
1–2 tsp crumbled dried oregano leaves
1 clove garlic
freshly ground black pepper to taste
hot pepper sauce to taste

To make the onion pulp, cut an onion in half horizontally, then scrape the cut surface with a sharp-edged teaspoon. (The other half of the onion can be refrigerated and used later.)

Combine all the ingredients in a clean, dry screw-top jar.

Pour as much of the dressing as you like over warm, chopped or cubed cooked new or waxy potato slices and mix gently until they are coated with the dressing. If desired, add some lightly cooked chopped green beans to the dressed potatoes, then toss gently again.

Sprinkle the salad with finely chopped parsley, coriander, and spring onions or chives. Cover and leave to stand at room temperature for about 30 minutes before serving with a tomato salad and barbecued meat, sliced ham, or cold roast meat.

Hot-Smoked Salmon with Potato Salad

Celebrate the arrival of summer with this delicious, warm salad. The combination of smoked salmon and new potatoes works particularly well and makes for a surprisingly substantial salad.

You can smoke your own salmon (see below), but a 200g pack of commercially hot-smoked salmon is just as good.

FOR 2 SERVINGS:

2 slices, each about 150g, fresh skinless salmon
1 Tbsp brown sugar
1 tsp salt

250g–300g new or waxy potatoes
about 150g small green beans
¼ cup olive oil
2 Tbsp lemon juice
1 Tbsp Dijon or other mustard
2 Tbsp capers
2 spring onions, sliced
salt, pepper and sugar to taste
¼ cup mayonnaise
1 Tbsp each lemon juice and warm water
1 tsp finely grated lemon rind
salad greens

To smoke the salmon, place it (skin-side down) on a sheet of doubled tin foil with the corners twisted to hold in the juices. Thoroughly mix the sugar and salt and sprinkle it over the salmon. Place the salmon, still in the foil, in the smoker and follow the manufacturer's instructions. We fuel ours with ¼–½ cup methylated spirits, and use 1 cup manuka chips dampened with ¼ cup of water. Smoke for about 15–20 minutes.

Halve the potatoes if large, then simmer in lightly salted water until tender, adding the whole beans in the last 5 minutes. Drain the vegetables and immediately cool the beans under cold water, then cool, skin and slice the potatoes. Set aside while you make the dressing and finish the mayonnaise.

Combine the oil and the next four ingredients in a screw-top jar. Shake to mix, then season to taste. In a separate container combine the mayonnaise with the lemon juice and warm water, then stir in the lemon rind.

Gently mix the sliced potatoes and beans in the mustard dressing. Arrange the salad greens on two plates. Top with the dressed potatoes and beans, finishing with some salmon. Drizzle with lemon mayonnaise and serve immediately.

Hot Potato Salad

If you like the idea of warm food with a tangy sauce or dressing, try this recipe which is perfect for cooler late spring or early summer days when the idea of a salad is appealing, but it is not quite warm enough for a cold meal. Because freshly dug new potatoes are among our favourite foods, we often cook more than we need – leftovers are delicious served like this!

FOR 2–3 SERVINGS:

2–3 bacon rashers
1 onion, finely chopped
2 tsp flour
about 1 tsp sugar
about ½ tsp each salt and dry mustard
about ½ cup water
2–3 Tbsp white wine vinegar
4 medium cooked new or waxy potatoes
2 gherkins or dill pickles
chopped parsley to garnish
pinch of paprika, optional

Cook the bacon in a medium frypan until crisp, then remove it from the pan and let it cool on a folded paper towel.

Add the onion to the bacon drippings in the pan and cook, covered, until the onion is transparent and straw-coloured.

Stir the flour, sugar, salt and mustard into the onion in the pan, then add the water and bring to the boil, stirring constantly, until the sauce thickens. Add 2 tablespoons of the vinegar and stir over low heat until the dressing comes back to the boil. Taste and add the extra vinegar if you like a more tangy dressing, and more water if the sauce has thickened too much to coat the potatoes thinly. Adjust the seasonings as required – the strongly flavoured sauce should taste both sweet and sour.

Slice the cooked potatoes and the gherkins into the dressing. Set aside, covered, until ready to serve.

Just before serving reheat the mixture, stirring occasionally, taking care not to break up the potato pieces.

Serve in a shallow bowl, sprinkled with the chopped bacon, chopped parsley, and a sprinkling of paprika if desired.

Serve with hot frankfurters or sausages, or cold meat such as corned beef, roast lamb or pork.

Potato salads are always popular! Vary them, trying thin dressings as well as creamy ones. For best flavour, add the dressing ahead of time to allow the flavours in the dressing to be absorbed by the potatoes.

Peanutty Potato Salad ▶

This high-protein peanutty dressing is an Indonesian specialty, known as 'gado gado'.

It turns cold, cooked potatoes – and other vegetables – into a very satisfying meal.

DRESSING:

2 tsp canola or other oil
1 onion, finely chopped
1 large garlic clove, finely chopped
2 tsp brown sugar
2 tsp Kikkoman soy sauce
2 tsp lemon juice
¼ cup of crunchy or smooth peanut butter
water or coconut cream
hot pepper sauce to taste

cooked waxy or new potatoes, quartered or sliced
cooked beans, chopped into 5cm lengths
cucumber, peeled and thickly sliced
spring onions, chopped
hard-boiled eggs, peeled and quartered
tofu, cubed and fried
beansprouts
crisp lettuce leaves

Heat the oil in a frypan and cook the onion and garlic until tender. Stir in the brown sugar, soy sauce, lemon juice and peanut butter. Stir over low heat, then add enough water and/or coconut cream to thin the sauce to pouring consistency. Add enough pepper sauce to taste. Pour the sauce into a jug and set aside.

Arrange the first seven ingredients for the salad accompaniments in bowls on the table with the jug of peanutty sauce. Place 1–2 lettuce leaves on individual plates, then encourage diners to help themselves to the accompaniments, finishing up with some sauce poured over the salad.

Spicy Yoghurt Potato Salad Dressing

We are great believers in cooking more potatoes than we need for a meal because having a ziplock bag of cooked potatoes in the refrigerator is like having money in the bank – always useful!

In warm weather we use cold, cooked new potatoes to make this low-calorie creamy salad with its spicy flavour, and serve it with barbecued butterflied lamb, lamb kebabs, steak or interesting sausages. During colder weather we make it from leftover, firm-textured main crop potatoes – it is marvellous as a side dish for curries.

MAKES ABOUT 1 CUP:

1 large clove garlic, peeled
½–1 small green chilli, deseeded and roughly chopped
¼ cup fresh coriander leaves, roughly chopped
2 spring onions, roughly chopped
1 tsp ground cumin
½ tsp sugar
½ tsp salt
1 cup plain unsweetened yoghurt

Combine the first seven ingredients in a food processor, then process until finely chopped. Add the yoghurt and pulse just enough to combine.

Gently mix the dressing through leftover cubed potatoes using proportions to suit yourself.

To retain nutrients when boiling potatoes, keep the pieces large and don't use more water than you need. Always have a lid on the pot.

If you have one, use a steamer above another pot to cook potatoes. Steaming retains nutrients which are otherwise lost.

Snacking
on Spuds

The following recipes are a really mixed bunch! Some make tasty finger food, others are very

good for breakfasts, while some will especially please those who like interesting spicy dishes.

Potato Pancakes

A cross between hash browns and fritters, these are especially popular with children who enjoy their crisp texture and mild flavour. The bacon adds interest, but you can leave it out, especially if you are serving the pancakes with meat and a salad.

FOR 6–8 SERVINGS (16 PANCAKES):

2 large eggs, unbeaten
2 Tbsp milk
2 rashers lean bacon or ham, very finely chopped
1 onion, very finely chopped
1 tsp curry powder
1 tsp celery salt
3–4 medium (about 500g) all purpose or floury potatoes, scrubbed or peeled
¼ cup flour
vegetable oil for frying

Mix together the eggs, milk, bacon, onion and seasonings in a large bowl.

Just before cooking, grate the potatoes into the mixture, then add the flour.

Put just enough oil in a frypan to cover the bottom. Heat until a small test amount of the pancake mixture bubbles when put in. Drop in dessertspoonsful of the mixture, four at a time, using a second spoon to stop the mixture from sticking to the first spoon. Try to make even-shaped pancakes, flattening them a little if necessary. Cook each pancake for 3–4 minutes per side, until golden brown and cooked through to the centre. As they are cooked, transfer the pancakes to a paper towel on a flat plate and place in a warm oven.

Serve alone, or with tomatoes and/or mushrooms etc. for a light meal. Or, serve as finger food, topped with sour cream and a little smoked salmon (or other topping/s).

VARIATION: Omit the bacon or ham and serve the pancakes with chops, steak, sausages and cooked vegetables or your favourite salad for dinner.

Pea Flour Patties

In this eggless recipe, small pieces of raw vegetables are incorporated into an Indian spice-flavoured batter. Try them served hot alongside a yoghurt-based dip.

FOR 4 SERVINGS:

1 cup pea flour
about ½ cup water
1 tsp turmeric
2 tsp ground cumin
2 tsp ground coriander seed
2 tsp garam masala
2 medium (about 300g) waxy or all purpose potatoes
1 onion
1 cup frozen peas or other vegetables
oil for frying

Mix the pea flour with the water and the next four ingredients to make a fairly stiff paste. Leave to stand for 5 minutes or longer, while you prepare the vegetables.

Scrub the potatoes using a 'green scratchy' (see page 98). Cut the potatoes and the other vegetables into pea-sized cubes.

Mix the vegetables into the batter just before you intend to start making the patties; you may need to thicken the batter by adding extra pea flour to make it thick enough to keep the vegetables together.

Pour the oil into a frypan to a depth of 2cm. Heat, then drop in teaspoonfuls of mixture, a few at a time. Adjust the heat so the patties cook and brown nicely in about 4 minutes, then turn and cook the other side for the same time. Faster cooking will result in raw vegetables inside the batter. As the patties are cooked, transfer them to a shallow plate covered with absorbent paper napkins. Alternatively serve them as finger food with your favourite toppings.

Serve immediately as finger food, with a herby dip made by combining plain unsweetened yoghurt, lemon juice, chopped mint, salt and a little sugar to suit your taste.

Did you know that 54% of Kiwis eat potatoes four times a week?

For an easy lunch at work, take a potato to microwave, and a small can of flavoured tuna. How easy is that!

Filo Samosas

Everyone enjoys the interesting contrast of a light flaky crust with the dense, well-seasoned potato filling of these little pastries. Although they are a simplified version of a traditional Indian vegetarian snack, they still contain quite a few ingredients. Use as many as possible, but if you have to leave out a few seasonings, we are sure you will still enjoy them.

FOR 8 SMALL SAMOSAS (4 SERVINGS):

2 medium (about 300g) all purpose or floury potatoes
1 Tbsp oil
1 medium onion, finely chopped
1½ tsp curry powder
1 tsp ground cumin
½ tsp garam masala
½ tsp ground coriander seeds
¾ cup frozen peas
2 Tbsp water
1 tsp salt
½ tsp sugar
juice of ½ lemon
2 Tbsp chopped mint or fresh coriander leaves
6 sheets filo pastry
25g butter, melted

Scrub and cut the potatoes into 1cm cubes. Cook in a lidded microwave container (see page 98) or in a pot in a little water until tender.

Heat the oil in a large frypan. Gently cook the onion and all the seasonings until the onion is tender. Add the peas and the water, cover and cook for 2 minutes. Add the drained, cooked potatoes, salt, sugar and lemon juice, and mix thoroughly, without breaking up the potato too much. Taste and add extra salt and lemon juice if required. Stir in the chopped herbs.

Preheat the oven to 200°C.

Stack together three lightly buttered sheets of filo. Cut crosswise into four even strips. Put a good tablespoon of filling at the end of one strip and fold into a triangular parcel (see diagram below).

Repeat this step with the remaining filo sheets and filling mixture. Lightly brush the top of each samosa with melted butter. Place on a baking tray.

Bake the samosas for 10 minutes then reduce the heat to 180°C and bake for a further 15–20 minutes until golden brown.

Serve warm, as a snack or a light meal, at any time of the day.

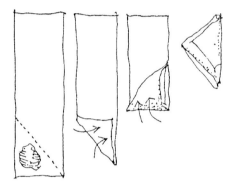

Jacket Wedges

These jacket wedges make great snacks that are popular with all age groups. Keep wedges interesting by experimenting and adding different spices and flavourings to the coating mixture so they are never exactly the same twice. Serve straight from the oven, in a shallow basket or bowl lined with paper towels, or serve them on a large platter, surrounding one or more bought or homemade dips – the sky's the limit!

FOR 3–4 SERVINGS:

4 large (1kg) all purpose or floury potatoes
3 Tbsp olive or canola oil
1 Tbsp light soya sauce
1 tsp very finely chopped garlic
1 Tbsp finely grated parmesan cheese
½ tsp salt

Preheat the oven to 200°C.

Scrub the potatoes with a 'green scratchy' (see page 98), but do not peel them. Cut each potato lengthwise into about 8 wedges and place them in a bowl of cold water as you go. Once all the potatoes have been scrubbed and chopped, drain off the water and pat the wedges dry.

Mix together the oil, soya sauce, garlic, parmesan cheese and salt in a shallow bowl. Using your fingers, gently turn the potato wedges in this mixture to coat. As each wedge is coated, stand it skin-side down on a shallow baking tray lined with a piece of baking paper.

Bake for 35–40 minutes or until the wedges are tender and golden brown.

VARIATIONS: Mix different seasonings with the oil. Use your favourites or try one or more of the following: curry powder, cumin, plain or smoked paprika, flavoured salts, crumbled dried oregano, thyme or sage.

Omit the parmesan cheese and sprinkle some grated cheddar cheese over each wedge a few minutes before they have finished baking.

Serve hot or warm with dips such as guacamole, salsa, satay sauce, or sour cream, as snacks or appetisers.

Skordalia

We've seen this delicious dish served in much the same way as mashed potatoes, but it is traditionally served as a dip.

FOR 4–6 SERVINGS:

4 medium (about 700g) all purpose or floury potatoes
6 cloves garlic
½ cup olive oil
6 Tbsp wine vinegar or a lemon juice and vinegar mixture
about ½ tsp salt
pinch of paprika to garnish, optional

Peel the potatoes. Gently boil until tender. Drain well, then mash.

Peel and finely chop or grind the garlic to a paste. Place the garlic, mashed potato, oil and vinegar in a food processor. Process until smooth, then season to taste with salt.

Garnish with the paprika if desired and serve immediately with vegetable crudités or refrigerate in a covered container until required.

Fat-Free Potato Wedges

These easy-to-prepare potato wedges make excellent, wonderfully easy and very popular snacks to serve alone, or with one or more dips, as a snack. They are best eaten as soon as they are cooked.

Preheat oven to 200–225°C, (fan-bake) with a rack in the middle of the oven.

Wash, rub with a "green scratchy" (see page 98) and dry several medium to large potatoes. For preference use evenly shaped, oval potatoes, each of which weigh 250–300g. (Agria are our favourites but you can use others too.)

Cut the potatoes lengthwise into six long wedges.

Lay each wedge, skin-side down, on an oven tray lined with baking paper, or a non-stick liner. Sprinkle the cut surfaces with pepper if you like, or leave them exactly as they are.

Bake for 60 minutes at the lower temperature, or 45 minutes at the higher temperature, until the wedges are an even light brown.

Serve the wedges hot, on paper napkins.

VARIATIONS: Cook the potato wedges exactly as above, and serve as a side dish, with meat and other vegetables.

Boiling and salad potatoes have a waxy texture which is smooth and holds together beautifully during cooking. All new potatoes come into this category. Other potatoes with this texture are Nadine, Draga, Frisia, and limited or local supplies of Jersey Benne, Liseta, Red King Edward, and Tiffany.

Baking, roasting and mashing potatoes have a soft, floury texture. Varieties include Ilam Hardy, Red Rascal, Agria, Fianna, and localised supplies of White Delight.

Some potato varieties fit somewhere between Waxy and Floury and are all-purpose potatoes. Look for Rua, Desiree, Karaka, and Moonlight, and limited and local supplies of Red Ruby, Rocket and Maris Anchor.

Potato Puffs

Potato puffs are small, tasty savouries that are always very popular for morning tea savouries, at parties, for suppers, and at 'ladies a plate' functions, as long as there is an oven in which they can be reheated. They are also enormously popular with hungry teenagers, and will disappear from the plate like magic if you are nice enough to make them for your children and their friends as an after-school treat. They are also very good served with soup at lunchtime.

We do, however, have to add a word of warning. Straight from the oven, they are dangerously hot and can burn the inside of your mouth! Leave them to cool a little before serving.

FOR 12 SAVOURIES:

3 slices sandwich bread
butter for spreading
1 cup cold mashed potato
1 cup grated tasty cheese
1 egg
1–2 Tbsp onion pulp (see below)
1–2 rashers bacon, chopped
salt or seasoned salt
pinch of paprika, optional

Lightly butter each slice of bread. Cut off the crusts if you are fussy, then cut each slice into four small squares. Press the squares into patty or muffin pans, butter-side down.

Preheat the oven to 190°C.

Mix the mashed potato with the cheese, egg, onion pulp and bacon (the less bacon you use, the more salt you'll need).

Spoon the mixture into the uncooked bread cases (best done with two dessertspoons; use the tip of the second one to help slide the potato mixture off the first spoon). Sprinkle the potato mixture with a little paprika for extra colour if desired.

Bake for 20–30 minutes until the bread cases are light brown.

Eat when hot (but not too hot), or cool on a rack, then freeze for reheating later.

NOTE: To make onion pulp, cut an unpeeled onion through its equator, i.e. horizontally, then scrape the surface with the edge of an upside-down teaspoon.

VARIATION: Make four giant savouries, using four slices of bread to fill each of four round individual pie tins/moulds. Divide the potato filling between the four pie shells, and bake as above.

Swiss Potato Cake

We love this recipe and although Alison feels her untraditional version might well horrify a traditional Swiss cook, her family has always enjoyed it. For Alison, it brings back wonderful memories, when she and Peter enjoyed these cakes on a perfect summer's evening, on the top of a perfect Swiss mountain, outside a perfect Swiss chalet, surrounded by perfect Swiss cows. It could not have been nicer!

FOR 1 SERVING:

2 medium (about 300g) all purpose or floury potatoes, grated
about 25g butter, melted
about 2 tsp oil
about ½ cup grated cheese
2 tsp finely chopped herbs
½ cup sautéed mushrooms

Scrub and coarsely shred the potatoes with a sharp cutter, e.g. using the shredding blade in a food processor. Plunge the shreds into a bowl of cold water and leave for at least 5 minutes. Drain the shreds in a colander, then pat dry using folded paper towels or a clean teatowel.

Melt the butter in a large pot, then add the potato and toss to coat.

Heat the oil in a small non-stick frypan, ensuring the base and sides are well coated. Add the potato, pressing down on the mass quite firmly. Place the lid on the pan at an angle so it is ajar and cook over moderate heat for about 15 minutes or until the cake is evenly golden brown on the underside. Slide the cake out of the pan onto the lid or a plate, then flip it back into the pan, uncooked side down. Cook for a further 10 minutes, again with the lid ajar. During the last 3 minutes sprinkle over the grated cheese mixed with the herbs, top with the sautéed mushrooms, then let the cheese melt slightly. Slide the potato cake onto a plate, with the cheese and mushroom topping uppermost.

Serve immediately with a side salad, and a bread roll if desired.

Baked Baby Potatoes

Baked baby potatoes make an interesting and simple twist on finger food. They're delicious filled with a little blue cheese, or sour cream and chives, or sour cream and smoked salmon.

Brining the potatoes first may seem like an unusual step, but it's easy and really does give the skins a different texture.

For up to 1kg baby new potatoes, make a brine solution by dissolving 3 teaspoons of salt in 4 cups of hot water. Place the potatoes in a large bowl or pot, then pour the brine over them and leave them to stand for 30–60 minutes.

Preheat the oven to 180°C.

Drain the potatoes, then arrange them on a baking tray. Position the tray in the middle of the oven and bake for 30–40 minutes or until the potatoes are soft when gently squeezed.

Remove the potatoes from the oven, then leave them to stand until they are cool enough to handle.

Cut a cross in the top of each potato, then squeeze gently to open them up. Fill each with a small wedge of blue cheese or 1 teaspoon of sour cream, then top with a sprinkle of chives, a small piece of smoked salmon or even a small blob of salmon caviar.

Serve while still warm.

NOTE: While butter is always good with baked potatoes, it is best avoided if you plan to serve these as finger food as it becomes a little drippy when it melts.

Potato & Kumara Cakes with Mango Salsa

These crisp little potato and kumara cakes really come to life when served with this delicious mango salsa!

FOR 2–3 SERVINGS:

200g all purpose or floury potatoes
150g kumara
2 spring onions
1 large egg
½ tsp salt
black pepper
about ¼ cup oil for cooking

SALSA:

400g can mango slices in light syrup or 1 cup finely
    chopped fresh mango
1 spring onion
1 Tbsp lemon (or lime) juice
½ tsp minced red chilli
½ tsp salt
1–2 Tbsp chopped coriander leaf

Scrub the potatoes and kumara, then grate with the skins on. Place the grated mixture in a bowl and cover with water. Leave to stand for 1–2 minutes, then drain in a sieve, squeezing out as much water as you can. Transfer back to the dried bowl.

Thinly slice the spring onions and add these to the grated mixture along with the egg, salt and a generous grind of black pepper, then stir lightly with a fork to combine (do not over-mix). Leave the mixture to stand while you prepare the salsa.

Drain the mango slices and cut the flesh into 5mm cubes. Thinly slice the spring onion then mix this together with the cubed mango, lemon or lime juice, chilli, salt and chopped coriander in a small bowl.

Heat the oil in a large non-stick pan, gently drop generous dessertspoons of the kumara-potato mixture into the pan, flattening them into cakes about 1cm thick. Cook over a medium-high heat for 3–4 minutes per side, or until crisp and golden brown.

Drain the cooked cakes briefly on several layers of paper towels, then arrange on plates and serve topped with a generous dollop of the salsa and a green salad.

Did you know that Kiwis get around 30% of their vitamin C from potatoes?

Be creative with your toppings for baked or microwaved potatoes! As well as sour cream and grated cheeses, try lighter options of baked beans, chilli, tuna and salsa. Serve them with a salad as a complete meal!

Mediterranean Potatoes ▶

This recipe turns everyday potatoes into something that will delight everyone. Depending on the flavourings added, the potatoes can be served on the side or as the main part of a casual meal.

FOR 2 MAIN COURSE SERVINGS:

6 medium (about 900g) all purpose or floury potatoes
2–3 Tbsp olive or other oil
1–2 large cloves finely chopped garlic
pinch of chilli powder or cayenne pepper
several sprigs of fresh thyme, rosemary and/or sage
½ tsp salt or 2 tsp chopped capers
1 Tbsp chopped anchovies
2 Tbsp caper vinegar
about ¼ cup chopped parsley
black olives, optional

Scrub the potatoes to remove all dirt, then cut them lengthwise into large chunky wedges or chip shapes. Rinse or stand in cold water for a few minutes before patting dry.

Heat the oil in a large frypan. Add the prepared potatoes and toss to coat evenly. Cover the pan and cook over a moderate heat, turning every 5 minutes for about 20 minutes until the potatoes are barely tender and are lightly browned on most sides.

After about 10 minutes stir through the garlic, then sprinkle the potatoes with chilli powder or cayenne pepper. Mix well. Add the herb sprigs and the salt or capers to the pan, then cover again.

When the potatoes are tender, remove the herbs. Mix in the anchovies and the caper vinegar and cook for about 10 minutes further, uncovered, turning occasionally. Taste and adjust the seasonings as desired.

Just before serving, mix through the chopped parsley. Pile the potatoes into a serving dish and scatter the olives – if using – over the top.

Serve with poached or fried eggs and a green salad or a chunky tomato and basil salad.

Bubble & Squeak

Alison and her sisters loved Bubble and Squeak when they were growing up. Their mother always cooked large amounts of potatoes and other vegetables to accompany the evening meal and leftovers would be stirred together before being put away in a cool place overnight.

Next morning, the vegetables would be mixed with a little milk, put into a preheated frying pan with a knob of butter, then pushed down to form a cake. As the mixture browned on both sides until it became crusty, the pan made popping noises (or bubbled and squeaked?) and the smell of browned potatoes became more and more inviting. Each serving was topped with a fried egg – the perfect accompaniment. But none of the girls put on weight, probably because as well as walking some distance to school every day, they would also play outside with their friends after school.

Although you may not want Bubble and Squeak for breakfast, it makes a good weekend lunch or easy dinner if you have the ingredients on hand. Quantities need not be precise, but the potatoes and cabbage are vital ingredients.

FOR 4 SERVINGS:

2–3 cups cooked potatoes, mashed or chopped
about 1 cup well-drained, shredded cooked cabbage
about 2 cups cooked or leftover vegetables, optional
milk to mix
2 Tbsp butter

Mix the mashed potatoes with the cabbage. Chop the vegetables into smallish pieces if using, then add to the potato. Mix well, adding a little milk if the vegetable mixture is too dry.

Heat a frypan, preferably with a non-stick finish. Add the butter and before it browns, tip in the vegetable mixture, firmly pushing it into the pan. Cook over a low to medium heat for about 10 minutes until the mixture is crusty and golden brown. Slide the mixture from the pan onto a plate, turn it back into the pan, browned-side up, and cook until the other side is browned, and it is hot in the middle.

To serve, cut into wedges and top with a fried egg if desired or with a mixed salad alongside.

VARIATION: Some older English recipes call for cold roast meat to be chopped and added to the uncooked mixture.

 Make potatoes one or more servings towards your "five plus vegetables a day".

A Side
of Potatoes

We are sure that you will enjoy this section as much as our families do! Interesting potatoes, served beside "run of the mill" meat, poultry or fish, can turn dinner into something special. We hope that you will work your way through all of our recipes, because there are so many that are especially good. If you are not sure what quantity you should cook, take our advice and make plenty. It is astounding how many of the following recipes will "steal the show", and become family favourites!

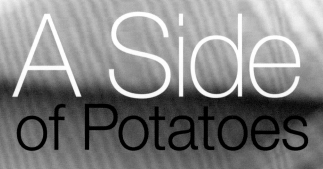

How to Cook Potatoes

Here are the basic instructions for cooking potatoes absolutely plainly. You may like to refer to these outlines when making a recipe which tells you to start with cooked potatoes.

All Purpose and Floury Potatoes (plus 'Main Crop' Waxy Varieties)

- Wash or scrub the potatoes you are going to cook.

- Peel them thinly, using a sharp vegetable knife or a potato peeler, or rub them all over with a 'green scratchy' – a plastic pad with a rough texture, usually sold in bundles, and meant for cleaning food particles off pots. Scrubbing them like this is fast and there's much less wastage than when peeling potatoes, especially with a knife.

- Cut out and discard any damaged parts of the potato.

- Cut the peeled potatoes into even-sized pieces.

- Bring a pot of lightly salted water to the boil. Drop in all the potatoes and check that the water barely covers the potatoes. Cover with a lid so the potatoes are surrounded by water or steam.

- When the water returns to the boil, lower the heat so the water is simmering.

- Cooking time will vary – anything from 15–30 minutes – and will depend on the variety of potato used, their size and the heat source. Check by piercing a large piece of potato with the sharp point of a knife. The potato is cooked when there is little resistance.

- Drain the cooked potatoes, saving the cooking water for use in gravy, sauce or to add to a pot of soup. It is quite surprising how much flavour there is in potato cooking liquid.

Early Season Waxy or 'New' Potatoes

- Using a vegetable knife or 'green scratchy' (see above), scrape off the thin, delicate skin of new potatoes. Cut out any imperfections, leaving the potatoes whole if they are small or cutting them in pieces of similar size.

- Bring a pot of lightly salted water to the boil. Drop in all the potatoes and check that the water covers the potatoes. Cover with a lid so the potatoes are surrounded by water or steam.

- Add a little sugar, salt, garlic, some mint sprigs or herbs of your choice to the water.

- After the water boils, cook them at a gentle simmer until tender when pierced.

- Cooking time will probably be a little shorter than the time required for main crop potatoes. Drain the cooked potatoes, then turn them in a little melted butter. If you have cooked them with mint, you can serve the edible leaves with the potatoes.

Stove-Top Mashed Potatoes

Mashed potatoes are comfort food with a capital M! A pile of light, fluffy, creamy mashed potatoes can be the highlight of a meal, whether you are cooking for yourself, your family, or guests.

It's worth taking a little time and trouble over their preparation, so they finish up absolutely perfect.

Start with all purpose or floury potatoes, since new or waxy potatoes will not turn out to be fluffy.

Wash or scrub the potatoes you are going to cook. Cut them into even-sized pieces.

Bring a pot of lightly salted water to the boil. Drop in all the potatoes and check that the water barely covers the potatoes. Cover with a lid so the potatoes are surrounded by water or steam.

Drain the potatoes when they are tender right through when tested with a pointed knife. Pour off the cooking liquid, saving it for later use in a gravy or sauce. If you have time, allow the drained potatoes to stand in the dry pot for 2–3 minutes.

Mash with a potato masher or push the potatoes through a potato ricer. Add 1 teaspoon of butter per serving. Lastly, beat the mashed potatoes with a fork, adding milk until they are light, smooth and creamy. Season as needed.

Serve immediately or leave to stand in a warm place for a few minutes before serving.

Microwaved Mashed Potatoes

It is hard to give accurate timing for cooking potatoes in the microwave because of the difference in cooking time between potato varieties and the varying levels of power in microwave ovens. Keep a note of how long it takes to cook a certain weight of potatoes, especially if you buy in bulk. After a little experimenting and accurate timing, you should be able to produce consistently good results.

Cut peeled all purpose or floury potatoes in 1–2cm cubes and put them in a microwave bag, dish or bowl.

Add 1 teaspoon butter and 1 tablespoon water per serving.

Cover and cook at 100% power in a microwave oven for 2–3 minutes per serving, shaking to reposition the potato cubes about halfway through the cooking time.

Leave to stand for 5 minutes after cooking, then test to make sure all the cubes are cooked through completely.

Mash without draining, adding milk, salt and pepper to taste. Then beat with a fork until they are light, smooth and creamy.

NOTE: Should the potato cubes appear to be slightly shrunken when you check them after cooking, you have cooked them too long. Next time you cook the same variety, allow half a minute less per serving.

Oven-Baked Potatoes

Baked potatoes are easy to prepare and cook. They may be served plainly as part of a meal or stuffed with a variety of interesting fillings and served as the main part of a meal.

To Bake Traditionally: Scrub medium to large potatoes, then brush or rub with oil (this will keep the skins soft). Bake on a rack, rather than on a solid surface, in a preheated 200°C oven for 50–60 minutes or at 180°C for 60–75 minutes until the potato flesh gives when pressed.

Microwave-Baked Potatoes

Scrub medium to large potatoes (try to choose potatoes roughly the same size for even cooking), then prick each one several times before cooking. Turn potatoes over halfway through cooking time.

For 100g of potatoes allow 3 minutes at high power

For 200g of potatoes allow 5½ minutes at high power

For 300g of potatoes allow 7½–8 minutes at high power

For 400g of potatoes allow 10 minutes at high power

Leave microwaved potatoes to stand for 3–5 minutes then cut a cross in the top of each one. Press down gently between the cuts to open out the cross. Put a little butter, sour cream or cheese in the cut.

A small number of potatoes will microwave faster than boiled potatoes. However, it is easy to overcook them, in which case they will be slightly shrivelled. You can avoid this next time by cooking them for a shorter period.

NOTE: Cooking times will vary with different microwave ovens, depending on their wattage. Use less time if you have a high powered oven.

Slow Cooked Baked Potatoes

Did you know that you can cook baked potatoes in a slow cooker? It is very handy to be able to fill up your slow cooker with foil-wrapped potatoes in the morning, then return to the kitchen hours later to find them ready and waiting! It's so easy too – all you need are potatoes, some foil and, of course, a slow cooker.

Choose potatoes that are labelled as 'suitable for baking'. Larger potatoes will take longer to cook all the way through so for best results select potatoes of similar size.

Wrap as many as you will need individually in foil (to stop them drying out) and arrange them in the cooker. Cover, turn the slow cooker to LOW, and in 6–8 hours you should have delicious baked potatoes!

Serve the baked potatoes with butter and/or sour cream as a side dish. Or they can be stuffed, e.g. with baked beans and grated cheese, leftover mince mixtures, etc., and served as a main dish, in which case it is best to reheat them, either in a microwave or regular oven, until the filling is heated through.

Sometimes potatoes that have been pressed against the sides of the cooker bowl can brown a bit. To prevent this happening, turn or rearrange them after 4–5 hours.

Twice Baked Potato Skins

Twice baked potato skins were very popular some years ago. Although they are seldom seen in restaurants these days, they remain a delicious treat so why not make them at home. They offer plenty of scope to experiment with different spices and dips or toppings.

Cut as many baked potatoes as required into quarters lengthwise as soon as they are cool enough to handle. Scoop out most of the cooked flesh, leaving a 5mm shell. (Refrigerate the flesh to use at a later time.) Brush both sides of the skins with canola or olive oil, then sprinkle one side with salt, pepper, and two or three of your favourite dried spices.

Bake, uncovered, in a shallow metal dish, in a preheated 230°C oven for 15–20 minutes or until crisp and browned around the edges. Top with – or dip into – salsa, pesto, or grated cheese, etc.

Checkerboard Potatoes

Sometimes it's good to cook potatoes in a way that is just a little different. Checkerboard potatoes are worth trying – they cook more quickly than regular baked potatoes, they look more colourful and they don't require any last minute attention.

Scrub some fairly large, oval potatoes – as many as are required – and cut each one in half lengthwise. Using a sharp vegetable knife make a series of parallel cuts lengthwise, 5mm apart, cutting down as deeply as you can without cutting through the skin. Then cut similar lines crosswise so you finish up with a checkerboard design.

Blot the cut surface with a paper towel, pressing down firmly, then lightly brush the same surface with melted butter or oil. Sprinkle evenly with paprika. (You will get a nice even result if you shake the paprika through a fine sieve.)

Bake the potatoes, cut side up, in a preheated 200°C oven for 35–40 minutes or until the potatoes feel soft when squeezed. The cuts should open slightly during the cooking process. Serve immediately.

Roast Potatoes

Roasted potatoes that cook in a roasting pan with a joint of meat or a chicken need very little attention as they cook. They will brown better and crisp up more if they are not packed in the pan too tightly and are cooked in a large shallow roasting pan rather than in a small deep roasting pan. And because the roasting meat spatters a bit as it cooks, the potatoes get naturally basted. Then there are the pan drippings, which add flavour and colour to the potatoes.

Although large potatoes can be cut in half or into quarters for roasting, oval-shaped, whole, smallish potatoes look particularly good. We think the heat circulates round them better too, since only a small part of an oval potato lies against the roasting pan surface.

Main crop potatoes (see pages 99 & 187) take about 60–75 minutes at 180°C, depending on their size. We think it is a good idea to turn potatoes over occasionally, so they become golden brown and crisp on as many surfaces as possible.

NOTE: New potatoes do not roast well.

Crusty Roast Potatoes

Peel the required number of potatoes – main crop (see pages 99 & 187) are best – and cut them into even-sized pieces. Parboil (partly cook) in boiling water for 15 minutes.

Pat dry, coat lightly with flour then roast as above. Some people like to roughen the surface of the parboiled potatoes with a fork so they brown better, but it's not really necessary.

Garlic Roast Potatoes

Peel the required number of potatoes, ideally oval-shaped, smallish, whole potatoes.

Bring a pot of lightly salted water to the boil. Drop in all the potatoes and check that the water covers them. Cover and cook for 15 minutes.

Drain the potatoes, pat dry, then stand them on a board until they are cool enough to handle.

While the potatoes are cooking, mash 2 cloves of garlic in ¼ cup oil using a pestle and mortar or a small grinder or blender.

When the potatoes are cool enough to handle, make some deep crosswise cuts, 5mm apart, on each potato taking care not to cut them right through. Thoroughly brush each potato with the garlic oil, ensuring that the oil gets into the cuts.

Put the potatoes in a shallow baking dish and cook in an oven preheated to 200°C for about 1 hour, brushing with more garlic oil at intervals.

Cubed Roast Vegetables ▲

A platter of seasoned roasted vegetables makes an interesting addition to almost any dinner. A good combination of vegetables includes some all-purpose potatoes, orange kumara, pumpkin, carrots, parsnip, beetroot, red onions, red, green and/or orange peppers, mushrooms, etc.

FOR 8 SERVINGS:
8–10 cups prepared vegetables (see above)
4 tsp garlic-infused or plain olive oil
handful of fresh rosemary leaves

Seasoning Mix:
1 Tbsp ground cumin
1 tsp each curry powder, plain or smoked paprika, celery
    salt and garlic salt
½–1 tsp chilli powder, optional

Combine all the ingredients for the seasoning mix into a screw-topped jar. Shake to mix.

Preheat the oven to 220°C.

Prepare the vegetables. Remove the skin from the pumpkin and onions and wash the other vegetables. Cut everything except the onions and mushrooms into 2–3cm cubes. Cut the onions into quarters through the root. Leave the mushrooms whole.

Put all the vegetables except the mushrooms in a large plastic bag (supermarket bags are good for this). Drizzle three-quarters of the oil over them, then toss to coat. Sprinkle into the bag about 3–4 teaspoons of the seasoning mix (save the rest for future use) and toss the vegetables again. Lastly, add the rosemary leaves and toss again. Brush the mushrooms with the rest of the oil.

Place a Teflon liner or some non-stick baking paper into each of two large roasting pans. Tip in the vegetables and spread them out so they are no more than two deep.

Bake for about 1 hour.

VARIATION: Toss in some chopped fresh herbs or toasted pinenuts, black olives or grilled cherry tomatoes after the vegetables have been roasted.

Bird's Nest Potatoes

This recipe has been popular with Alison's family for more than 40 years. A food processor makes light work of grating the raw potatoes and a large electric frypan will do a great job of cooking them (you need a large pan unless you are just cooking for one or two people).

Scrub, then grate 1 large all purpose or floury potato per person. Pile the shredded potato in the centre of a clean teatowel. Squeeze the teatowel to remove most of the liquid from the shredded potato. Heat a little canola or olive oil in a very hot frypan, then drop handfuls of potato into the pan. Flatten each 'cake' lightly, but do not pack the shreds too tightly. Turn the cakes over when they are golden brown, adding more oil when cooking the second side if necessary.

NOTE: Work fast, putting the grated potato into the pan soon after grating it or the raw potato will turn brown on standing.

Potatoes are easy to grow – see pages 186 and 187 for everything you need to know.

Kiwis love potatoes!

97% of New Zealanders eat potatoes

54% of the population eat fresh potatoes four or more times a week

42% of New Zealanders eat processed potatoes at home fortnightly or more

20% of the population eat fresh potatoes each day

New Zealanders eat 7 million portions of hot chips per week

Skillet Potatoes ▷

These potatoes are always very popular. Our extended family thinks that they are particularly good served in warm weather, with cold meat and a tomato salad or a mixed salad. If you have an electric frypan with a non-stick finish, you will find the recipe is particularly easy to make, otherwise use a large frypan – but don't forget to keep an eye on the potatoes as they cook.

FOR 3–4 SERVINGS:

Scrub or peel 4–5 medium-size potatoes (about 600g). Cut the potatoes into 5mm thick slices and drop them into a bowl of cold water as you go.

Cook 2 sliced onions in 3–4 tablespoons butter (or 1 tablespoon each of butter and oil) in a large non-stick electric frypan with a lid.

Drain the raw potato slices, pat them dry and add to the onion in the pan. Turn to coat with butter, then cover and cook on low heat for 15 minutes, turning occasionally.

Uncover, then turn up the heat a little and allow the vegetables to brown slightly, cooking for a further 10–15 minutes.

Just before serving, drain off any excess butter/oil, season the potatoes with salt and pepper or any other seasonings you think would be good, and sprinkle with 2 tablespoons of finely chopped fresh herbs.

Sautéed Potatoes

Simple though they may be, sautéed potatoes are always really popular with everybody. Because of this, in our house we often cook more potatoes than we need for a meal – so there will be leftovers to sauté later on! Perfect, baby new potatoes are not suitable, but they are good after they have matured a bit and are not quite so waxy when cooked.

FOR 2 SERVINGS:

Slice 3–4 medium cold, cooked potatoes into chunky pieces. Heat 3–4 tablespoons of butter or oil (or a mixture of the two) in a non-stick frypan which is large enough for the potatoes to be easily turned. When the pan is hot, add the potatoes and cook, uncovered, turning every few minutes for 20–30 minutes until they are evenly crisp and golden. Sprinkle with chopped parsley before serving.

VARIATION: Bring to the boil in a small pot 2 tablespoons of wine vinegar, 1 chopped garlic clove, 1 teaspoon of finely grated lemon rind and 2 tablespoons of olive oil. Drizzle over the sautéed potatoes just before serving.

It pays to cook more potatoes than you need for dinner – for example, sauté leftovers for breakfast, or make a potato salad for lunch!

Potatoes of the same variety are not always identical. As a potato grows it is affected by the weather, climate, soil and the time of year.

Hash Browns

Alison and her family were first introduced to hash browns in San Francisco nearly 40 years ago. On their arrival they staggered off the plane with their two preschoolers, found a downtown hotel, and next morning went looking for a nearby place to eat breakfast. Alison suspects the dark-suited businessmen enjoying their quiet breakfast were not impressed with the family's rather noisy company, but all the Holsts thought the hash browns, bacon and 'easy over' fried eggs, cooked on a large hot plate in front of them were wonderful!

Boil or microwave as many large, floury potatoes as required until they are just tender (it's not necessary to peel them first). Refrigerate for at least 8 hours, then grate coarsely.

Heat a large frypan with just enough butter to form a film. When the butter is a light straw colour, spoon in the grated potatoes. Fill the pan to form a layer of potato about 2cm thick. Pat down evenly with a fish slice or turner so it forms a large, flat-topped cake. Brown over moderate heat for 10–15 minutes or until a crisp, golden brown crust forms underneath.

Slide the potato cake onto a plate, then flip it back into the pan, uncooked side down. Add a little extra butter down the sides of the pan and cook until crisp underneath.

Remove from the pan and cut into wedges. Serve with bacon, eggs, tomatoes, and/or mushrooms.

VARIATIONS:

Cook hash browns on a preheated, solid barbecue plate which has had a little oil drizzled onto it first. Hash browns are also popular when served with barbecued foods such as chops, steaks or sausages, with barbecued mushrooms and/or tomatoes and a green salad.

Shape then cook individual servings of hash browns if you are using a large square electric frypan.

NOTE: When we cook hash browns on a barbecue plate, we use oil instead of butter, keeping it in a squirt bottle for speed, accuracy and ease of use.

Potato Cakes

Deservedly popular, these potato cakes don't need much time nor do they need to be made to an exact formula – vary their seasonings and additions each time you make them, using what is available. You'll need to cook the cakes immediately because the mixture will turn sticky if left to stand.

FOR 1–2 SERVINGS:

1 cup grated or mashed cold cooked potato
½ cup self-raising flour or scone mix
½ tsp celery salt
½ tsp green herb instant stock powder
about 2 Tbsp chopped parsley or other herb/s
⅓–½ cup chopped cooked vegetables, chicken or meat,
     optional
milk
flour
oil

Mix the potato with the rest of the ingredients except the milk. Add enough milk to mix to a firm dough. Form into a cylinder on a wooden board, using a little flour to prevent the dough from sticking.

Cut into 1cm slices using a sharp serrated knife. Lightly flour both sides of each potato cake.

Pour the oil into a frypan to a depth of 5mm and heat. Cook the potato cakes in the hot oil for 4–5 minutes on each side until they are evenly browned. Do not shorten the cooking time or the centres of the potato cakes will be pasty.

Serve hot for breakfast or lunch or with salad or steamed vegetables for dinner.

VARIATIONS: Add the contents of a can of tuna or salmon, reserving the liquid. Omit the celery salt and instant stock powder and use the reserved liquid to mix the dough before adding any milk. For a milder flavour discard the liquid from the can and use flavourings and milk as above.

Potatoes are rich in vitamins and minerals, contain protective antioxidants and are virtually fat free.

Always remember how versatile potatoes are – they taste great when baked, stuffed, pan-fried, sautéed, roasted and barbecued, and of course, boiled then mashed! Yum!

Microwaved Cubed Potatoes

This is a very useful way to precook potatoes for salads and other recipes. Vary the seasonings and the size of the pieces to suit yourself.

The cubed potatoes will cook more quickly and evenly if they are coated with the oil or melted butter before they are microwaved.

PER SERVING:

1 medium waxy or all purpose potato, cubed
½ tsp butter or oil
2 tsp water
½ clove garlic, chopped, or 2 tsp chopped parsley, or
    1 chopped spring onion or 1 sprig of mint

Scrub or peel the potato. Cut into 1.5cm cubes, dropping them into a bowl of cold water as you go.

Drain the raw potato cubes and put in an oven bag or small microwave dish. Add the remaining ingredients, using oil if the potatoes are to be used in a salad. The potatoes will cook fastest and most evenly if they almost fill the container or bag they are in. If using an oven bag, loosely close it with a rubber band leaving a fingertip-sized gap through which steam can escape during cooking (without this gap, the bag may blow up and burst).

Approximate cooking times on 100% power:

1 serving (125–150g) 3–3½ minutes
2 servings (250–300g) 4–4½ minutes
4 servings (500–600g) 5–6½ minutes

After a couple of minutes of cooking, shake the container to coat the potato pieces evenly with the butter or oil and the seasonings.

Carefully squeeze the potatoes through the bag to see if they give a little to check if they are done.

Leave the potatoes to stand for 3–4 minutes after cooking.

NOTE: Should the potato cubes appear to be slightly shrunken when you check them, they have been overcooked. Next time you cook the same variety, allow half a minute less per serving.

Crunchy Brown Microwaved Potatoes

These are as close as we can get to fried potatoes using a microwave. You will need a microwave browning dish, which can sometimes be found in second-hand shops. These dishes are made by Corning, an American company, and they have a special coating on the bottom which gets very hot when it is heated in a microwave, allowing the potatoes to brown.

Change the seasonings to suit yourself, but a combination of curry powder and paprika results in a good colour.

FOR 2 SERVINGS:

2 medium (about 300g) all purpose or floury potatoes
1 Tbsp flour
1 tsp salt
1 tsp paprika
¼ tsp curry powder
1 Tbsp butter
1 Tbsp oil

Scrub or peel the potatoes. Cut into 1cm cubes, then pat dry with a paper towel. Measure the flour and seasonings into a dry plastic bag, shake to mix, then add the potato cubes and shake well to coat thoroughly.

Heat the empty browning dish on 100% power for 6 minutes. Have the butter and potatoes ready to go in as soon as the dish has heated.

As soon as the dish has finished heating, pour the oil into the dish without removing it from the microwave. Add the butter in several pieces, then quickly add the potatoes. Microwave, uncovered, at 100% power for 3 minutes. Again without removing the dish from the microwave, turn the potato using a spoon then cook for a further 2–3 minutes until a potato cube is tender when tested.

Serve hot as an accompaniment to a main meal or serve with pan-cooked bacon, tomato or mushrooms for a weekend breakfast or brunch.

Potatoes keep best in a cool place, out of direct light, in a ventilated paper or cardboard container, so you can buy enough for several weeks in large quantities.

When you make mashed potatoes, try different additions at times. Don't always use milk and butter! Try yoghurt or olive oil. Add extra flavours for a change – chopped fresh herbs, chopped spring onions, sautéed onions or sautéed chopped mushrooms.

Microwaved Herbed Potato Cake

This tasty and impressive dish is easy when made in a microwave oven, especially if you have a food processor and if you use a microwave ring pan.

FOR 4–5 SERVINGS:

about 25g butter
4 medium (about 600g) all purpose or floury potatoes
2 small onions or spring onions, very finely chopped
½ cup chopped fresh parsley or other fresh herbs
2 tsp instant green herb stock powder
½ cup grated cheese (mild or tasty to taste)
pinch of paprika

Melt the butter in a 6-cup microwave ring pan in which you will cook the potatoes.

Scrub the potatoes, ideally using a 'green scratchy' (see page 125). Coarsely shred the scrubbed potatoes, preferably using the shredding blade of a food processor, then place them in a bowl of cold water as soon as possible to prevent browning.

Drain the shredded potato in a sieve, squeezing them well to remove excess water (or pile the shredded potato in the centre of a clean teatowel, then gather up the edges and squeeze the teatowel to remove most of the liquid from the shredded potato).

In a bowl mix the potato with the onion, herbs, stock powder and the melted butter. Press the mixture into the microwave ring pan, cover with a lid or plastic film and microwave at 100% power for 10 minutes or until the potato cake is tender. Leave it to stand for 2 minutes, then turn it out onto a flat plate.

Scatter the grated cheese over the top, sprinkle with paprika and microwave for about 30 seconds or until the cheese melts.

Cut the potato cake into large chunky pieces and serve with meat or poultry and other vegetables.

NOTE: If you want to prepare this ahead of time, turn the cooked cake out onto a microwavable dinner plate, remove the centre cone, but leave the microwave dish over the potato cake on the plate. A few minutes before serving dinner, microwave it on 100% power until the cake is hot right through. Remove the dish before serving.

Microwaved Potatoes in Coconut Cream

Over the years Alison has made this recipe many times in various supermarkets. She is always surprised by the number of people who taste it and enjoy it so much that they rush off to buy the ingredients so they can make it themselves – as soon as they get home.

FOR 1–2 SERVINGS:

1 onion, chopped
4 small waxy or new potatoes (about 200g), unpeeled and cut into quarters
½–¾ cup canned coconut cream
1 tsp curry powder
¼ tsp salt
½ tsp sugar
1 cup frozen peas
about 100g cauliflorets, optional
1 cup chopped cabbage, optional

Put the onion and the potatoes in a microwaveproof dish with the coconut cream, curry powder, salt and sugar. (Use less coconut cream if peas are the only vegetable.)

Cover and microwave at 100% power for 5 minutes or until the potatoes are barely tender, then shake to mix.

Add the frozen peas and stir to coat the vegetables. Microwave for 3 minutes (use fewer peas if you are also adding cauliflower and cabbage but cook for 5 minutes, rather than 3), stirring at least once during the cooking time.

When the cauliflower and cabbage are cooked to the tender-crisp stage, taste and adjust the seasonings as required.

Serve immediately or leave to stand and reheat when required. This easy vegetable curry is good served alone or with grilled or barbecued meat or chicken.

NOTE: Alison uses new potatoes from her garden in summer, or small, pearly white Nadine potatoes at other times.

Buy smaller cans of coconut cream or look for dried coconut cream which can be reconstituted.

A microwaved potato cooks quickly and easily. Split it and add a topping of salsa and cottage cheese or tomatoes and tuna and you have an almost instant, low fat meal, at home or in the lunchroom at work!

A microwaved or baked potato in its skin contains more fibre than two slices of wholemeal bread.

Scalloped Potatoes ▶

Although we often use the microwave oven to make scalloped potatoes for two, we tend to cook a family-sized dish in the oven, often alongside a meat loaf or similar. If you aren't in the habit of making scalloped potatoes, do try this recipe because we think it will win you over!

FOR 4 SERVINGS:

600g medium all purpose or floury potatoes
2 Tbsp (25g) butter
1–2 cloves garlic or 2 small onions, finely chopped
1 tsp salt
pepper to taste
1 cup milk

Preheat the oven to 200–220°C, positioning the rack just above the centre. (Set the temperature to 220° if you plan to cook something else at the same time; 200° if the potatoes will be on their own.)

Choose even shaped potatoes which will look more attractive when layered and thinly peel or scrub them with a 'green scratchy' (see page 98). Cut the potatoes into thin crosswise slices, and put them in a bowl of cold water.

Lightly coat the inside of a shallow ovenware dish with non-stick spray.

Heat the butter in a small pot, but don't let it brown. Add the garlic, stirring until it heats through. Add the salt, pepper and milk.

While the milk heats, drain the potatoes and arrange them in the prepared dish. Flatten them with your hand or with a fish slice top, then evenly pour over the hot milk mixture.

Cover with a lid, a sheet of foil or baking paper folded over loosely at the edges, and bake for 20–30 minutes. Uncover, and bake for a further 15–30 minutes until the top is golden brown, and the potatoes feel tender when pierced with a sharp knife.

Serve with a meat loaf, chops or sausages, etc., and vegetables.

Microwaved Scalloped Potatoes For Two

This remarkably good, quick and easy (taking less than 20 minutes from start to finish) dish looks impressive, and is sure to stand you in good stead on those occasions when you want to turn an ordinary meal into something much nicer!

FOR 2 SERVINGS:

2–3 medium all purpose or floury potatoes (about 300–450g)
1 small onion, thinly sliced
1 clove garlic, chopped, optional
2 tsp butter
1 Tbsp water
1 Tbsp flour
½ cup milk
flavoured or plain salt, e.g. celery, onion or garlic
½ cup grated cheddar cheese
1 Tbsp chopped parsley
about ¼ tsp paprika

Scrub the potatoes and cut them into 5mm thick slices. Combine with the onion and garlic and place in layers in a 20cm microwaveproof shallow casserole dish.

Add the butter and water, cover, and cook at 100% power for 5 minutes until the potatoes are barely tender, shaking the dish after 2–3 minutes.

Remove the dish from the microwave and sprinkle with the flour. Add the milk, and a little salt. Shake the dish or turn the potatoes over several times to mix the ingredients. Cover and cook for a further 2–3 minutes until the sauce thickens and the potatoes are perfectly tender.

Remove from the microwave again and sprinkle the top layer evenly with the cheese, parsley and paprika. Microwave, uncovered for about 1 minute or less until the cheese melts.

Serve with grilled meat and plainly cooked vegetables.

Potatoes are really versatile – big piles of creamy mashed potatoes will be "wolfed down" in student flats, and duchesse potatoes (also made from mashed potatoes) can grace the most elegant dinner parties!

Easy Oven-Baked 'Chips'

Deep-frying chips happens very rarely in either of our households. We're not comfortable with the high fat content, we don't like clearing up the mess made by oil spattered over the stove as the chips cook, and we hate getting rid of the large quantities of stale oil involved. We have solved the problem by baking chips rather than frying them, which uses much less oil and makes very little mess. These baked chips always disappear very quickly, and as we don't get any complaints we feel that our families are hardly disadvantaged!

P.S. Just before the chips are done, we sometimes cut fish fillets into strips, dip them in flour, then into a beer batter made by mixing together 1 egg, ½ cup each of beer and flour, with seasonings to taste, and cook them in a pan of hot oil 2–3cm deep, turning them once.

FOR 2–3 SERVINGS OF CHIPS:

Preheat the oven to 230°C, positioning the tray in the centre.

Peel or scrub 2–3 large all purpose or floury potatoes and thinly slice into 5–7mm thick chips. Drop the chips into a bowl of cold water as you go and leave them to stand in the water for 5 minutes after you have finished to avoid browning.

Rinse the potatoes under cold running water, then thoroughly pat or blot them dry, using a clean teatowel or paper towels. Dry the bowl, too.

Return the chips to the dry bowl and pour 2–3 tablespoons of canola or other flavourless oil over them and mix with your fingers until they are completely coated with a thin film of oil.

Line a roasting pan or sponge roll tin with baking paper. Place the chips in the dish in one layer.

Bake in a preheated 230°C oven for 20 minutes until the chips are tender, turning once. If they do not brown enough in this time, slide out the baking paper and brown the chips under the grill.

Just before serving, sprinkle the chips with a little plain or seasoned salt. Serve immediately.

Sinfully Good Potato Wedges

These rich but absolutely delicious potatoes should be served only as an occasional treat. Coated with a heavily herbed and spiced mixture and baked until crisp, they are wonderful! We wouldn't feel so guilty eating them if we could stop after a couple, but (for us at least) it's impossible.

It is a good idea to line your baking dish with a non-stick Teflon liner or with baking paper so that the edges of the liner go up the sides a little. This will stop the wedges from sticking and make the clean-up minimal.

FOR 3–4 SERVINGS:

4 large (about 1kg) all purpose or floury potatoes
25g butter, melted
½ tsp salt
3 Tbsp olive oil
2 tsp finely chopped garlic
2 tsp ground cumin
1 tsp dried oregano
¼–½ tsp chilli powder

Scrub, then microwave or boil the potatoes whole until they are barely tender. Cool them if you have time, then cut each one lengthwise into 8 wedges.

Preheat the oven to 180°C.

Warm the butter in a large roasting pan until it is liquid but not hot. Add the salt, olive oil, garlic, cumin, oregano and chilli and mix well.

Using your hands, turn the potato wedges in the pan, mixing gently but thoroughly until all surfaces are well coated. Spread them out in a single layer, then bake for 1–1½ hours until crispy, turning once.

VARIATION: Vary the amounts and types of herbs and spices to suit yourself.

Serve warm, as a snack, for dipping into your favourite tomato-based salsa (or with the delicious green pea pesto from our Diabetes book).

 Not sure how much a serving of potatoes (and other vegetables) is? It's about a handful – how easy is that to remember!

Nelson Potatoes

This is a really good recipe that Alison dreamed up one stormy night in a motel in Collingwood after a very long drive with two pre-teens in the back seat. They had hoped to feast on fresh fish from fishing boats, but it was not to be. They dashed out, bought sausages, apples and apple cider, shut themselves in their motel, forgot about the weather outside, and had a very good time (probably because she and Peter drank the rest of the cider instead of having any green vegetables!)

You should always cook much more of this mixture than you think you need because it disappears so fast!

FOR 4 SERVINGS:

2 medium onions
2 Tbsp butter or oil
3 medium Granny Smith or Braeburn apples
3 large (about 600g) all purpose or floury potatoes,
    scrubbed and sliced
½ cup liquid such as apple juice, cider, stock or wine
freshly ground pepper and salt
chopped fresh herbs, e.g. sage, thyme or oregano

Peel and slice the onions. Cook them in a large frypan in the butter or oil until they are transparent and browned on the edges. Raise the heat, add the sliced apples and cook, uncovered, stirring often, until the apples have also slightly browned.

Mix in the sliced potatoes, then add the liquid. Cover tightly and cook for about 20 minutes until the potatoes are tender. Lift the lid from time to time and turn the apples and vegetables, adding extra liquid if the mixture becomes too dry.

Add pepper, salt and herbs to taste just before serving.

Served with sausages or pork chops, this combination is especially good, but we like it with any grilled meat as well as ham and smoked chicken.

Duchesse Potatoes

These potatoes always look impressive, and can be served alongside most meat, poultry or fish dishes for special occasions. They are made by adding egg to firm, lump-free mashed potatoes, which can then be piped into any shape you like, e.g. large rosettes or circular nests which can then be filled with a colourful vegetable mixture. Another attractive option is to pipe the potato mixture around the edge of scallop shells or individual dishes of similar size which you can later fill with seafood in a creamy sauce. For best results use floury potatoes.

Duchesse potatoes can be prepared ahead, browned attractively in the oven, and reheated in a low oven just before serving. However, it is really important to ensure that the mashed potato mixture is completely smooth – any lumps can block the piping bag. To make lump-free mashed potato, use a potato ricer (a metal cylinder with holey sides – a bit like a giant garlic crusher), available from most speciality kitchen shops. Fill it with boiled, floury potatoes, then put the presser in place and push down until all the potato has been squeezed out the small holes. If you do not want to invest in a potato ricer, simply press the cooked potatoes through a sieve to get rid of any lumps – it takes a bit longer, but it works!

For 4 servings, peel and chop 500g floury potatoes into even-size pieces. Boil until tender, but not mushy. Press the drained, cooked potato through a sieve or potato ricer, then mash with 25g butter and 1 large beaten egg (and an extra yolk if possible). Keep the mixture firm. Season to taste, then transfer the mashed potatoes into a forcer bag

with a star-shaped nozzle. Pipe out the mixture into shapes of your choice on to a sheet of baking paper on a baking tray, e.g. rosettes or circles that can later be filled with a vegetable mixture.

Bake the piped shapes in a preheated 200ºC oven for 20 minutes or until the edges turn brown.

NOTE: The rosettes always spread a little when they are baked.

Party Potatoes

Here is a shortcut recipe that is ideal for those times when you have to prepare a meal for a crowd. The buttery herbed coating disguises the flavour and appearance of the canned potatoes. Allow about 2–3 potatoes per person, depending on the age and appetites of your guests.

FOR 40 SERVINGS:

about 15 x 410g cans of small potatoes
6–8 Tbsp melted butter
about 1 cup finely chopped fresh herbs, e.g. a
    combination of parsley, chives, thyme and oregano,
    or parsley, chives and dill (chop herbs in food
    processor for best results)

Drain the potatoes from the cans, reserving the liquid. Put them in a covered microwave dish or in a large oven bag with ½ cup of the reserved liquid and heat at 100% power for 9–10 minutes. If using an oven bag, use a rubber band rather than a metal twist to loosely seal it.

Drain the potatoes, turn them in a third of the melted butter, then sprinkle generously with about ¼ cup of the herbs. Mix gently to coat evenly.

Repeat this process with the remaining potatoes.

If it is not possible to microwave the potatoes just before you need them, microwave them ahead of time then put them while they are still hot in oven bags and place the bags in an insulated container, e.g. a chilly bin, for up to 1 hour. Transfer the prepared potatoes to serving dishes just before they are required.

Serve as part of a buffet meal, as you would freshly cooked new potatoes. Use leftovers in potato salads, in scalloped potato dishes, or as sautéed potatoes.

NOTES: You can buy large catering-size cans of vegetables from cash-and-carry outlets. If you can get these, use 2–3 x 3kg size cans of potatoes in brine instead of the smaller cans. Large cans each contain about 45 small potatoes.

410g cans each hold about 6 fairly small potatoes – enough for two fairly generous servings.

Leftover canned potatoes may be refrigerated in plastic bags for 3–4 days.

Cooked potatoes should never be left standing around for long without refrigeration, especially in warm weather.

Friggione

This is a great vegetable mixture which you can make in the morning and bring out to serve with barbecued meat on a warm summer evening. For this to be at its best, do not scrimp on the cooking time. And although it loses its bright colour, it tastes better as the liquid disappears and the mixture darkens in colour.

FOR 4–6 SERVINGS:

about ¼ cup olive oil
5 medium (about 750g) all purpose or floury potatoes,
    scrubbed
2 large red onions
2 red and yellow peppers
1 x 425g can Italian seasoned tomatoes
1–1½ tsp salt
1 tsp sugar
freshly ground black pepper
chopped parsley, optional

Heat the oil in a large frypan, preferably with a non-stick surface. Cut the scrubbed potatoes into 1cm cubes and slice the onion and peppers.

Add the prepared potato, onion and pepper combination to the hot oil. Cover and cook over a moderate heat for 20 minutes, stirring several times, until the vegetables are tender and lightly browned.

Add the tomatoes and their juice. Cook, uncovered, over a medium heat for 15–30 minutes until the mixture darkens in colour and the liquid has reduced to just a small amount around the vegetables. Season to taste and sprinkle with the chopped parsley, if using, before serving.

Serve warm or hot, or reheat later in the frypan or in a microwave oven. Serve with barbecued meat, crusty rolls and a leafy green salad.

 Have you ever wondered why nutritionists are impressed by potatoes? It's because they contain Vitamin C, potassium, iron, magnesium, B group vitamins, antioxidants, fibre and carbohydrates!

Filo Surprise Packages

The potatoes on your dinner plate gain new importance when they are enclosed in crisp filo pastry! Make edible ties from long chive leaves or bacon or ham rinds to wrap up the packages but if this is not possible use string, in which case it should be removed before serving.

FOR 2 SERVINGS:

2 medium waxy or all purpose potatoes (about 300g), cooked
2 Tbsp sour cream or grated cheese
1–2 tsp fresh chopped herbs
¼ tsp salt
4 sheets filo pastry
edible ties or string (see above)

Slice the potatoes and mix with the sour cream, herbs and salt, varying the proportions to taste.

Preheat the oven to 180–190°C.

Lay two of the filo sheets on a clean dry surface. Brush each of these lightly with oil or melted butter, then cover each with a second sheet of filo. Cut each of the sandwiched sheets in half cross-ways giving four, almost square sheets. Stack the 'sandwiches' so you have two piles, four layers thick, turning the top layer so that each stack resembles an eight pointed star. Pile the potato mixture in the middle, then gather up all four corners to enclose the potato. Tie up the corners with your choice of fastening so the package looks like a pouch. Gently fan out the corners.

Place the packages in a buttered sponge roll tin, then bake for 20–30 minutes until evenly browned.

Salmon Surprise Packages

Serve these filo packages as a light lunch for two with an interesting green salad that includes dill leaves and cucumber or with lightly cooked, buttered asparagus spears.

Follow the recipe for Filo Surprise Packages (see above), but use fresh dill or spring onion as the herb.

Cut into small pieces 4–6 slices of smoked salmon and 2 slices of brie or camembert cheese. Fold these extra ingredients through the rest of the filling along with 2 teaspoons of horseradish sauce.

Colcannon

Although we enjoyed our original colcannon recipe, made by stirring lightly cooked cabbage through mashed potatoes flavoured with a little nutmeg, we have now decided that we like it even better with sizzled bacon and bacon drippings stirred through.

Potatoes (all purpose or floury)
Cabbage
Salt
Butter
Bacon
Oil
Milk
Nutmeg

Cook potatoes in the usual way (see page 125).

When the potatoes are about half cooked, put the tender young cabbage which has been cut in 5mm slices, then cut crosswise into fairly short lengths in a large frypan (in which you will later cook the bacon). Add a little salt and just enough butter (about ¼ teaspoon per serving) to stop the cabbage burning. Cover tightly and cook on high heat, watching until it is tender but still bright green, and all the water has evaporated. Set aside in a sieve.

Chop the bacon (one or two rashers per person) and put it in the pan in which the cabbage was cooked with 1 teaspoon of oil. Heat gradually over low heat, then raise the heat as bacon fat forms in the pan.

Meanwhile, drain and mash the potatoes. Add a little butter, some milk, pepper and freshly grated nutmeg. Beat with a fork until creamy and smooth.

When the bacon is light brown and crunchy, add the mashed potatoes and cabbage to the pan, and fold together. Taste and adjust the seasonings as required, then serve with baked or roast chicken or grilled sausages, etc.

Berrichonne Potatoes ▲

These are so good we would almost eat them as a meal in themselves, but they also make a delicious side dish.

Effectively the potatoes are braised as they cook, which means they are a wonderful combination of soft and moist with brown crispy tops. Yum!

FOR 4–6 SERVINGS:

1 Tbsp olive or other oil
1 medium onion, peeled and diced
4–5 bacon rashers (about 125g), chopped
1kg all purpose or floury potatoes
1 tsp instant chicken stock powder
¾ cup hot water
2–3 Tbsp olive oil, extra
pepper to taste
¼ cup hot water, extra

Preheat the oven to 200°C.

Heat the first measure of oil in a large frypan. Add the onion and cook, stirring occasionally, until the onion has softened, then add the bacon. Continue to cook, stirring frequently until the bacon begins to brown, then remove the pan from the heat.

Scrub the potatoes well using a 'green scratchy' (see page 98). Quarter them lengthwise, then cut the quarters in half crosswise.

Coat the inside of a shallow 3 litre casserole dish with nonstick spray. Sprinkle the cooked onion and bacon into the dish, then scatter the potatoes over. Dissolve the stock powder in the first measure of hot water, then pour it over the potatoes. Drizzle the surface with the remaining measure of oil, and add pepper to taste.

Place the potatoes in the oven and bake for 40–45 minutes, gently turning the potatoes once after about 30 minutes. If the mixture begins to look too dry, add the extra hot water.

When the potatoes are golden brown and tender, remove from the oven and leave to stand for 5 minutes before serving.

Curried New Potatoes

Serve new potatoes in a curry sauce alongside grilled chops, pan-cooked sausages or a plain steak to make your meal more interesting.

FOR 4 SERVINGS:

2 Tbsp butter
1–2 tsp curry powder or to taste
1 onion, chopped
6 medium (about 600g) new or waxy potatoes
1 tsp instant chicken or vegetable stock powder
1 tsp sugar
½ cup hot water
½ cup coconut cream or ¼ cup sour cream
extra water if needed
½ cup thawed green peas, optional
¼ cup sour cream, optional
4–6 hardboiled eggs, optional
freshly chopped coriander leaves, optional

Melt the butter in a medium frypan. Add the curry powder and onion and cook gently for a few minutes.

Scrape or thoroughly scrub the potatoes, then cut into halves or quarter them lengthwise for quicker cooking. Add to the curry mixture, along with the instant stock and sugar dissolved in the hot water, and the coconut cream. Cover tightly and gently simmer for 15 minutes or until the potatoes are tender and the liquid is thick. Add extra water or raise the heat so you finish up with sauce thick enough to coat the potatoes.

Serve beside the plainly cooked meat or proceed as below.

VARIATION: Add ½ cup thawed green peas when the potatoes are nearly done, and cook until the peas are tender. If using sour cream rather than coconut cream, the sauce will be thinner. Cook uncovered until the sauce thickens to the desired consistency.

MAIN COURSE VARIATION: To make a main course for 2–3 people, make the sauce using the coconut cream. Add 4–6 hard-boiled eggs, sliced lengthwise, cut side up. Heat them through, covered, over very low heat. Serve the curried potatoes, peas and eggs on rice. Sprinkle with the coriander leaves if using.

NOTES: Do not use both sour cream and coconut cream.

Joginder Kaur Basi's Dry Potato Curry

This delicious curried potato recipe was given to Alison for use in this book by an experienced Indian cook who, with her daughters, set up Aashiayana, one of New Zealand's first Indian restaurants, in the late 1970s. We feel very honoured to have been given this recipe to share – over the years many people have asked for it but up until now, it has never been put to paper.

FOR 4 SERVINGS:

6 medium (about 600g) all purpose or floury potatoes
2 Tbsp vegetable oil or ghee
½ tsp asafoetida, optional*
1 Tbsp sesame seeds
1 Tbsp coriander seeds
1 Tbsp cumin seeds
4 garlic cloves, peeled but left whole
2–3cm piece root ginger, finely chopped or grated
2 green chillies, deseeded and finely chopped, optional
1 tsp sugar
1 tsp salt
1 Tbsp turmeric
1 tsp lemon juice
1 tsp garam masala
2 Tbsp fresh coriander leaves, chopped

*asafoetida is a spice with a rather strong odour, mainly used in Indian cooking. You may need to look in a speciality store for this.

Peel or scrub the potatoes and cut into 1.5cm cubes. Set aside.

Heat the oil in a large frypan with a lid. Add the asafoetida, if using, and brown for about 30 seconds over moderate heat.

Stir in the seeds and cover the pan until you hear the seeds begin to pop. Remove the lid and add the garlic, ginger, chilli if using, and the potato, sugar, salt and turmeric. Stir well. Reduce the heat to low, cover and cook for 10 minutes. Add the lemon juice, cover again, and cook for a further 10–20 minutes until the potatoes are tender. Stir in the garam masala and sprinkle with the coriander.

Serve with another curry, a salad if desired, and with naan or other Indian bread.

When you roast potatoes, spray them with a light but even oil coating rather than standing them in an oil bath!

Spicy Potatoes ▷

A great accompaniment for any Indian-style meal, these look more complicated to make than they actually are. Curry leaves, which can sometimes be found in the produce department of your supermarket (and keep well frozen in an airtight bag) make an interesting addition if you can get them, but they're not essential.

FOR 4 SERVINGS:

600–800g waxy or all purpose potatoes
1 tsp turmeric
1 tsp salt
2 Tbsp canola oil
1 tsp mustard seed
1 tsp cumin seeds
1 tsp each paprika, ground coriander and garam masala
handful of curry leaves, optional
½–1 tsp minced red chilli, optional
2 Tbsp lemon juice
salt to taste

Scrub the potatoes and cut into 2cm cubes. Place them in a large pot and add just enough hot water to cover, then add the turmeric and salt. Bring to the boil and cook for 8–10 minutes until tender. Drain well and set aside.

Heat the oil in a large non-stick frypan. Add the mustard and cumin seeds and cook until the seeds begin to pop. Stir in the cooked potato, ground spices, curry leaves and chilli if using, and the lemon juice. Cook for 4–5 minutes, stirring frequently.

Remove from the heat, season to taste and serve immediately.

Greek-style Garlic & Lemon Potatoes

It's amazing how the flavours and aromas of food can bring the memories flooding back. The smell of these potatoes always evokes for Simon vivid memories of the Greek beach where he first tried these. They make a great accompaniment for fish or chicken dishes.

FOR 3–4 SERVINGS:

1kg all purpose or floury potatoes
2 cloves garlic, crushed
½ cup chicken stock
1–2 Tbsp lemon juice
2–3 Tbsp olive oil
salt and pepper to taste

Preheat the oven to 225°C.

Scrub the potatoes and cut into 2cm cubes. Coat the inside of a shallow 20 x 30cm casserole dish with non-stick spray. Add the potatoes, garlic, stock, lemon juice and the oil, then toss gently to combine. Season to taste with the salt and pepper.

Place the dish in the middle of the oven and cook for 20–25 minutes until golden brown, turning the potatoes gently once after about 10 minutes.

Leave the skin on potatoes used for roasting, boiling, or in salads! You can even mash potatoes with their skin on – then you can be trendy and call them "smashed" potatoes!

Potato Gnocchi

These little potato gnocchi (Italian-style dumplings) are moist and delicious, with just a hint of nutmeg – serve them tossed in melted butter and topped with freshly grated parmesan cheese.

FOR 4–6 SERVINGS:

3 medium (750g) all purpose or floury potatoes
1 egg
½ tsp salt
¼ tsp freshly ground nutmeg
freshly ground black pepper
1–1½ cups flour
flour for dusting
knob of butter
freshly grated parmesan cheese
freshly chopped herbs to garnish

Microwave or boil the whole unpeeled potatoes until cooked but still firm. Drain and cool enough to handle.

Halve the potatoes and scoop out the flesh from the skins. Place the flesh in a large bowl or food processor. Mash or briefly process until lump-free.

Add the egg, salt, nutmeg and pepper to taste. Measure in 1 cup of flour, then mix together to form a smooth non-sticky dough. If it seems too wet, add a quarter cup more flour and mix again, adding more flour if necessary.

Knead the dough for about 1 minute, then divide it into four roughly equal balls. Roll the balls into 35–40cm long and 1.5cm thick lengths. Using a sharp knife, cut the dough into a number of smaller lengths measuring about 2.5–3cm. Shape by rolling each small piece lightly under your fingers, then pressing it against the back of a grater or rolling it under the tines of a lightly floured fork. Arrange the prepared gnocchi on a floured baking sheet or tray.

Bring a large pot of water to the boil. Tip 20 or so gnocchi into the water and boil for 2–3 minutes until they rise to the surface. Leave in the water for a further 30 seconds, then remove with a slotted spoon. Transfer the cooked gnocchi to a prewarmed dish and place the butter on top. Cook the remaining gnocchi in several batches, adding them to the warmed dish and tossing them in the melted butter as they are done.

Serve on warmed plates and top with parmesan cheese and the herbs if using.

Potato Bread

If you like to make bread, you may like to try this recipe. The addition of potato makes it seem more substantial, and it also helps to hold in moisture, keeping the bread fresh for longer.

MAKES A LARGE COTTAGE LOAF:

3 tsp Surebake yeast
1¾ cups warm water
3 Tbsp lecithin granules or oil
1 Tbsp sugar
1½ tsp salt
1 cup wholemeal flour
2 cups high-grade flour
1 cup instant potato flakes

Bread Machine Instructions: Carefully measure all the ingredients in the order specified by the manufacturer into a 750g capacity bread machine.

For a cooked loaf, set the machine to the NORMAL/WHITE bread cycle, MEDIUM crust and START, (or set to the DOUGH cycle, then shape, rise and bake the loaf by hand as described below.)

Hand-made Bread Instructions: Measure the first six ingredients into a large bowl and mix thoroughly. Cover and leave for 15 minutes or longer in a warm place.

Stir in the flour and potato flakes and stir to make a soft dough, adding a little extra flour if necessary, to make a dough which is just firm enough to turn out and knead.

Knead using the dough hook of an electric mixer or by hand on a lightly floured surface for 10 minutes, adding extra flour if necessary, until the dough forms a soft ball that springs back when gently pressed.

Turn the dough in 2–3 teaspoons of oil in a clean, dry bowl, then cover with plastic film and leave in a warm, draught-free place for 30 minutes.

Shaping and Baking: Knead the oiled dough lightly in the bowl for 1 minute, then turn out on a Teflon or baking paper-lined oven tray. Gently form into a large ball and leave to rise again in the same warm draught-free place for about 1 hour or until the dough has doubled in size.

Preheat the oven to 225°C. Lightly spray the top of the loaf with water and evenly sprinkle it with flour. Using a very sharp knife, make several shallow, parallel cuts about 2cm apart across the top of the loaf, then repeat this action at right angles to the original cuts to make a checkerboard pattern.

Bake for 20–30 minutes or until the loaf is evenly browned top and bottom, and sounds hollow when the bottom is tapped.

NOTE: Leave to cool before eating as the potato flakes can impart an unusual flavour which disappears on cooling.

Mainly
Potatoes

Have fun with the recipes in this section, where potatoes are generously used in the main meal of the day. Many of these ideas come into the "Comfort Food" category. There are pies that are perfect for picnics or packed lunches, some of our favourite fish and potato dishes, and a good range of aromatic, bubbling casseroles to welcome family members when they come home at the end of a cold day. We hope you will try them all!

Minted Green Pea & Potato Frittata

This easy-to-make frittata is baked rather than cooked in a frypan, so you don't need to worry about it browning too much on the bottom as it cooks. It makes wonderful picnic food, is excellent for packed lunches for work or school, and is also popular as an informal weekend evening meal, served with a salad.

FOR 4–6 SERVINGS (12 SLICES):

500–600g new potatoes or washed white waxy potatoes
2 cups frozen minted peas
2–3 spring onions, finely sliced
4 medium firm tomatoes, deseeded and chopped into
    1cm cubes
2 cups grated tasty cheese
4 large eggs
1 cup evaporated milk
1 tsp salt
pepper to taste

Line a rectangular metal baking pan, about 20 x 30cm with sides about 5–6cm tall, with a sheet of baking paper. The paper should fit neatly in the base of the pan and up the sides, with the corners folded (but not cut). Coat the baking paper with non-stick spray.

Preheat the oven to 220°C (or 210°C fanbake) with the rack positioned in or just below the middle.

Scrape the new potatoes, or rub them if they are the white variety, then cut in half lengthwise, then in quarters crosswise. Cook in about 2cm of lightly salted water in a medium-sized pot, covered, for about 20 minutes or until the potatoes are almost tender. Add the peas and cook for

5–10 minutes longer. Drain the vegetables and spread them out on a shallow tray or dish to cool.

When the potatoes are cool enough to handle, cut the quarters into small chunks. Mix together the spring onion, tomato, peas and potatoes, then spread half the vegetable mixture over the paper-lined base of the pan. Sprinkle over half the cheese, then top with the remaining vegetable mixture.

In a bowl beat together the eggs, milk, and salt and pepper to taste. Pour evenly over the vegetable and cheese layers and sprinkle the remaining cheese over the top.

Bake for 40–45 minutes until the egg mixture is set and the cheese topping has browned attractively. Leave to cool for at least half an hour before cutting with a serrated knife into about 12 slices, three portions crosswise and four lengthwise.

Eat immediately or cover and refrigerate for up to two days until required.

VARIATIONS:

Add chopped ham or cooked chicken to the prepared vegetable mixture.

Replace the peas with mixed frozen vegetables adding any suitable chopped fresh herbs to replace the mint flavour.

Replace the chopped tomatoes with 1 or 2 chopped red peppers, and add them to the partly cooked potatoes with the peas.

NOTE: Using evaporated milk gives body and extra richness to the frittata.

Twice-Baked Stuffed Potatoes

As well as making a substantial meal, this recipe also lends itself to many different and tasty versions.

FOR 4 SERVINGS:

4 large (about 800–900g) all purpose or floury potatoes
about ¼ cup milk
½–1 cup grated cheese
salt and pepper to taste
1 x 440g can filling, e.g. spaghetti, baked beans, chilli
    beans or chilli con carne
relish or sour cream, optional

Scrub the potatoes, then bake or microwave until tender (see Ways to Bake Potatoes, page 126). Cut off the top third lengthwise from each potato and scoop out most of the flesh, leaving a shell. Mash half of the potato flesh with the milk, grated cheese, and salt and pepper. Use the other half at a later date.

Pile the potato mixture into the shells and top each one with a generous amount of canned filling. At this stage you can set aside the prepared potatoes for reheating later.

Reheat the stuffed potatoes in the oven or microwave.

Put the potatoes on an oven tray and bake for about 20–30 minutes at 180°C in a preheated oven until the shells and their filling are hot right through or allow 3–4 minutes per potato at 70% power in a microwave oven. Depending on the canned filling, top each potato with a spoonful of your favourite relish or with a teaspoon of sour cream.

Serve for lunch or as a main meal with a salad or cooked vegetables.

NOTE: Reheated potatoes can be very hot, so take care when you dive in.

Spanish Omelet ▶

This is such an excellent recipe we think you should teach your children and grandchildren how to make it, too! This dish can be found throughout Spain – but with slight variations. So feel free to modify this recipe yourself.

FOR 2 SERVINGS:

3 large waxy or all purpose potatoes (about 600g)
3 Tbsp oil
2 large eggs
½ tsp salt

Scrub and cut the potatoes into cubes.

Heat the oil in a smallish non-stick frypan, then tip in the potatoes. Cover and cook until tender, about 5–10 minutes (the potatoes need not brown).

Beat the eggs and salt with a fork. Tip the cooked potatoes into the beaten egg, then tip the mixture back into the hot pan after adding a dribble of extra oil.

Cook, uncovered, tilting the pan occasionally, until the omelet is nearly set. Slide it from the pan onto a plate, and flip it back into the pan to brown the uncooked side.

Serve the omelet alone, or with salad vegetables.

VARIATIONS: Add a chopped onion to the pan with the potatoes. Mix a chopped red and/or green pepper or chopped cooked vegetables into the potato and uncooked egg mixture.

NOTE: The omelet works best when the mixture almost fills the pan it is made in.

Patata Frittata

A frittata is a cross between an omelet and a crustless quiche. Make it when you want something quick and easy, or when you haven't bought any special ingredients, and want to use up small amounts of various quick-cooking vegetables from your fridge or garden.

FOR 4–6 SERVINGS:

50g butter
3 onions, sliced
3–4 medium (about 450–600g) all purpose potatoes, scrubbed and sliced
2–3 zucchini or other vegetable, sliced
4 eggs, preferably large
2 Tbsp water
½ cup grated parmesan cheese

Melt the butter in a large non-stick frypan or use a heavy iron pan. Cook the onions in the butter over a moderate heat until they are lightly, but evenly browned. Add the potato, stir well, then cover the pan and cook for 15–20 minutes, stirring occasionally. After 10–15 minutes, add the zucchini. Firmly press the vegetable mixture down into the pan.

In a bowl beat the eggs with the water and half the cheese. Pour over the vegetable mixture, jiggling the pan to get rid of any air pockets under the egg mixture, then cook over a gentle heat for 10 minutes or until the sides and bottom have set.

Sprinkle the remaining cheese over the top, then brown the frittata, still in the pan, under a grill until the top is set, nicely puffed and lightly browned.

Leave to stand for a few minutes until the frittata firms up, then carefully cut it into slices taking care not to damage the non-stick surface of the pan. Alternatively, slide the frittata out of the pan onto a large round plate before cutting it.

NOTE: It is not always easy to stop a frittata (or other food) sticking to a heavy iron pan. When cleaning the pan, always get rid of any stuck-on food particles (steel wool is good for this). Rinse the pan well, then rub canola or other oil over the inner surface then heat until it is very hot. When it has cooled down, rub it with a paper towel then coat it with non-stick spray. Finally, rub it gently one more time, again with a paper towel.

 Potatoes start off with no fat in them. Chips are enormously popular, but, of course, they have added fat! Chips which are cut so they are thick and chunky, and cooked at a good, high temperature (about 185°C for 3–4 minutes) contain considerably less fat than finely cut (shoe-string) potato chips.

Jane's Potato Flan

Jane, a friend of many years' standing, gave Alison this recipe. She found it to be very popular when it was served for lunch with a salad, as well as being a good addition to a buffet meal.

FOR 3–4 SERVINGS:

400g ready-made flaky pastry
1 cup cottage cheese
1 egg, beaten
¼ cup sour cream
1 tsp salt
2 tsp spring onions, finely chopped
1 cup mashed potato
about 2 Tbsp grated parmesan cheese

Preheat the oven to 220°C.

Roll out the pastry until it is nice and thin and use it to line a 20cm flan tin or pie plate.

Combine the cottage cheese, egg and sour cream in a food processor or blender (press them through a sieve if you want a really smooth mixture).

Add the salt, spring onion and mashed potato and process again until combined.

Turn the potato mixture into the unbaked crust and sprinkle liberally with the cheese. Bake for 30–40 minutes until the pastry and the top are lightly browned.

Serve warm with one or more salads such as cubed tomatoes and marinated green beans.

Hot-smoked Fish and Potato Flan

Alison often makes a fishy variation of Jane's Potato Flan (see above) using a side of hot-smoked, locally caught fish from the fish counter at her local supermarket. She flakes about a cup of flesh, carefully removing all skin and bones. Next, she chops the flesh with a sharp knife and folds it through the flan filling, along with a few dashes of Tabasco or a similar hot pepper sauce before putting the fishy mixture into a 23cm flan tin or pie plate, lined with pastry as in the main recipe, and bakes it at the same temperature, for the same length of time.

Picnic Pie

Celebrate summer! Line a picnic basket with a cheerfully checked teatowel, pack inside it this pie, some fresh fruit and something cold to drink, and set off for a picnic at your favourite beach or park. It's even more enjoyable if you arrange for another family to meet you there. Perhaps they could take something different – such as a rotisseried or roast chicken, bread rolls and tomatoes. It is always more fun when you put the contents of two picnic baskets together! Enjoy!

FOR ABOUT 6 SERVINGS:

400g flaky pastry
3–4 eggs
3 Tbsp milk
2 ham steaks, cubed, or 4–6 slices bacon, cooked and chopped
2 sprigs mint, chopped
4 spring onions, finely chopped
4 medium (about 300g) waxy or new potatoes, cooked, cooled and cut into cubes
1 cup cold cooked peas or 1½ cups cooked green beans

Preheat the oven to 200°C.

Roll out the pastry on a floured board into two thin rounds or rectangles, reserving scraps to decorate. Set one round aside and use the other to line a 23cm pie plate or a shallow, rectangular baking dish. Trim edges level with the edge of the plate or baking dish.

In a large bowl mix the eggs with the milk to combine whites and yolks. Reserve 1 tablespoonful to use for a glaze.

Add the ham or bacon, mint and spring onion, the potato and the peas or beans. Mix well.

Tip the filling into the pastry-lined plate. Dampen the edges of the second sheet of pastry and place it on top of the filling. Pinch the edges together and fold them under. Press around the edge with a fork if you like. Decorate the top with the pastry scraps and glaze with the reserved egg. Cut a few steam vents in the centre.

Bake for 30 minutes, lowering the heat if the pastry browns too quickly. Cool on a rack and wrap in a teatowel, rather than in plastic or foil, to keep the pastry crisp.

NOTE: You can vary the filling of a pie like this as much as you like except for the number of eggs. They are particularly important because they hold everything together. Although we prefer not to add any salt when bacon or ham is included, and only cook the potatoes in lightly salted water, you may like to add some extra. Don't include any raw ingredients that need long cooking.

Self-crusting Vegetable Quiche

A crustless quiche is a very good addition to any cook's repertoire. It is much easier than making a pastry-based pie, and it looks and tastes good. We serve these quiches for lunch, hoping there will be leftovers for packed lunches the next day. Our favourite quiches contain new (or fairly new) potatoes, and fresh green vegetables such as asparagus, broccoli or tender little green beans. We sometimes add some red pepper or arrange tomato slices on top for extra colour (tomatoes actually in the quiche can make it a bit sloppy). If not over-beaten, this mixture should separate during cooking, forming a firmer layer, or crust, below the well-flavoured filling. You can make it in a loaf tin or a square tin instead of a round one, which is good if you want to cut the quiche into squares or rectangles instead of wedges.

FOR 4–6 SERVINGS:

1 Tbsp butter
1 large onion, chopped
2 cloves garlic, chopped
3 medium (about 300–450g) waxy or all purpose
    potatoes, cooked
3 large eggs
¾ tsp salt
1 cup milk
½ cup self-raising flour

1 cup cooked asparagus, spinach, mushrooms or
    broccoli, well drained and chopped
1 cup grated tasty cheese
1–2 tomatoes, thinly sliced, optional

Position a rack in the middle of the oven and preheat to 220°C.

Melt the butter in a frypan. Cook the onion and garlic in the butter until tender. Cut the potatoes into 1cm cubes. Add to the pan and cook for 1 minute further, then set aside to cool.

Beat the eggs, salt and milk together with a fork. Pour the egg mixture into a large bowl containing the flour, stirring with a fork or whisk until just combined. Add the potato, the drained vegetables and the cheese. Stir gently to mix before pouring into a lightly sprayed or buttered 20–23cm non-stick metal pan or another suitable pan of similar size, but do not use a springform pan with a removable base. Garnish with the tomato if using.

Bake for 20–30 minutes until the quiche is lightly browned and set in the centre. Remove from the oven and leave to stand for at least 5 minutes.

Serve hot, warm or cold, with a tomato or green salad, or cut into small rectangles and serve as finger food.

Cheesy Onion Flan

This tasty flan makes a popular and economical family meal. Leftovers go well in school lunches, too. It is also a useful dish to make if you are cooking for vegetarians.

FOR 4–6 SERVINGS:

50g very cold butter
¾ cup flour
¼ cup grated cheese
2–3 Tbsp cold water
1 Tbsp oil
1 large onion, chopped
1 large clove garlic, chopped
1 tsp cumin
½ tsp oregano
3 large new potatoes (about 300g), cooked and cubed
3 large eggs
¼ cup milk
½ tsp salt
1 cup tasty grated cheddar cheese
pinch of paprika

Using a food processor, chop the butter into the flour. Add the first measure of cheese, then with the motor running add the cold water, drop by drop, until the mixture forms a ball.

Transfer the ball of dough to the lightly floured bench and roll out thinly. Line a 23cm pie plate or flan tin with the resulting pastry and chill until the filling is ready.

Preheat the oven to 220ºC.

Heat the oil in a frypan and add the onion and garlic. Cover and cook gently over moderate heat until the onion is transparent and lightly browned. Stir in the seasonings, then the potatoes. Mix well and cook, uncovered, until the potatoes start to sizzle. Remove from the heat.

Break the eggs into a bowl. Add the milk and salt and mix with a fork to blend. Add the potato mixture and stir to mix. Tip the filling into the chilled pie crust.

Sprinkle the surface of the filling with the second measure of cheese and the paprika. Bake for 20 minutes or until the pastry is golden brown and the filling has set.

Cut the flan into pieces for easy serving. It may be eaten cold or reheated, preferably with a salad.

Minted Holiday Pie

Feeding a houseful of hollow-legged children? Carry this pie to the nearest park, beach or playground or, if the weather does not co-operate, into your TV room!

FOR 8–12 SERVINGS:

400g flaky pastry
6 frankfurters
5 medium (about 750g) waxy or all purpose potatoes, cooked
2 cups cooked peas, beans or leeks
1 Tbsp chopped mint
6 eggs
½ tsp salt
4–6 tomatoes, fresh or canned (if using canned tomatoes, ensure they are well drained)

Roll out a little more than half of the pastry until it is very thin. Use it to line a large roasting pan, allowing the pastry to overhang by a few centimetres. Roll out the remaining pastry even more thinly so it is large enough to cover the filling and set aside.

Preheat the oven to 220°C. Cut the frankfurters into small chunks and slice the potatoes. Spread half the potato, peas and mint and all the chopped frankfurters over the pastry in the pan.

Break the eggs, one at a time, onto a saucer. Using a fork, beat each one enough to break the yolk, then pour it around the chopped frankfurters. Reserve about 1 teaspoon of beaten egg to glaze the pastry top later. Scatter the remaining vegetables evenly over the egg, then sprinkle with salt.

Slice or chop the tomatoes and arrange them evenly over the pie filling.

Spread the second pastry sheet over the filling. Dampen the overhanging edges with water and gently lift them, then press them down over the top. Pinch the edges together and shape attractively if desired. Brush the reserved egg over the surface and pierce the top to make about 12 holes. Bake for 15 minutes or until golden brown, then reduce the heat to 150°C and bake for a further 15 minutes.

Serve the pie warm or cold, cut in squares, with carrot and celery sticks and bread rolls to fill any gaps.

Neptune's Potato Pie

Alison dreamed up the name of this pie, which combines inexpensive canned smoked fish fillets and potatoes, to make it seem more inviting to her children.

FOR ABOUT 6 SERVINGS:

400g flaky pastry
2 large (about 500g) all purpose potatoes, cooked
1 x 300–425g can smoked fish fillets, drained and flaked
3 large eggs
½ cup chopped spring onions
1 cup grated tasty cheese

Preheat the oven to 200°C. Roll out the pastry on a floured board into two 23cm circles. Line a pie plate of the same size with one of the circles.

Cut the potatoes into 1cm thick slices and place in a large, shallow mixing bowl. Add the flaked fish, unbeaten eggs, spring onion and grated cheese. Mix carefully, stirring the eggs through the mixture without breaking up the potatoes too much.

Tip the filling into the pie plate. Dampen the surface of the remaining pastry circle with cold water. Place, damp side down, over the pie filling. Press the outer edges of the pastry together, then trim 2cm beyond the pie plate edge. Fold the overhang under the edge of the lower crust and crimp if desired. Cut a vent in the middle of the pie.

Bake for 30–40 minutes or until the pastry has browned evenly and the centre is firm when pressed gently.

Serve wedges cold or warm as part of a summer meal with one or more salads.

Always handle potatoes carefully – although they may seem tough, they bruise easily if you drop them or treat them roughly, so for best flavour and less waste, look after them!

Cottage Pie

This recipe makes a delicious cottage pie, but with a twist in that it can be cooked in a slow cooker or, if you prefer, it can be baked traditionally in the oven.

This recipe can be doubled but do check that your slow cooker – and the container in which the pie will cook – is large enough.

FOR 2–3 SERVINGS:

600–700g floury or all purpose potatoes
1 onion
1–2 carrots
1 stalk celery
250g minced beef
1 Tbsp flour
1 Tbsp tomato concentrate
1 Tbsp Worcestershire sauce
½ cup stock or 1 tsp instant stock powder dissolved in
    ½ cup water
2 tsp butter
milk as required
¼ cup grated cheese
pinch of ground paprika, optional

(If using your slow cooker, select a heatproof dish that is big enough to hold minced meat for 2–3 servings and which will fit inside.)

Peel and quarter the potatoes. Cook, covered, in lightly salted water until tender.

Finely chop the onion, carrot and celery in a food processor or grate them. Put the prepared raw vegetables and mince into a large non-stick frypan. Brown the mixture, stirring regularly, adding a little oil if necessary to avoid it sticking. Stir in the flour, tomato concentrate, Worcestershire sauce and stock, and bring to the boil. Take the mixture off the heat and spoon it into the non-stick sprayed prepared dish.

Drain the cooked potato and mash with the butter. Beat with a fork, adding enough milk to make a smooth creamy mixture. Spread over the top of the meat and vegetable mixture, swirling the surface attractively. Sprinkle with the grated cheese and add a little paprika for extra colour if desired. (Refrigerate for up to 24 hours at this point).

To cook in a slow cooker: Place the prepared cottage pie in the slow cooker. Add enough cool water to come 1cm up the side of the pie plate. Cover and cook on LOW for 8–10 hours.

To cook conventionally: Place in a preheated 180°C oven and bake for 30–40 minutes.

Serve with a green salad.

Potato Pan Pizza

This useful, quick recipe can be made with some leftover cooked potato (or microwave about 350g potato, but let it cool first) that's great for a quick weekend lunch. Once you are familiar with the recipe, you can make additions and variations of your own.

FOR 2 LARGE OR 4 SMALLER SERVINGS:

1¼–1½ cups cooked all purpose or floury potatoes
1 large egg
1–2 spring onions, chopped
oil for frying
½ cup self-raising flour

TOPPINGS:

½–1 cup grated cheese
1 large or 2 small firm tomatoes
about ¼ cup chopped salami or bacon
sliced black olives, optional

Chop the cooked potatoes, then mash them roughly with a fork.

Using a fork, beat the egg in a bowl and add the spring onion. Add the prepared potato and stir it through the egg mixture.

Put a large frypan on low heat. Just before you are ready to add the flour to the potato dough, raise the heat under the pan to medium heat and brush the surface with a little oil, spreading it evenly over the surface.

Stir the flour into the potato, then shape the mixture into a ball and roll out on a piece of baking paper sprinkled with just enough extra flour to stop the dough sticking until it is the same size as the base of the frypan (the potato dough should be uncracked and even around the outside edge). Discard any flour left on the baking paper and reserve. Slide the pizza base into the hot pan.

Cook the base for 3–4 minutes until the underside is an even golden brown. Slide it out of the pan onto the baking paper, then slip a large plate underneath the pizza. Add a little more oil to the pan and when hot flip the pizza back into the pan, browned side up.

Preheat the grill.

Spread the toppings on top of the pizza while it is still in the pan. When the underside has browned, put the pan under the grill to melt and lightly brown the cheese.

Slide the cooked pizza from the pan onto a rack or serving board. Cut into the required number of portions and eat while warm.

Mushroom & Potato Pie

This single crust pie is simple to make and makes a great winter meal. Its impressive appearance is matched only by its delicious flavour!

FOR 4 SERVINGS:

3–4 medium (about 500g) waxy or all purpose potatoes
1 medium onion
2 Tbsp olive or canola oil
1 tsp minced garlic
200g brown mushrooms
½ tsp dried basil or 1 Tbsp basil pesto
¼ tsp dried thyme
½ tsp salt
black pepper to taste
1 cup sour cream
½ tsp salt
black pepper
1–2 sheets pre-rolled flaky pastry
milk or lightly beaten egg to glaze

Preheat the oven to 220°C.

Scrub the potatoes, then cut into 5mm slices. Place in an oven bag or in a covered microwave dish and cook at 100% power for 10 minutes, stirring gently after 5 minutes.

Alternatively, boil the sliced potato until just tender, handling them gently to avoid breaking them up.

Peel and slice the onion while the oil heats in a large frypan. Add the onion and garlic and sauté until the onion is soft and transparent.

While the onion cooks, slice the mushrooms, then add them to the pan along with the herbs, salt and pepper. Cook, stirring frequently, until the mushrooms have wilted.

Lightly oil or spray with non-stick spray a 20x25cm casserole or deep pie plate. Arrange half the potato slices evenly over the bottom of the dish, then cover with the mushroom mixture and top with the remaining potato slices. Stir together the sour cream and a little extra salt and pepper and spoon over the potato-mushroom mixture in an even layer.

Roll out the pastry (if necessary), until it will cover the casserole/pie plate. Lay the pastry gently over the filling mixture, trimming off any excess. Decorate the edge by patterning it with the tines of a fork and puncture the pastry at 5cm intervals over the surface. Brush with a little milk or beaten egg to glaze, then bake at 220°C for about 15 minutes until the pastry is golden brown.

Serve with a salad or cooked vegetables and some crusty bread.

Curried Sausage & Potato Pie

This recipe has been a favourite in Alison's house for many years. The woman who sent it to her wrote at the time that she had several teenage sons – making it easy for us to imagine them sitting round the table, happily tucking in! We hope their families now enjoy the same recipe just as much as their fathers did!

FOR 4–6 SERVINGS:

5–6 medium (about 1kg) floury or all-purpose potatoes
2 medium onions
1kg sausage meat
1 Tbsp curry powder
2–3 Tbsp brown sugar
1 x 400g can apple sauce or 2 cups cooked and drained apple
pinch of ground cumin, oregano, and salt, optional
1 Tbsp butter
freshly ground black pepper
½ cup milk
½–1 cup grated cheese

Thinly peel the potatoes and cut into even-sized pieces. Cook, covered, in lightly salted water until tender.

While the potatoes are cooking, finely chop the onions.

Next, coat the inside of a small roasting pan or a large, shallow baking dish with non-stick spray. Layer three-quarters of the chopped onion in the bottom of the dish. Working with wet hands, form the sausage meat into sausage shapes and arrange them over the onion. Sprinkle the remaining onion on top.

Preheat the oven to 180°C.

Mix together the curry powder and brown sugar and sprinkle evenly over the sausage and onion layers, then spread over the apple sauce. Sprinkle over the cumin, oregano, and salt if using.

Drain and mash the potatoes with the butter, pepper and milk, then beat with a fork until creamy. Spread over the sausages, swirl or roughen the top attractively, then sprinkle with the grated cheese.

Bake, uncovered, for 1 hour.

Serve as a main meal with several cooked vegetables or a green leafy salad.

Smoked Fish Pie

This useful pie, popular with all age groups at any time of year, is mostly made from store-cupboard ingredients. Adding a vegetable in the sauce with the fish, and a mixed or green salad served alongside the pie adds contrasting colours and textures.

FOR 3–4 SERVINGS:

600g floury or all purpose potatoes, scrubbed
2 large eggs
3 Tbsp butter
3 Tbsp flour
1 cup milk
½ cup liquid from the canned fish (see below) or extra milk
1 x 310g can smoked fish fillets or larger can salmon, drained and flaked
1 can whole kernel corn or mushrooms in brine
½ spring onion, chopped
¼ cup chopped parsley
salt
butter and milk for mashing potatoes
2–3 Tbsp grated cheese
paprika

Choose a heatproof 4 cup capacity baking dish that you can use to serve the pie and which will fit in your slow cooker (if using). Coat the inside of the dish with non-stick spray.

Quarter the unpeeled potatoes lengthwise. Place in a pot with the eggs and cook, covered, in lightly salted water until the eggs are hard-boiled and the potatoes are tender. Drain the potatoes and remove their skins. Cool the cooked eggs in cold water, then peel and chop.

Melt the butter in a pot over moderate heat and stir in the flour. Let the mixture bubble, then add the milk. Stir the sauce until it thickens. Add the extra liquid to the white sauce and stir until it comes to the boil again.

Stir the flaked fish, corn, spring onion, parsley and chopped egg into the sauce. Add salt to taste. Turn the mixture into the prepared heatproof dish.

Mash the potatoes with a little butter and milk. Beat with a fork to a creamy consistency. Spoon onto the fish mixture, swirling the top attractively. Sprinkle with the grated cheese and a little paprika. Refrigerate if not cooking immediately.

To cook in a slow cooker: Place the prepared fish pie in the slow cooker. Add enough water to come 1cm up the side of the pie plate. Cover and cook on LOW for 4–8 hours, taking it out when it suits you.

To cook conventionally: Place in a preheated 180°C oven and bake, uncovered, for 30–40 minutes.

Serve with a green salad or coleslaw.

VARIATIONS: Add a variety of cooked vegetables, e.g. cooked peas, corn, diced carrots, etc, to the sauce.

Potatoes to Die For

Alison's friend Sharon gave her this recipe some years ago and although she always feels a certain degree of guilt as she pours in the sour cream, she justifies it by the fact that she makes it only as an occasional treat.

FOR 4 MAIN COURSE SERVINGS:

10 medium (about 1.5 kg) floury potatoes
3 large cloves garlic
¼ cup flour
½ tsp salt
2 cups low fat sour cream
½ cup milk
200g gruyère cheese

Scrub the potatoes and cut into 5mm slices, dropping them into a large container of cold water as they are prepared. Ensure all the slices are separated, in order to remove the starchy liquid on the cut surfaces. Transfer the drained potatoes to a microwave dish or oven bag, cover the bowl or tie the bag loosely, and cook for about 15 minutes at 100% power in a microwave oven until tender.

Make the sauce while the potatoes cook. Finely chop the garlic, then add it to a medium-sized bowl, mixing until smooth with the flour, salt, sour cream and milk.

Preheat the oven to 180°C.

Butter or spray a 23x30cm ovenproof dish. Make an overlapping layer of half of the potatoes in the dish. Drizzle half the sour cream mixture over, then grate on almost half the cheese. Repeat with the remaining ingredients, then grate the rest of the cheese evenly all over the top.

Bake, uncovered, for about 30 minutes until the mixture feels firm and the topping is golden brown. Remove from the oven and leave to stand in a warm place for 5–10 minutes before serving.

Serve as a main meal with a mixed green salad in a tart, mustardy dressing.

VARIATION: For an extra-special treat, top with 200–300g hot-smoked salmon, broken into flakes and spread over the central part of the browned surface of the potatoes as soon as the pie is removed from the oven.

Oakhill Potatoes ▶

Alison learnt how to make this recipe when she was one of a group of university students, planning, then cooking a pre-ball dinner on a very limited budget. Different members of our family have made it over the years, and it still keeps stealing the show, disappearing before other dishes at many a party over the years! Although it requires some time and effort, you can double or triple the recipe, make it a day in advance, and refrigerate it until needed.

FOR 4–6 SERVINGS:

4 large (about 800g) cooked, all purpose or floury potatoes
2 hard-boiled eggs, peeled and roughly chopped
2 rashers bacon
1 medium onion
50g butter
¼ cup flour
1 tsp dry mustard
1 tsp salt
2 cups milk
½ cup grated tasty cheddar cheese
1 Tbsp butter
1 cup fresh breadcrumbs

Slice the cooked potatoes into a shallow, sprayed or buttered baking dish. Add the eggs.

Chop the bacon and onion and cook them together in the first measure of butter in a large pot until the onion is transparent. Stir in the flour, mustard and salt, half of the milk then bring to the boil, stirring constantly. Add the remaining milk and bring to the boil again. Take off the heat and stir in the grated cheese straight away. If the sauce seems too thick to pour easily, thin it with some extra milk. Pour the sauce over the potatoes, covering the entire surface.

Top the sauce with buttered crumbs made by melting the second measure of butter and stirring it into the crumbs.

Refrigerate for up to 24 hours or bake immediately, in the middle of the oven, at 180°C for 30–45 minutes until the potato mixture has heated through and the crumb topping is golden brown.

Serve as part of a buffet dinner or as a family meal, with a salad and small bread rolls.

VARIATION: For a vegetarian meal, leave out the bacon and use twice as much cheese.

Potato, Bean & Bacon One-pan Dinner

This is our version of a dish which is based on a Swiss recipe given to us by our friend, Chris, who has made it regularly for her family over the years. It's wonderful to go out in the garden, just as Chris does, to dig up smallish new potatoes, then to pick young green beans, and be eating the meal just half an hour later.

You can also make it using small white washed potatoes and beans from the supermarket.

FOR 2 SERVINGS:

2 Tbsp oil
1 medium onion
350–400g new or waxy white washed potatoes
200–250g green beans
1 thickly sliced ham steak, about 200g
salt and pepper

Gently heat a large frypan, preferably with a non-stick finish, and with a close-fitting lid. Add the oil and swirl it round so the bottom of the pan is covered.

Chop the onion into small squares and sprinkle the pieces over the bottom of the pan. Cover.

Wash or scrub the potatoes and cut the smallest ones into quarters lengthwise or larger potatoes into 2cm cubes. Arrange them over the onions and replace the lid.

Top and tail the beans and cut them into pieces about 5cm long and arrange over the potatoes.

Cut the ham steak into 1cm cubes and sprinkle them over the beans. Sprinkle a little salt and pepper over, and replace the lid.

Cook over gentle to moderate heat. Any resulting liquid turns to steam and cooks the vegetables in about half an hour. At the end of the cooking time there should be no liquid left.

Serve in two shallow bowls as a complete meal.

VARIATION: The ham steak can be replaced with a similar weight of bacon end, or thickly sliced bacon, either of which should be finely chopped and added to the pan after putting in the oil.

Holiday Hash

We don't think it's necessary to feel apologetic when we cook something like this for a holiday meal.

This is a good one-pan meal, perfect to cook if you're away from your kitchen, on holiday perhaps, and although you don't need to peel the potatoes (see page 98), you do need to precook them.

Alison remembers cooking this mixture in a campground kitchen, impressing the other campers by her foresight in bringing with her in a chilly bin her precooked potatoes. They were also very impressed by the final product!

FOR 4 SERVINGS:

4 large (about 800g) all purpose or floury potatoes, cooked
1–2 cups cubed meat, e.g. corned beef, ham steaks, luncheon sausage, canned Spam, frankfurters or cooked sausages
about ¼ cup chopped gherkins, cucumber or other pickle
4 spring onions, chopped
¼ cup chopped parsley
milk
butter or oil for frying

Roughly chop or mash the cooked potatoes with a fork. Mix with the cubed meat, chopped gherkins, spring onion and parsley. If the potato and meat mixture looks a little dry at this point, add just enough milk to dampen it so it will stay together during cooking.

Heat a 20–23cm non-stick frypan or electric frypan. Add enough butter or oil to coat the base and sides, then add the potato mixture. Cover and cook on a low-to-moderate heat until a crust forms around the bottom and sides (about 20–30 minutes). Carefully run a knife around the edge so it does not stick, then slide out the hash cake onto a plate. Add a little more butter or oil, then slide the hash cake back into the pan again, cooked side up.

To serve, cut into quarters. It is particularly nice served with tomatoes and coleslaw or a lettuce salad.

Fish Cakes

Everyone loves fish cakes. They may not be glamour food, but serve them up and watch them disappear!

FOR 2–4 SERVINGS:

2 cups cold mashed potato
1 large egg
1 cup self-raising flour or scone mix
about 1 cup canned tuna, salmon or smoked fish, drained with liquid reserved
about 2 Tbsp chopped parsley or fresh herb of choice
milk to mix
extra flour
oil for frying

Using a fork or a potato masher, mix the mashed potato and egg with the flour or scone mix. Add the drained fish and the chopped herbs. Mix with a knife or stirrer (see page 192), using some of the reserved liquid from the can and a little milk if necessary, until the mixture is firm enough to shape into cakes. Add extra flour or scone mix if the mixture is too soft.

Using wet hands, form the mixture into 8 cakes, then lightly dredge them in the extra flour.

Heat the oil to a depth of 3–5mm in a heavy-bottomed frypan or electric frypan. When the oil is hot, cook the cakes for 4–5 minutes on each side until they are evenly browned and cooked in the centre. Do not shorten the cooking time or the centres of the fish cakes will be pasty.

Serve with Thai sweet chilli sauce and a salad.

VARIATIONS:

Make without the egg.

Replace the fish with chopped ham etc.

Add chopped spring onions or fresh herbs etc.

Buy potatoes in big bags to get most for your money! Keep them in a cool, dark place (but not in the refrigerator) in a paper bag or cardboard box – not in a plastic bag.

Thai Green Chicken & Potato Curry ▶

With a little practice, it's possible to make this quick, tasty and popular curry – Thai curry paste is available at most supermarkets – in less than half an hour! Because we especially like the flavour of kaffir lime leaves, we grow the trees from which they come at home, but they are available at Asian food stores and markets and can be frozen for later use. However, if you can't find them, just make the curry without them, or add ordinary lemon or lime leaves.

FOR 4 SERVINGS:

2 Tbsp canola oil
2 Tbsp Thai Green Curry Paste
2 medium onions, quartered then sliced
4 medium (about 450g) new or waxy white washed
    potatoes, scrubbed and cut into 1.5cm cubes
4 kaffir lime leaves, optional
2 zucchini, sliced
500g boneless and skinless chicken thighs or breasts,
    cubed
1 x 400ml can regular or light coconut cream
200g green beans, cut into 3cm lengths
2 Tbsp fish sauce
2 tsp sugar
salt to taste
handful of fresh basil leaves, optional

Heat the oil in a large frypan, wok or pot with a lid. Stir in the curry paste and cook for about 2 minutes, then add the onion, potato and lime leaves and stir-fry for 5 minutes.

Stir in the chicken, then add the coconut cream. Cover and simmer for 10 minutes.

Add the prepared vegetables. Cover and simmer for about 10 minutes until the chicken and potatoes are cooked and the vegetables are tender. Add the fish sauce and sugar, with salt to taste, then stir in the basil leaves just before serving.

Layered Lamb & Potato Bake

Simon's wife Sam labelled this as one of the most delicious dishes he has ever turned out of his slow cooker. Not a bad compliment, considering how easy it is to make. It's so good we've given conventional cooking instructions too, for those who don't yet have a slow cooker.

FOR 6 SERVINGS:

800g all purpose or floury potatoes
½ tsp salt
1 large onion
1 large clove garlic
1 Tbsp oil
1.2–1.5kg (about 8) lamb shoulder chops
1 x 400g can diced tomatoes in juice
2 Tbsp tomato paste
1 Tbsp balsamic vinegar
1 tsp dried oreganum
salt and pepper
chopped basil or parsley to serve, optional

Turn a medium-to-large slow cooker to LOW and coat with non-stick spray. (If baking conventionally, non-stick spray a 3-litre casserole dish.) Peel and thinly slice the potatoes. Arrange the potatoes in a layer in the slow cooker or casserole dish and sprinkle with the salt.

Peel and chop the onion and garlic. Heat the oil in a medium frypan, add the onion and garlic and cook until the onion has softened.

While the onion cooks, arrange the lamb chops in a layer on top of the potatoes.

When the onion is ready, stir the tomatoes and juice, tomato paste, vinegar, and oreganum into the pan. Season to taste, then bring the sauce to the boil.

Pour the onion and tomato mixture over the lamb.

To cook in a slow cooker: Cover and cook on LOW for 8–10 hours.

To cook conventionally: Cover the casserole dish with a close-fitting lid or sheet of foil, then bake in a preheated oven for 2–2½ hours at 150°C or until the lamb chops are almost falling off the bone.

To serve, carefully move the chops to one side. Divide the potatoes between plates, place a chop on top of each and spoon over some of the sauce. Garnish with a little chopped basil or parsley if desired.

Peppery Chickpea & Potato Curry

The spiciness in this simple curry comes largely from black pepper, which gives an interesting heat that is quite different from chilli. We make it using a fairly mild curry powder, which gives flavour but does not mask the pepper effect.

FOR 3 SERVINGS:

1 tsp black peppercorns
2 large cloves garlic, peeled
2–3 Tbsp chopped coriander leaves
1 Tbsp canola oil
1 Tbsp mild curry powder
2 medium (300–500g) waxy or new potatoes, scrubbed and diced
1 x 400g can chickpeas, rinsed and drained
2 medium tomatoes, diced
¾ cup coconut cream
½ cup hot water
1 Tbsp soy sauce
½ tsp sugar
salt to taste
1–2 Tbsp chopped coriander leaves, extra

Measure the peppercorns into a blender or mortar and pestle. Add the garlic and the coriander leaves and blend or pound to a paste. Add the oil and mix well.

Transfer the paste to a medium large non-stick frypan and cook over a medium heat, stirring frequently, for 2–3 minutes or until fragrant. Stir in the curry powder and cook for a further 1–2 minutes.

Add the prepared potatoes, chickpeas and tomatoes. Stir to coat with the spice mixture, then add the coconut cream, hot water, soy sauce and sugar. Bring to the boil, then reduce the heat to a gentle simmer and cook, stirring frequently, for 10–15 minutes or until the potato cubes are cooked through.

Season to taste with salt, garnish with the chopped coriander and serve. A cucumber salad and some naan bread make great accompaniments.

NOTE: If preferred, replace the coconut cream with ¾ cup light and creamy evaporated milk plus ¼ tsp coconut essence.

Scalloped Potatoes with Tuna

Scalloped potato mixtures are always popular. Using a packet soup mix creates a particularly flavourful mixture, and adding tuna turns it into a substantial meal. This recipe works remarkably well in a slow cooker but we've given instructions for either baking or slow cooking.

FOR 4 SERVINGS:

1kg floury or all purpose potatoes, scrubbed
2 medium onions, diced
1 x 220g can tuna, drained and flaked
250g sour cream
½ cup milk
37g packet onion or bacon and onion soup mix
1 cup grated cheese
pinch of paprika to dust

Cut the scrubbed potatoes into 2–3mm thick slices.

Thoroughly coat the bowl of the slow cooker or a shallow casserole dish with non-stick spray. Sprinkle half the diced onion into the bowl. Cover with half the sliced potatoes, then crumble over the tuna. Sprinkle in the remaining onion and arrange the rest of the potato in another layer on top.

Combine the sour cream, milk and soup mix in a small bowl. Pour evenly over the layered potato mixture, then sprinkle the top with the grated cheese and dust lightly with paprika.

To cook in a slow cooker: Set the slow cooker to HIGH and cook for 4–5 hours.

To cook conventionally: Preheat the oven to 220°C. Cover the casserole dish (use the lid or a sheet of foil folded loosely over the edges) and bake for 30 minutes. Uncover and bake for a further 30 minutes until the cheesy topping is evenly golden brown and the potatoes in the centre are tender.

VARIATION: Make without the tuna and serve as a side dish for 6 people.

 Did you know that potatoes have been given the Heart Foundation's tick of approval? For heart health, watch that you don't add too much fat or salt to your potatoes.

Vegetarian Shepherd's Pie ▼

This recipe must be one of the most popular recipes in our book Meals Without Meat. So many people tell us that everyone in their family really enjoys it, often without realising that it contains beans rather than meat!

FOR 4–6 SERVINGS:

6 large (about 1kg) all purpose or floury potatoes
2 Tbsp butter
1 cup grated cheese
milk
2 large onions, roughly chopped
2 Tbsp butter
1 red or green pepper, deseeded and chopped
3 Tbsp flour
1 tsp instant vegetable stock powder
1 tsp each basil, oregano, paprika and soya sauce
1½ cups water, beer, wine, bean liquid and/or the potato cooking liquid.
2 Tbsp tomato concentrate
1 x 440g can red kidney beans, drained

Thinly peel the potatoes, then cut into chunks. Simmer in lightly salted water until tender. Drain, reserving the cooking liquid.

Mash the potatoes with the first measure of butter, half the grated cheese, and enough milk to make a fairly soft consistency. After mashing, beat the potatoes with a fork until they are light and fluffy.

In a large pot cook the onions in the second measure of butter until they are tender and well browned. Add the pepper and flour and stir until the flour is lightly browned. Add the remaining ingredients except the beans, then bring to the boil, stirring constantly. Add the beans, either whole or roughly chopped or mashed. Taste and adjust the seasoning as required.

Spread the bean mixture into a lightly sprayed 20x25cm baking dish. Cover with spoonfuls of the mashed potato, spreading it to cover the beans. Sprinkle the remaining grated cheese over the surface.

Cook, uncovered, at 180ºC for 20–30 minutes or in a microwave oven (about 5 minutes on High, 100% power) until the bottom centre feels hot. Brown the top under a grill after microwaving, if necessary.

VARIATIONS: For a traditional Shepherd's Pie, replace the beans with about 2 cups of roughly chopped cold roast lamb or hogget.

Irish Stew

Although it is not traditional, we like to precook the onion and garlic for this stew. A mixture of fresh herbs, as well as the traditional parsley, gives it a very good flavour. Like others in this chapter, we originally developed this version for a slow cooker, but it can be cooked as a casserole.

FOR 3–4 SERVINGS:

2 tsp oil
2 large onions, cut into 1cm cubes
1 large clove garlic, chopped
500g all purpose or floury potatoes scrubbed
¼ cup chopped fresh herbs (parsley, sage, thyme etc.)
about 600g trimmed lamb shoulder meat, cubed
1 tsp salt
½ tsp pepper
¼ cup flour
1 tsp balsamic vinegar
½ cup chicken stock or ½ cup water and ½ tsp instant
    stock powder
extra chopped fresh parsley to garnish
cornflour mixed with a little water to make a paste,
    optional

Thoroughly coat the bowl of the slow cooker or a large casserole dish with non-stick spray. Turn the slow cooker on to HIGH or preheat the oven to 160°C.

Heat the oil in a non-stick frypan with a lid. Add the onion and garlic and cook for about 5 minutes, stirring occasionally.

Cut the potatoes into 2cm cubes. Put half the onion in the bottom of the prepared slow cooker or casserole dish. Layer half the potato cubes on top, and sprinkle with half the chopped herbs. Repeat the layers using the rest of the onion, potato and herbs.

Toss the cubed lamb with the salt, pepper and flour, then place the lamb on top of the vegetables. Pour over the vinegar and stock.

To cook in a slow cooker: Cover and cook on HIGH for 5–7 hours. After 4 hours, gently fold the meat through the vegetables. This should be nicely cooked after 5 hours, but the meat becomes even more tender on longer cooking.

To cook conventionally: Tightly cover the casserole dish, then place in the oven and cook for 2½–3 hours, stirring the stew gently after about 2 hours.

Add the cornflour paste to the liquid to thicken if desired.

Serve, generously sprinkled with the chopped parsley, with green beans or broccoli, and carrots.

NOTE: Although it is not traditional, you can add cubed carrots to this stew.

Pizza Potatoes

Because most children love the flavour of pizza, you can use the same combination of flavours here producing a stuffed potato that can be served as the main part of a meal. Most of the ingredients are optional – the only really vital one is the cheese!

FOR 1–2 SERVINGS:

1 large (about 200g) evenly shaped floury potato
1 cup grated cheese
2 spring onions, chopped
1 rasher bacon, chopped and sautéed
¼ cup chopped, sautéed mushrooms or red peppers
¼ tsp dried oregano
1 Tbsp tomato paste
yoghurt, milk, mayonnaise or sour cream to thin
extra bacon and/or chopped olives or anchovies to
    garnish, optional

Scrub, oil, then bake the potato either in a preheated 200°C oven for 1–1½ hours or at 100% power for 5–6 minutes in a microwave oven, turning it once during the cooking time. Allow 3–4 minutes' standing time after microwaving. Check if it is cooked through by pressing it gently, if cooked the potato should give a little.

While the potato cooks, mix together in a bowl the cheese, spring onion, bacon, mushroom or red pepper, and oregano. Add the tomato paste.

When the potato is cooked, allow it to cool enough to handle then cut in half lengthwise and scoop out the flesh with a spoon. Mash the flesh with the remaining ingredients. Add a little yoghurt or other dairy product if the mixture is dry.

Pile the filling into the potato halves and garnish as desired.

Reheat in a preheated 180°C oven for 15–20 minutes or microwave for 3–4 minutes at 100% power.

Serve alone or with a salad.

The way potatoes are stored and cooked can affect their nutritional content. To retain most nutrients, prepare potatoes just before you are going to cook them. Don't leave them standing in water or exposed to the air for longer than you have to.

Bacon, Potato and Prune Cake ▶

Based on a Swiss alpine recipe, this unusual filling and delicious main course can be made in a large slow cooker or in a large pot with some space to spare.

FOR 6 SERVINGS:

enough strips of shoulder bacon to line the bowl
2 large onions, sliced into lengthwise slivers
3 cloves garlic, crushed and chopped
2 tsp olive oil
2 large eggs
¾ cup crème fraiche or plain cream plus 2 Tbsp lemon juice
250g pitted prunes
1kg all purpose or floury potatoes

If you are making this in a slow cooker, turn it to HIGH. Choose a 7-cup capacity heatproof bowl that will fit in the slow cooker and coat the inside with non-stick spray.

Line the bottom and sides of the bowl with the bacon, leaving enough hanging over the sides to fold over the filling.

In a frypan, gently cook the onion and garlic in the oil for about 5 minutes.

Mix the eggs and crème fraiche in a separate large bowl. Chop the prunes into pea-size pieces, then add, along with the sautéed onion and garlic, to the egg mixture.

Scrub, then grate the potatoes. Tip into a clean teatowel and squeeze out most of the liquid. Stir the grated potato through the egg mixture, then press into the bacon-lined bowl and fold the ends of the bacon over the top. Cover with foil.

To cook in a slow cooker: Lower the bowl into the slow cooker (use long strips of folded foil as 'lifters'). Add enough warm water to come halfway up the bowl. Cook on HIGH for 4–5 hours or on LOW for 8 hours, checking the water level occasionally.

To cook conventionally: Place the foil-covered bowl in a large pot, adding enough warm water to come halfway up the bowl. Cover the pot and cook for 3–4 hours, checking the water level occasionally to make sure the pot does not boil dry.

When cooked, carefully remove from the slow cooker or large pot and take off the foil lid. Turn out onto a rack as you would a cake. Using a serrated knife, cut into 6 wedges and serve immediately with several lightly cooked vegetables or an interesting leafy salad, depending on the season.

Slow Cooker 'Lazy Daisy' One-pot Dinner

We all have days when we feel exhausted, when something easy and basic for dinner is called for. This fast, easy 'everything in one bowl' dinner will, we hope, make your day easier so you can put your feet up a little sooner. We originally wrote this recipe with slow cookers in mind, but you can cook it in the oven if desired.

FOR 4 SERVINGS:

about 600g chuck steak
2 bay leaves
1 rounded tsp Marmite or other similar spread or 1 Tbsp instant beef stock powder
½ cup boiling water
2 Tbsp balsamic or red wine vinegar
1 medium onion, cut into 1cm cubes
2 large carrots, chopped into 2cm cubes
1 cup sliced celery, optional
4 medium waxy or new potatoes (about 600g), scrubbed and cut into 2cm cubes
2 cups frozen peas
brown sugar and salt to taste
arrowroot, potato starch or cornflour to thicken

Coat the inside of the bowl of a medium-to-large slow cooker with non-stick spray.

Cut the steak into 2cm cubes and add to the slow cooker along with the bay leaves.

In a bowl or measuring jug dissolve the Marmite or instant beef stock in the boiling water and stir well. Add the vinegar, stir again, then drizzle it over the meat. Add the vegetables except the frozen peas.

Cover and cook on LOW for about 8 hours or until everything is tender. About half an hour before serving, turn the slow cooker to HIGH. Put the frozen peas in a large sieve over the sink and run boiling water over them to heat them up. Add them to the cooker and stir. There will be considerably more liquid than you started off with.

Taste the liquid, and add about 1 tablespoon of brown sugar and up to 1 teaspoon of salt to round off the flavour as desired. Then thicken with 1–2 tablespoons of arrowroot or other starch paste mixed with a little water. Cook for a few more minutes until the gravy thickens, then serve in bowls.

VARIATION: Proceed as above, but put everything in a large casserole dish instead of a slow cooker. Bake at 150°C for 1½–2 hours until the meat is very tender.

Murphy's Potato Moussaka ▼

A moussaka is a baked, layered meat and vegetable mixture. Its ingredients vary from country to country, but we love this version with a cheesy, eggy mixture baked on top of layers of tomato-flavoured mince and potatoes. Alison has always found it to be wonderful family food, especially enjoyed by teenagers. Although not traditional, we make it with sliced cooked potatoes and sometimes we'll use a can of tomatoes already flavoured with Italian-style herbs, rather than plain canned tomatoes. The choice is yours.

FOR 6 SERVINGS:

500g mince
2 large onions, finely chopped
2 Tbsp oil
½ tsp salt
2 Tbsp flour
1 x 440g can Italian seasoned tomatoes
5 large (750–800g) all purpose potatoes, peeled and
    cooked

SAUCE:

2 Tbsp butter
2 Tbsp flour
½ tsp freshly grated nutmeg
1 cup milk
1 cup grated cheese
1 egg, beaten

In a large frypan over high heat brown the mince and onion in the oil, stirring frequently. Stir in the salt and flour and cook for 1–2 minutes before stirring in the tomatoes. Continue cooking, stirring, until the mixture boils and thickens.

Cut the cooked potatoes lengthwise into 5mm thick slices. Set aside.

Make the sauce next. Melt the butter, add the flour and nutmeg and cook briefly, stirring constantly. Add half the milk and stir continuously until the sauce thickens. Add the rest of the milk and continue to stir until the sauce boils and thickens. After it boils, take it off the heat and stir in the grated cheese and the egg.

Preheat the oven to 180°C.

Spray or butter a 10–12 cup capacity shallow ovenproof dish and spread with one-third of the potato. Cover with half the mince, one-third of the potato, then the rest of the mince. Top with the remaining potato. Press down the top layer of potatoes to flatten. Pour the cheese sauce evenly over the top layer of potato and bake, uncovered, for about 30 minutes.

Remove from the oven and leave to stand for a few minutes before serving as the main meal of the day with a cooked green vegetable or a green salad.

Sherrean's Bacon, Bean & Potato Savoury

Sherrean, a Californian friend of Alison's, has made this recipe for 50 years. Her daughters, now adults with children of their own, also make it because everyone always enjoys it so much! When Alison makes it using fresh produce from her garden, she's worked out that if she moves fast, she can dig the potatoes while the bacon browns, then pick the beans while the potatoes are starting to cook!

FOR 1 SERVING:

2–3 rashers bacon, rind removed and cut into 2cm long strips
1 small onion, chopped
1 tsp butter
2–3 medium (about 300g) waxy or new potatoes, scrubbed
about 2 Tbsp water
½ tsp chicken or green herb instant stock powder or ¼ tsp salt
oregano and ground cumin to taste
about 100g young scarlet runners or green beans of choice, cut into 5cm lengths
about 1 tsp cornflour mixed to a paste with a little water

Cook the bacon strips in a pan until crisp. Remove and set aside most of it to use as a garnish later on. Add to the remaining bacon and bacon drippings in the pan the onion and butter. Cook until the onion is transparent and just beginning to brown.

Cut the potatoes into quarters and add to the pan along with the water, stock powder or salt and herbs. Simmer for about 10 minutes until the potatoes are almost tender.

Add the beans and cook for a further 10 minutes. If necessary, add a little extra water during the cooking time with the aim of finishing up with about 2 tablespoons of liquid. Thicken the liquid with just enough cornflour paste to coat and glaze the vegetables. Taste and adjust the seasonings if necessary.

Serve in a shallow bowl, sprinkled with the reserved cooked bacon with a tomato salad alongside if you like.

NOTE: Multiply the ingredients to suit the number of people for whom you are cooking.

Potatoes Plus

Most of the recipes in this section are favourites of ours, where potatoes cook happily alongside the meat we are cooking for dinner. As well, there is one of our favourite vegetarian curries, and last but not least, delicious home-made fish and chips, made easy! We hope that you will enjoy all of these as much as we do, and that they make your life a little easier!

Chickpea, Spinach & Potato Curry

This makes a great vegetarian meal, easy and delicious on its own, but even more interesting when served with an array of Indian condiments.

FOR 4 LARGE SERVINGS:

2 Tbsp canola oil
1 large onion, diced
2 cloves garlic, crushed, peeled and chopped
1 Tbsp finely chopped root ginger
2–3 medium (about 300g) waxy potatoes, cut into 1cm cubes
2–3 tsp curry powder (mild or hot to taste)
½–1 tsp cumin seeds, optional
2–3 bay leaves
1 x 250g package frozen spinach, thawed
1 x 400g can whole tomatoes in juice
1 x 310g can chickpeas, drained
¼–½ cup water, if required
2 tsp garam masala
salt and pepper to taste
2 Tbsp chopped fresh coriander

Heat the oil in a large pot. Add the onion, garlic and ginger and stir-fry until the onion has softened and is turning clear. Add the potatoes, curry powder, cumin seeds if using, and the bay leaves. Cook for 1–2 minutes then add the spinach with its liquid and the tomatoes in juice. Crush the tomatoes, then stir in the chickpeas.

Gently simmer for 15 minutes or until the potato cubes are tender, adding a little water if the mixture begins to look too dry. When the potatoes are cooked, add the garam masala and season to taste with salt and pepper. Add the chopped coriander.

For a simple meal serve in bowls as is. Alternatively serve with rice, naan bread or poppadums and assorted chutneys and relishes.

Slow Cooked Glazed 'Roast' Lamb with Potatoes

Alison thinks that this reasonably priced and rectangularly shaped small forequarter lamb roast with some rib bones on its underside is one of the nicest and easiest meat dishes she has ever cooked in her slow cooker. Its coating makes a very attractive and tasty glaze as the meat cooks, while the bones are easy to remove when the meat is cooked to the well-done stage, resulting in boneless meat that can be carved into slices from top to bottom.

FOR 24 SERVINGS:

700–1100g lamb forequarter roast
1–2 Tbsp dark soy sauce
1–2 Tbsp Wattie's Asian Chilli Sauce
1 tsp sesame oil
4–8 small (about 500g) waxy or washed white potatoes
2 large carrots or other root vegetables, cut in large chunks
2–3 tsp cornflour
½–¾ cup boiling water

Coat the inside of the bowl of a medium-to-large slow cooker with non-stick spray and turn to LOW.

Locate the top part of the front leg bone (or the shoulder blade), so you know where to find it when it's time to remove it after cooking.

Mix together the dark soy sauce, chilli sauce and sesame oil. Rub the mixture all over the meat, then place in the slow cooker, rib-side down.

Rub the vegetables with any remaining coating and arrange around the meat. Cover and cook for 7–8 hours, by which time the meat should have an attractive brown glaze.

Lift out the cooked meat and place on a board. Lift away the rib bones first then, using a knife, remove the bone surrounded by meat. Slice the meat and set aside to keep warm while you make the gravy.

Lift out the vegetables and set aside while you make the gravy. Stir the cornflour into the dark pan drippings, then stir in the boiling water. Don't forget to turn off the slow cooker after this step.

Serve the sliced lamb with the roasted vegetables and gravy, and with green peas or another green vegetable of your choice.

VARIATION: To cook conventionally, roast the lamb shoulder in a roasting pan, loosely covered with a tent of tin foil. Cook at 160°C for 2–3 hours, or according to individual preference.

Easy Beef Pot Roast with Potatoes ▶

This excellent pot roast is very easy to make because you don't need to brown anything first. You will need to ask your butcher to tie the meat into a neat roll because you are unlikely to find chuck steak rolled and tied at the supermarket – or even in most New Zealand butcher shops. Alison's helpful butcher says that the shoulder end of the chuck makes a more tender pot roast than the neck end.

FOR 6 SERVINGS:

1.5–2kg chuck steak, about 12cm x 18cm, tied
dark soy sauce
2 tsp garlic salt
½ tsp oregano
½ tsp ground cumin
½ tsp paprika, preferably smoked
6–8 medium (about 700g) waxy or new white washed
    potatoes
2 stalks celery, cut into 5cm lengths
3 large carrots, each cut into thirds
2 large onions, quartered
1 x 400g can tomatoes in juice
salt and pepper
½ tsp sugar
1 cup beef stock (if cooking in the oven)

Coat the inside of the bowl of a medium-to-large slow cooker (or a large casserole dish with a close-fitting lid) with non-stick spray. Turn the slow cooker to LOW (or preheat the oven to 130°C–140°C).

Pat the meat dry with a paper towel and rub it all over with the soy sauce. Combine the next four ingredients in a bowl and mix thoroughly. Sprinkle over the top of the meat and then transfer to the slow cooker or casserole dish.

Arrange the prepared vegetables round the meat. Add the tomatoes and juice.

To cook in a slow cooker: Cover and cook on LOW for 8 hours. At the end of this time, turn the cooker to HIGH. Lift out the cooked meat and vegetables and set aside to keep warm while you thicken the liquid in the cooker with arrowroot or potato starch mixed to a paste with a little cold water. Season to taste, including the sugar.

To cook conventionally: Add the stock to the casserole dish, then cover tightly. Bake for 3–4 hours or until the meat is tender, checking once or twice during this time to ensure there is always some liquid in the casserole dish.

Slice the meat and serve with the slow-cooked vegetables, the thickened gravy and a briefly cooked green vegetable.

NOTE: The size and weight of a rolled chuck roast should not make a difference to its cooking time.

Pork & Paprika Casserole

Alison created this easy casserole many years ago when Simon was a baby and Kirsten was not much older. Alison remembers waiting for the butcher to cube the shoulder pork for her, while Kirsten would be busy investigating everything within reach.

If the paprika in your store cupboard is stale and brown rather than red, throw it out and buy a fresh lot.

FOR 4 SERVINGS:

2 tsp canola or olive oil
2 medium onions, chopped
2 cloves garlic, chopped
600g lean shoulder pork, cubed
200g button mushrooms, halved
1 red pepper, deseeded and chopped, optional
1 cup sliced celery, optional
1 Tbsp paprika
1 Tbsp instant chicken stock powder
½ cup water or white wine
4–6 medium all purpose or floury potatoes
cornflour, arrowroot or potato starch to thicken
chopped parsley leaves to garnish

To cook in a slow cooker: Heat the oil in a frypan. Add the onion and garlic and cook over low to moderate heat until the onion is lightly browned and has turned clear.

Cut the cubed pork into smaller pieces if desired, then tip into the slow cooker. Add the mushrooms, and the pepper and celery if using, and then the onion mixture. Sprinkle the paprika and instant stock over the bowl and toss the contents to mix. Add the water.

Scrub or peel the potatoes, then halve them and arrange round the inside of the slow cooker, with the cut surfaces closest to the edge. Cover and cook on LOW for about 8 hours or on HIGH for about 4 hours. A few minutes before you turn off the cooker, thicken the liquid with some cornflour, arrowroot or potato starch paste (made by adding a little water), stirring it in gently.

To cook conventionally: Preheat the oven to 180°C. Heat the oil in a large casserole dish. Add the onion and garlic and cook over low to moderate heat until the onion is lightly browned and turned clear. Add the remaining ingredients and stir gently, then cover tightly and bake for 1½ –2 hours.

Sprinkle with chopped parsley just before serving alongside a quickly cooked green vegetable or a green salad.

Malay Beef & Potato Curry ▶

Although this curry requires long slow cooking, the actual 'hands on' preparation time is quite short. Don't be put off by the long list of ingredients, either. They are mostly spices, which are added in two batches. If you don't have all of them on hand, just leave them out – with the exception of the five-spice it will make little difference in the end.

FOR 4–6 SERVINGS:

1kg gravy beef
2 Tbsp ground coriander
1 Tbsp ground cumin
2 tsp five-spice powder
1 tsp each chilli powder, turmeric and ground cinnamon
½ tsp ground cloves
3 Tbsp canola oil
1 medium onion, quartered and sliced
4 cardamom pods, crushed
2.5-5cm piece cinnamon stick
1 whole star anise star
6 cloves
2 cups water
1 x 400g can coconut cream
4 medium (about 600–700g) all purpose potatoes, cubed
1–1½ cups fresh or frozen green beans, optional
2–3 Tbsp lemon juice
1–2 tsp salt

Trim any obvious fat from the meat, then cut into cubes. Place the meat in a medium sized bowl. Measure in the first seven spices and toss to coat.

Heat the oil in a large heavy pot or casserole dish. Add the onion, cardamom, cinnamon stick, star anise and cloves and cook over moderate heat until the onion is soft and golden brown.

Add the spice-coated meat to the pot and cook, stirring frequently, for about 10 minutes. Stir in the water, increase the heat and bring the contents of the pot to the boil. Reduce the heat to a gentle simmer, cover, and cook, stirring occasionally, for 1 hour.

Pour in the coconut cream and add the potatoes. Stir well, cover and cook for a further 45–60 minutes, or until the beef is very tender. Add the beans if using, lemon juice and salt to taste. Simmer, uncovered, for 5 or so minutes until the beans are tender.

Serve on its own or over steamed rice, accompanied with Malaysian roti (bread).

Pork Sausages, Peppers & Potatoes

When we make this easy and really delicious recipe, we always use red, orange and yellow peppers, rather than green ones which can give the mixture a slightly bitter flavour. Their colour after slow cooking is also less than attractive.

FOR 4 SERVINGS:

8 good quality pure pork sausages
2 large onions
4 cloves garlic
4 plump, crisp peppers, preferably 2 red, 1 orange and 1 yellow
½ tsp salt
freshly ground pepper to taste
½ tsp dried thyme leaves
½–1 cup chicken stock or white wine
4 largish all purpose or floury potatoes
cornflour, potato starch or arrowroot to thicken, optional

To cook in a slow cooker: Coat the inside of the bowl of a medium slow cooker with non-stick spray. Evenly brown the sausages in a non-stick frypan over moderate heat, turning them often and pricking in a number of places to stop them bursting.

Cut the onions in half from top to bottom, and remove the skins. Cut the onion halves into lengthwise slivers and transfer to the slow cooker. Peel and chop the garlic and add to the onion.

Cut the peppers in half from top to bottom. Remove and discard the stems, seeds and membranes, then cut into long thin slices. Add to the onion and garlic in the slow cooker.

Sprinkle with the salt, pepper and thyme, then place the browned sausages on top and drizzle with ½ cup of stock.

Wash, thinly peel and quarter the potatoes. Place around the sausages, ensuring the cut surfaces touch the sides of the slow cooker.

Cover, turn to HIGH and cook for 4 hours or LOW for 7–8 hours. When the sausages are cooked, thicken the liquid if desired with some paste made from a little cornflour, potato starch or arrowroot mixed with cold water. It is easier to stir this evenly through the liquid if you remove the potatoes and sausages first.

To cook conventionally: Preheat the oven to 180°C. Put the prepared onions, garlic and potatoes in a large well-sprayed or oiled casserole dish with a tight-fitting lid. Top with the sliced peppers, then sprinkle with the flavourings and stock. Add all the stock, then arrange the browned sausages on top.

Cover the casserole dish tightly, putting a piece of tin foil under the lid if you think it is necessary to stop the liquid evaporating while it is in the oven. Cook for 1¼–1½ hours or until the potatoes are tender. Thicken any remaining liquid with a little cornflour paste just before serving.

Serve with a green side salad.

Lynley's 'Gingered Up' Corned Beef Dinner

It is always nice when a friend shares a recipe with you, especially one that's not only novel and easy to make, but also tastes very good!

FOR 6–8 SERVINGS:

1.5kg piece corned silverside, preferably evenly shaped
1.5 litres ginger ale (about ⅔ of a large bottle)
½ orange
1 cinnamon stick
4–6 cloves
2–3 cloves garlic, optional
6–8 medium waxy or new potatoes, peeled or scrubbed

Rinse the corned beef, then place in the slow cooker or a pot with a tight-fitting lid. Add enough ginger ale to half-cover the meat. If you have no other use for the remaining ginger ale, you can use the whole bottle without affecting the recipe.

Cut the orange into several slices and add to the beef, along with the cinnamon stick, broken into several pieces, and the cloves. Peel the garlic if using, then thoroughly squash each clove with a flat-bottomed glass bottle, then add them to the cooker or pot. Place the potatoes, whole or chopped according to your preference, around the corned beef.

To cook in a slow cooker: Cover and cook on LOW for about 8 hours.

To cook conventionally: Place the covered pot on the stove and bring to the boil over moderate heat, then simmer gently for about 2½ hours.

Sauce: Melt 25g of butter in a pot with 1 tablespoon of canola or other oil. Stir in 3 slightly rounded tablespoons of flour, then add, ½ a cup at a time, 1½ cups of the corned beef cooking liquid, stirring or whisking as you go, and bringing to the boil after each addition. To turn this into a mustard sauce, simply stir in 1 rounded teaspoon of Dijon or other mustard of your choice. It's even more delicious if you also add 1 tablespoon of cream or sour cream before bringing the sauce back to the boil.

To serve, mash the potatoes or leave whole. Slice the meat and serve hot with vegetables of your choice.

Roast Beef with Potatoes

Roasts don't get much simpler than this one, which requires just 10–15 minutes' preparation. Then you've just got to put it in the oven and come back in an hour.

FOR 4–6 SERVINGS:

1.2–1.5kg beef topside roast
2 cloves garlic, peeled and sliced
2 Tbsp Dijon mustard
1 Tbsp olive oil
1 Tbsp dark soy sauce
1–2 tsp fresh or dried thyme, optional
1–2 tsp fresh or dried rosemary, chopped, optional
1–1.2kg all purpose or floury potatoes, scrubbed
1 teaspoon instant chicken stock powder
1 cup boiling water
2 cloves garlic
2 Tbsp olive oil
salt and pepper to taste

Pierce the beef at intervals with a sharp knife and insert a sliver of garlic into each cut. Measure the mustard, oil, soy sauce and herbs, if using, into a large plastic bag. Massage the bag to mix the contents, then add the beef. Massage the bag again so the paste covers the entire roast. Leave to stand for at least 15 minutes but longer if possible (up to 24 hours if refrigerated).

Preheat the oven to 180°C.

Cut the potatoes into 1–1.5cm thick slices, then arrange them so they overlap in the bottom of a small roasting pan or shallow casserole dish. Add the stock powder to the boiling water and pour into the pan. Peel, crush and chop the garlic and add to the pan with the olive oil and salt and pepper to taste.

Place the meat on a wire rack and position it over the potatoes in the pan. Cook for 1–1¼ hours, depending on how well done you like your beef. (A meat thermometer is useful for checking doneness – the temperature at the thickest part should be 50°C for rare or 60°C for medium).

Stand the cooked beef in a warm place for 10–15 minutes before carving, collecting any juices to add to the gravy (see Note below).

Serve on warmed plates with gravy and one or more lightly cooked seasonal vegetables.

NOTE: To make a tangy gravy, combine and heat 1–2 tablespoons Dijon mustard (smooth or whole grain), ½ cup red wine and ½ cup other liquid (e.g. vegetable cooking liquid or stock) and any juices collected during resting or carving.

Lemon-Garlic Roasted Chicken & Vegetables

Roast chicken dinners are special for all sorts of reasons. This version is a favourite for two reasons: it tastes great and it's really easy!

FOR 4–6 SERVINGS:

1 chicken, about 1.5–1.8kg
1 large or 2 small lemons
3–4 cloves garlic
2–3 sprigs each fresh thyme and tarragon (or rosemary)
1–2 Tbsp olive oil
salt and pepper
1–1.5kg roasting vegetables, e.g. floury potatoes, kumara, parsnip, pumpkin, red/green/yellow peppers etc.
2–3 Tbsp olive oil
1–2 cloves garlic, extra
3–4 sprigs fresh thyme and tarragon or rosemary, optional

GRAVY

2 Tbsp flour
2 Tbsp olive oil
1–1½ cups chicken juices, stock, water or white wine
salt and pepper to taste

Preheat the oven to 200°C.

Rinse the chicken inside and out, removing any giblets etc. Pat dry. Pierce the lemon/s about six times with a sharp knife, then crush and peel the first quantity of garlic. Place the lemon and garlic inside the chicken along with the fresh herbs.

Place the chicken, breast side up, in a large roasting bag and add the olive oil. Massage the bag so the whole chicken is coated with the oil, then tie the bag leaving a finger-sized gap at the opening for the steam to escape. Place the bag in a large roasting pan and transfer to the oven to start cooking while you prepare the vegetables.

Scrub or peel the root vegetables, depending on your preference, then halve or quarter them lengthwise depending on their size. Cut the pumpkin into 4–5cm chunks and deseed and quarter the peppers. Crush, peel and chop the second quantity of garlic. Place all the prepared vegetables in a large unpunctured plastic bag, add the oil and toss to coat.

Remove the vegetables from the bag and arrange them, except the peppers, in the pan around the bagged chicken. Add the peppers 20–30 minutes later as they require less time to roast.

After about 1¼ –1½ hours, carefully remove the roasting pan from the oven. If the vegetables have not browned sufficiently, place them under the grill for a few minutes.

Snip a corner of the oven bag and collect any juices to make gravy (see below), then slit open the whole bag with a sharp knife and pierce the thickest part of the thigh with a sharp knife to check if the chicken is cooked, in which case the juices should run clear, not pink.

Carve or break up the chicken as required and arrange the meat and vegetables on a warmed platter or serving plates.

Measure the flour and oil into a non-stick frypan and mix to a smooth paste. Cook over a high heat until the mixture begins to colour, then gradually add the liquid and stir continuously to prevent lumps forming until the gravy boils and thickens. Season to taste.

Spray oils are fantastic for potatoes – you add much less oil but still get the wonderful crispy, crunchy result!

The water in which potatoes are cooked has a surprising amount of flavour. Use it, alone, or mixed with other vegetable cooking liquid, as liquid for gravy or to replace some of the milk in white or cheese sauce, or add it to stocks and soups.

Potatoes have so much flavour and nutrients in, or just under their skins, so it's a pity to throw it away. Try rubbing washed potatoes with "green scratchies" otherwise known as rectangular green plastic pot scrubs. These take off the dirt, leave most of the skin intact – and you finish up with more potato for your money.

If you MUST peel potatoes, use a sharp potato peeler in preference to a vegetable knife. The peeler removes a thinner layer than the knife does – so you save money too!

Oven-baked Fish & Chips

If your family likes fried fish and chips, but you don't like the last-minute work involved, try "oven frying" both the fish and the chips. As well as producing good results, it uses only a small amount of oil.

FOR 4 SERVINGS:

4 large (about 800g) all purpose or floury potatoes
1 Tbsp oil
4 boneless, skinless fish fillets (150g each)
½ cup self-raising flour
½ tsp salt
½ tsp sugar
½ tsp ground cumin (optional)
½ tsp dried oregano (optional)
½ tsp paprika (optional)
2 Tbsp oil
1 or 2 eggs

Turn the oven to 230°C with two shelves, one a little below the middle, the other above the first, near the top of the oven.

Scrub the potatoes and cut them lengthways first into halves, then into quarters, and then into eighths. Dry with a tea towel or paper towels. Put in a large plastic bag and drizzle with the first measure of oil. Shake gently, to lightly coat with the oil.

Place prepared potatoes in a large, shallow baking dish lined with baking paper and bake on the lower shelf for about 30 minutes, turning chips once or twice. Use the fan if your oven has this option.

While the chips cook, prepare the fish fillets. Mix the flour with the seasonings in a shallow bowl. Line another shallow metal dish, big enough to hold the fish in one layer, with baking paper and coat with non-stick spray. Beat the egg with a fork, just enough to combine the white and the yolk evenly.

When the chips are nearly cooked (about 12 minutes before you want to eat), put the prepared baking dish in the oven to heat for about 1 minute. While it heats, pat the fillets dry and coat first with the seasoned flour, then with the beaten egg, then again with the flour. Working fast, put the fillets in the preheated, sprayed dish and drizzle the remaining oil over them.

Cook the fish on the shelf above the chips for about 8 minutes altogether, turning with a fish slice after 5 minutes. Take the fish from oven as soon as the centre of each fillet seems cooked (it will be dry and tough if overcooked).

Serve the fish and chips promptly, with lemon or lime wedges and a side salad.

Growing your own potatoes

If you have the space, it is very satisfying to plant a few rows of potatoes in your back garden, watch them grow into healthy plants, and eventually to dig them up and find for each potato you planted you now have a dozen new healthy ones. We have always found that children or grandchildren enjoy helping with the harvest too!

Growing times

Depending on how long they take to grow, varieties are divided into early, early main and main crop. Choose varieties that suit your preferred time of harvest. (See below for a selection of varieties.) It's a good idea to experiment with new varieties to find the ones which best suit your growing conditions and taste preferences.

Height / spread

Potato plants grow about 50cm tall. Each plant can spread 80–90cm, depending on the variety.

Frost hardiness

Potato plants are not frost hardy but will usually re-sprout after a frost.

Sun, soil, water, food

Potatoes of all types grow best in open soils in a sunny, well-drained position. They also grow well in sandy soil if plenty of well decayed compost and manure has been mixed in before planting, and if they are watered regularly. Blood and bone or a balanced fertiliser also helps get good results.

Potatoes suitable for growing in the NZ home garden

EARLY POTATOES – these usually have a waxy texture, and are suitable for boiling and salads.

Early potatoes include:

Swift — Round, white skin and cream flesh. Very early.

Rocket — Round-oval, white skin and flesh.

Cliff's Kidney — An old, kidney shaped variety known for good quality.

Jersey Benne — Another old kidney shaped variety with good quality.

Liseta — oval, light yellow fleshed tubers.

EARLY MAIN CROP POTATOES – Most of these can be dug while the leaves are growing and bushy, or they can be left for longer until the plants become more mature and the leaves collapse and die.

Maris Anchor — Round-oval white fleshed tubers. Can be dug early or left to mature.

Ilam Hardy — Round-oval white skin and flesh. Vigorous grower which can be dug early or left until mature. They have a floury texture when mature.

Karaka — Round-oval white skin and flesh. Tendency to develop growth cracks in uneven growing conditions but exceptional flavour and are all-purpose potatoes.

Potatoes are usually grown, not from seeds, but from small "seed potatoes". Those suitable for planting should be 50–100g in weight with small sprouts starting to appear on them. Plant seed potatoes 5cm deep and 25–30cm apart, in rows 50–80cm apart. This makes the process of 'earthing up' easier (see below).

Care/maintenance

When the plants are 20cm high build up the soil ('earth up') around the plants, covering some of the new shoots and lower leaves but leaving about 10cm uncovered. Continue the process at two weekly intervals until the plants flower. Earthing up protects plants from late frost, warms the soil and helps retain moisture. It also prevents the tubers from turning green when they are exposed to light, thereby ensuring a better crop.

Growing potatoes in pots and tubs

Potatoes can be successfully grown in pots and tubs with drainage holes. Fill a large bucket with 10–15cm of free draining soil or potting mix and add a generous handful of a fertiliser containing a NPK of 5 / 7 / 4. Place a seed potato on top of this mix and cover it with soil. As the potato emerges add more soil mix every second week just leaving the top of the plant exposed until the bucket is full. Allow the plant to mature and flower. Simply tip out the potato plant and the soil to get the potatoes!

Harvesting potatoes

Potatoes can be harvested early while the tops are still green. At this stage, the tubers will be immature and small, but their flavour will justify the lower yields at this stage. Grow early maturing varieties for early harvest.

Pests and diseases

Those new to potato growing should ask the staff at garden centres for advice. Virus diseases are less likely if certified seed potatoes, produced especially for planting potatoes, are used.

Purple Passion — This is a new release, with purple skin and light yellow flesh. Exceptional flavour and texture when dug while tops are still green.

Nadine — Attractive round tubers with white skin and flesh. Sets high number of tubers which need regular watering to size up. Waxy texture but lacks flavour.

Katahdin or Chippewa — An old variety, round with white skin and flesh. Mainly suited to boiling.

Driver — Round tubers with white skin and flesh. Vigorous grower. Good for boiling and salads.

Heather — Oval tubers with purple skin and white flesh. Suitable for most end uses and can be left to mature.

MAIN CROP POTATOES — These are best when grown to full maturity. Suitable for storage.

Moonlight — Now the most popular variety in New Zealand. Oval with white skin and flesh. Easy to grow with high yield of good tasting tubers suitable for boiling and frying.

Agria — A popular variety with oval tubers and yellow flesh. Suitable for most purposes.

New potato varieties, with new names, are always being developed. Do not expect to see all the varieties mentioned here on sale. Some varieties do better in a particular part of the country, so will not be available everywhere.

Potato index

Mince index

Sausage index

Knives etc., by Mail Order

For about 20 years Alison has imported her favourite, very sharp kitchen knives from Switzerland. They keep their edges well, are easy to sharpen, a pleasure to use, and make excellent gifts.

VEGETABLE KNIFE $8.00
Ideal for cutting and peeling vegetables, these knives have a straight edged 85mm blade and black (dishwasher-proof) nylon handle. Each knife comes in an individual plastic sheath.

BONING/UTILITY KNIFE $9.50
Excellent for boning chicken and other meats, and/or for general kitchen duties. Featuring a 103mm blade that curves to a point and a dishwasher-proof, black nylon handle. Each knife comes in a plastic sheath.

SERRATED KNIFE $9.50
These knives are unbelievably useful. They are perfect for cutting cooked meats, ripe fruit and vegetables, and slicing bread and baking. Treated carefully, these blades stay sharp for years. The serrated 110mm blade is rounded at the end with a black (dishwasher-proof) nylon handle and each knife comes in an individual plastic sheath.

THREE-PIECE SET $22.00
This three-piece set includes a vegetable knife, a serrated knife (as described above) and a right-handed potato peeler with a matching black handle, presented in a white plastic wallet.

GIFT BOXED KNIFE SET $44.00
This set contains five knives plus a matching right-handed potato peeler. There is a straight bladed vegetable knife and a serrated knife (as above), as well as a handy 85mm serrated blade vegetable knife, a small (85mm) utility knife with a pointed tip and a smaller (85mm) serrated knife. These elegantly presented sets make ideal gifts.

SERRATED CARVING KNIFE $28.50
This fabulous knife cuts beautifully and is a pleasure to use; it's ideal for carving or cutting fresh bread. The 21cm serrated blade does not require sharpening. Once again the knife has a black moulded, dishwasher safe handle and comes in a plastic sheath.

COOK'S KNIFE $35.00
An excellent all-purpose kitchen knife. With a well balanced 19cm wedge-shaped blade and a contoured black nylon handle, these knives make short work of slicing and chopping, and have come out on top of their class in several comparative tests. Each dishwasher-safe knife comes with its own plastic sheath.

VICTORINOX MULTIPURPOSE KITCHEN SHEARS $29.50
Every kitchen should have a pair of these! With their comfortable nylon handles and sharp blades these quality shears make short work of everything from cutting a piece of string or sheet of paper to jointing a whole chicken. Note: Black handle only.

STEEL $20.00
These steels have a 20cm 'blade' and measure 33cm in total. With its matching black handle the steel is an ideal companion for your own knives, or as a gift. Alison gets excellent results using these steels. N.B. Not for use with serrated knives.

PROBUS SPREADER/SCRAPER $7.50
After her knives, these are the most used tools in Alison's kitchen! With a comfortable plastic handle, metal shank and flexible plastic blade (suitable for use on non-stick surfaces), these are excellent for mixing muffin batters, stirring and scraping bowls, spreading icings, turning pikelets etc., etc…

NON-STICK LINERS
Re-usable SureBrand PTFE non-stick liners are another essential kitchen item – they really help avoid the frustration of stuck-on baking, roasting or frying. Once you've used them, you'll wonder how you did without!

Round tin liner	(for 15-23cm tins)	$6.50
	(for 23-30cm tins)	$9.50
Square tin liner	(for 15-23cm tins)	$6.50
	(for 23-30cm tins)	$9.50
Ring tin liner	(for 23cm tins)	$6.95
Baking sheet liner	(33x44cm)	$13.95
Barbeque Liner	(Heavy duty 33x44cm)	$17.95
Frypan Liner	(Heavy duty round 30cm)	$10.95

All prices include GST. Prices current at time of publishing, subject to change without notice. Please add $5.00 post & packing to any order (any number of items).

Make cheques payable to Alison Holst Mail Orders and post to:

Alison Holst Mail Orders
FREEPOST 124807
PO Box 17016
Wellington

Or visit us at www.holst.co.nz